WHOLEFOODS

WHOLEFOODS

100 HEALTHY RECIPES SHOWN IN MORE THAN 300 PHOTOGRAPHS

NICOLA GRAIMES

southwater

This edition is published by Southwater
an imprint of Anness Publishing Ltd,
Blaby Road Wigston, Leicestershire
LE18 4SE; info@anness.com

www.southwaterbooks.com;
www.annesspublishing.com

If you like the images in this book and would
like to investigate using them for publishing,
promotions or advertising, please visit our
website www.practicalpictures.com
for more information.

© Anness Publishing Ltd 2013

A CIP catalogue record for this book is
available from the British Library.

Publisher: Joanna Lorenz
Editors: Kate Eddison and Siobhan O'Connor
Designer: Nigel Partridge
Photographers: Thomas Odulate (recipes)
and Amanda Heywood
Home Economists: Kate Jay and Annabel Ford
Production Controller: Stephen Lang

Main front cover image shows Creamy Lemon
Puy Lentils, for recipe see page 37

PUBLISHER'S NOTE
Although the advice and information in this
book are believed to be accurate and true at
the time of going to press, neither the authors
nor the publisher can accept any legal
responsibility or liability for any errors or
omissions that may have been made nor for
any inaccuracies nor for any loss, harm or
injury that comes about from following
instructions or advice in this book.

NOTES
• Bracketed terms are intended for
American readers.
• For all recipes, quantities are given in
both metric and imperial measures and,
where appropriate, measures are also
given in standard cups and spoons.
Follow one set, but not a mixture,
because they are not interchangeable.
• Standard spoon and cup measures are
level. 1 tsp = 5ml, 1 tbsp = 15ml, 1 cup
= 250ml/8fl oz
• Australian standard tablespoons are
20ml. Australian readers should use
3 tsp in place of 1 tbsp for measuring
small quantities.
• American pints are 16fl oz/2 cups.
American readers should use 20fl oz/
2.5 cups in place of 1 pint when
measuring liquids.
• Electric oven temperatures in this book
are for conventional ovens. When using
a fan oven, the temperature will
probably need to be reduced by about
10–20°C/20–40°F. Since ovens vary, you
should check with your manufacturer's
instruction book for guidance.
• The nutritional analysis given for each
recipe is calculated per portion (i.e.
serving or item), unless otherwise stated.
If the recipe gives a range, such as
Serves 4–6, then the nutritional analysis
will be for the smaller portion size, i.e. 6
servings. The analysis does not include
optional ingredients, such as salt added
to taste.
• Medium eggs (US large) are used
unless otherwise stated.

Contents

Introduction

Wholefoods are foods that have had nothing added or taken away – in other words, foods as close to their natural state as possible. They are foods that have not been unnecessarily processed or subjected to chemical treatments, or loaded with harmful additives, colourings or flavourings.

WHAT ARE WHOLEFOODS?

In the narrowest sense, wholefoods are specifically unrefined ingredients, such as grains, peas, beans, lentils, seeds, fruits and vegetables, but in this book we have taken the liberty of expanding the term to include all foods that should be included in a healthy diet. It is important to choose unrefined foods whenever you can, simply because they ensure the greatest intake of vitamins, minerals and fibre. When food is processed, precious nutrients are taken away as a result, although there are various degrees to which this occurs. Some people would argue, however, that a diet consisting entirely of wholefoods could be decidedly brown and boring.

A healthy wholefoods diet should always include a wide range of other ingredients, to add both variety and essential nutrients. Dairy products, fats and oils, and natural sweeteners are all needed to make wholefoods palatable and appealing. And there's no reason why, if you are making sure that you eat mainly wholefoods, you can't include a few refined foods here and there in your diet. A little white flour added to a wholemeal (whole-wheat) cake or pastry, for instance, will give a much lighter end result and will affect the nutritional value only marginally. And it is not such a sin to eat white rice instead of brown, or plain pasta rather than wholemeal occasionally, if the rest of the dish or meal is full of nutrient-packed, high-fibre foods.

ORGANIC FOODS

As food scares continue, many people are increasingly anxious about the type of food that they eat and how it is produced. The growing use of antibiotics, artificial additives and chemicals, as well as the introduction of irradiation and genetically modified foods, has added fuel to this concern.

People are looking for healthier, less processed foods, and the demand for organic foods is growing at a rate of about 30 per cent every year.

LEFT: *Coriander Omelette Parcels with Oriental Vegetables are satisfyingly tasty.*

ABOVE: *Try to eat at least five portions of fruits and vegetables a day.*

ABOVE: *Wholemeal bread provides more nutrients than refined white bread.*

ABOVE: *Carbohydrate-rich plantains, yams and potatoes supply steady energy.*

Organic foods were, until relatively recently, found only in health food stores, but now there is an expanding range of fresh and packaged organic foods in supermarkets. Reassuringly, products labelled as organic have to fulfil certain strict criteria. No artificial pesticides, fertilizers or other chemicals are allowed to be used in the growing or production of organic food, and genetically modified or irradiated ingredients are not permitted.

Traditional methods of agriculture, such as crop rotation, are often used, along with naturally occurring fertilizers. This preserves wildlife and minimizes pollution. Also, due to their shorter shelf-life, many organic fruits

and vegetables are less likely to have travelled a great distance before reaching stores. This has inspired a steady return to locally produced, seasonal foods. Whether organic food tastes better or is higher in nutrients is open to debate, but there is no denying that the environment and our health will undoubtedly benefit in the long term.

THE VEGETARIAN WHOLEFOOD DIET

We are often told to eat a balanced diet, but what does this mean in the context of a vegetarian diet? The key to maintaining good health is to eat a variety of foods that provide the right

proportion of protein, carbohydrates, fibre, fat, vitamins and minerals, as well as water. The ideal diet features enough calories to provide the body with vital energy – but not an excess, which leads to weight gain.

A vegetarian diet is not simply a matter of swapping meat and fish for cheese and eggs. Vegetarians need to ensure that they eat plenty of fruit and vegetables, legumes, nuts, seeds, rice, bread, pasta and potatoes, and some dairy foods. Focusing on wholefoods will help to achieve the optimum balance of nutrients. This book provides an array of delicious and nutritionally balanced vegetarian recipes using a variety of wholefood ingredients.

Breakfasts and Brunches

Start the day with a balanced breakfast.

High-carbohydrate wholefoods such as

cereals, grains or beans replenish nutrients

and energy stocks. What's more, research

suggests that those who eat a carbohydrate-

based breakfast are likely to eat less during

the day, perform better at school or work,

and find it easier to control their weight.

If you can't face solid food in the morning,

try a cleansing juice or fruit smoothie.

Orange and raspberry smoothie

This exquisite blend combines the sharp-sweet taste of raspberries and the zesty fruitiness of oranges with smooth yogurt. It tastes like creamy, fruit heaven in a glass. Even better, it takes just minutes to prepare, making it perfect as a quick breakfast juice for people in a hurry or, indeed, as a refreshing drink at any other time of day.

MAKES 2–3 GLASSES

250g/9oz/1¹⁄₃ cups raspberries, chilled
200ml/7fl oz/scant 1 cup natural (plain) yogurt, chilled
300ml/¹⁄₂ pint/1¹⁄₄ cups freshly squeezed orange juice, chilled

1 Put the raspberries and yogurt in a blender or food processor, and purée for about 1 minute until the mixture is smooth and creamy.

2 Add the orange juice to the raspberry and yogurt mixture, and process for another 30 seconds or until thoroughly combined.

3 Divide the smoothie among 2 or 3 tall glasses, and serve immediately.

COOK'S TIP
For a super-chilled version, use frozen raspberries instead of fresh ones. You may need to blend the raspberries and yogurt for a little longer to get a really smooth result.

Nutritional information per portion: Energy 94kcal/ 401kJ; Protein 5.1g; Carbohydrate 17.6g, of which sugars 17.6g; Fat 1g, of which saturates 0.4g; Cholesterol 1mg; Calcium 158mg; Fibre 2.2g; Sodium 68mg.

Hum-zinger

This tropical cleanser contains 100 per cent fruit. It will help to boost the digestive system and the kidneys, making your eyes sparkle, your hair shine and your skin glow. For best results, use really ripe fruit, otherwise the juice may be sharp and flavourless. If the fruit is not quite ripe when you buy it, leave it at room temperature for a day or two before juicing.

MAKES 1 GLASS

1/2 **pineapple, peeled**
1 **small mango, peeled and stoned (pitted)**
1/2 **small papaya, peeled and seeded**

1 Remove any 'eyes' left in the pineapple, then cut all the fruit into rough chunks. Using a juice extractor, juice all of the fruit.

2 Alternatively, use a blender or food processor, and purée the fruit for 2–3 minutes until very smooth.

3 Pour the juice into a tall glass, and serve immedlately.

COOK'S TIP
Pineapple and mango can produce a very thick juice when puréed in a blender or food processor. If using this method, you might want to thin it down with a little mineral water before serving. Or, if you prefer your juice well chilled, serve it with plenty of crushed ice instead.

Nutritional information per portion: Energy 322kcal/ 1378kJ; Protein 3.7g; Carbohydrate 79.1g, of which sugars 78.7g; Fat 1.3g, of which saturates 0.1g; Cholesterol 0mg; Calcium 136mg; Fibre 13.1g; Sodium 21mg.

Griddled pineapple and mango on panettone

Griddling concentrates the sweetness of both the pineapple and the mango, giving them a caramel flavour that is complemented by the vanilla yogurt and crisp toasted panettone.

SERVES 4

1 large pineapple
1 large mango
25g/1oz/2 tbsp unsalted butter, melted
4 thick slices panettone

FOR THE VANILLA YOGURT
250g/9oz/generous 1 cup Greek
    (US strained plain) yogurt
30ml/2 tbsp clear honey
2.5ml/¹/₂ tsp ground cinnamon
a few drops of natural vanilla extract,
    to taste

1 To prepare the pineapple, cut the bottom and the spiky top off the fruit. Carefully slice off the skin, removing all the spikes, then cut the pineapple into quarters; remove the core if it is hard. Cut the flesh into thick wedges.

2 To prepare the mango, cut away the two thick sides of the mango as close to the stone (pit) as possible. Peel the mango, then cut the remaining flesh from the stone. Slice the fruit and discard the stone.

3 Heat a griddle pan over a medium heat. Add the pineapple and mango (you may need to do this in batches). Brush with melted butter, and cook for 8 minutes, turning once, until soft and slightly golden. Alternatively, heat the grill (broiler) to high and line the rack with foil. Put the pineapple and mango on the foil, brush with butter and grill (broil) for 4 minutes on each side.

4 Meanwhile, put the yogurt in a bowl with the honey, cinnamon and vanilla. Stir well. Lightly toast the panettone, then serve, topped with the griddled pineapple and mango, and accompanied by the vanilla yogurt.

Nutritional information per portion: Energy 411kcal/1736kJ; Protein 9.9g; Carbohydrate 64.1g, of which sugars 42g; Fat 15.4g, of which saturates 7.7g; Cholesterol 14mg; Calcium 202mg; Fibre 4.7g; Sodium 278mg.

Apricot and **ginger compote**

The zing of fresh ginger adds warmth to this stimulating breakfast dish and complements the flavour of the plump, juicy apricots, which are a good source of iron and vitamins A and C.

SERVES 4

350g/12oz/1¹/₂ cups unsulphured ready-to-eat dried apricots

4cm/1¹/₂in piece fresh root ginger, finely chopped

200g/7oz/scant 1 cup natural (plain) live yogurt or low-fat fromage frais (low-fat cream cheese) or low-fat ricotta cheese

1 Cover the apricots with boiling water, then leave to soak overnight.

2 Put the apricots and soaking liquid in a pan, add the ginger and bring to the boil. Reduce the heat and simmer for 10 minutes until the fruit is soft and the liquid is syrupy. Strain the apricots, reserving the syrup; discard the ginger.

3 Serve the apricots warm with the reserved syrup, and a spoonful of yogurt, fromage frais or ricotta on top.

HEALTH BENEFITS
In traditional Chinese medicine, ginger is revered for its health-giving properties. It is antispasmodic, aids digestion and can help to treat colds and flu.

COOK'S TIP
Fresh ginger freezes well. Peel the root and store in a plastic bag in the freezer. You can grate it from frozen, then return the root to the freezer until next time you need it.

Nutritional information per portion: Energy 166kcal/708kJ; Protein 6.1g; Carbohydrate 35.7g, of which sugars 35.7g; Fat 1g, of which saturates 0.3g; Cholesterol 1mg; Calcium 159mg; Fibre 5.5g; Sodium 54mg.

Porridge with date purée and pistachio nuts

Full of valuable fibre and nutrients, dates give a natural sweet flavour to this warming winter breakfast dish. Oats, too, are good for you, and could help to lower cholesterol.

SERVES 4

250g/9oz/scant 2 cups fresh dates
225g/8oz/2 cups rolled oats
475ml/16fl oz/2 cups semi-skimmed (low-fat) milk
pinch of salt
50g/2oz/¹⁄₂ cup shelled, unsalted pistachio nuts, roughly chopped

1 First, make the date purée. Halve and stone (pit) the dates, and remove the stems. Cover the dates with boiling water and leave to soak for about 30 minutes until softened. Strain, reserving 90ml/3fl oz/¹⁄₃ cup of the soaking water.

2 Remove the skin from the dates, and put them in a food processor with the reserved soaking water. Process to a smooth paste.

3 Put the oats in a pan with the milk, 300ml/¹⁄₂ pint/1¹⁄₄ cups water and salt. Bring to the boil, then reduce the heat and simmer for 4–5 minutes until cooked and creamy, stirring frequently.

4 Serve the porridge immediately, in warm serving bowls, topped with a spoonful of the date purée and a sprinkling of the chopped pistachio nuts.

Nutritional information per portion: Energy 416kcal/1754kJ; Protein 13.6g; Carbohydrate 62.5g, of which sugars 21.2g; Fat 13.8g, of which saturates 1.3g; Cholesterol 0mg; Calcium 75mg; Fibre 5.7g; Sodium 127mg.

Luxury muesli

Commercially made muesli really can't compete with this home-made version. The combination of seeds, grains, nuts and dried fruits works particularly well, but you can experiment, if you like.

SERVES 4

50g/2oz/¹/₂ cup sunflower seeds
25g/1oz/¹/₄ cup pumpkin seeds
115g/4oz/1 cup rolled oats
115g/4oz/heaped 1 cup wheat flakes
115g/4oz/heaped 1 cup barley flakes
115g/4oz/1 cup raisins
115g/4oz/1 cup chopped
   hazelnuts, roasted
115g/4oz/¹/₂ cup unsulphured ready-
   to-eat dried apricots, chopped
50g/2oz/2 cups ready-to-eat dried
   apple slices, halved
25g/1oz/¹/₃ cup desiccated (dry
   unsweetened shredded) coconut

1 Dry-fry the sunflower and pumpkin seeds over medium heat for 3 minutes until golden, tossing the seeds regularly to prevent them burning.

2 Mix the toasted seeds with the remaining ingredients, and leave to cool. Store in an airtight container. Serve with semi-skimmed milk.

HEALTH BENEFIT
Sunflower seeds are rich in vitamin E, thought to reduce the risk of heart disease.

VARIATION
Serve the muesli in a long glass layered with fresh raspberries and fromage frais or mascarpone. Soak the muesli first in a little water or fruit juice to soften slightly.

Nutritional information per portion: Energy 813kcal/3411kJ; Protein 20.8g; Carbohydrate 100.9g, of which sugars 33.4g; Fat 39g, of which saturates 5.5g; Cholesterol 0mg; Calcium 145mg; Fibre 12.4g; Sodium 55mg.

Granola

Honey-coated nuts, seeds and oats, combined with sweet dried fruits, make an excellent and nutritious start to the day – without the additives often found in pre-packaged cereals.

SERVES 4

115g/4oz/1 cup rolled oats
115g/4oz/1 cup jumbo oats
50g/2oz/¹/₂ cup sunflower seeds
25g/1oz/2 tbsp sesame seeds
50g/2oz/¹/₂ cup hazelnuts, roasted
25g/1oz/¹/₄ cup almonds,
    roughly chopped
50ml/2fl oz/¹/₄ cup sunflower oil
50ml/2fl oz/¹/₄ cup clear honey
50g/2oz/¹/₂ cup raisins
50g/2oz/¹/₂ cup ready-to-eat dried
    sweetened cranberries

1 Preheat the oven to 140°C/ 275°F/Gas 1. Combine the oats, seeds and nuts in a bowl.

2 Heat the oil and honey in a large pan until melted, then remove from the heat. Add the oat, seed and nut mixture, and stir well to coat in the oil and honey. Spread out on one or two baking sheets.

3 Bake for about 50 minutes until crisp, stirring occasionally to prevent the mixture sticking. Remove it from the oven and mix in the raisins and cranberries. Leave to cool, then store in an airtight container.

4 Serve the granola with semi-skimmed milk or natural live yogurt and fresh fruit.

Nutritional information per portion: Energy 638kcal/2674kJ; Protein 14.4g; Carbohydrate 72.3g, of which sugars 27.9g; Fat 34.3g, of which saturates 2.9g; Cholesterol 0mg; Calcium 132mg; Fibre 6.9g; Sodium 39mg.

Oaty pancakes with caramel bananas and pecans

These pancakes are more like drop scones than the classic thin French crêpes. Bananas and pecan nuts, cooked in maple syrup, make a sweet and delicious topping.

SERVES 5

75g/3oz/²/₃ cup plain (all-purpose) flour

50g/2oz/¹/₂ cup wholemeal (whole-wheat) flour

50g/2oz/¹/₂ cup rolled oats

5ml/1 tsp baking powder

pinch of salt

25g/1oz/2 tbsp golden caster (superfine) sugar

1 egg

15ml/1 tbsp sunflower oil, plus extra for frying

250ml/8fl oz/1 cup semi-skimmed (low-fat) milk

FOR THE CARAMEL BANANAS AND PECAN NUTS

50g/2oz/4 tbsp butter

15ml/1 tbsp maple syrup

3 bananas, halved and quartered lengthways

25g/1oz/¹/₄ cup pecan nuts

1 To make the pancakes, combine the plain and wholemeal flours, oats, baking powder, salt and sugar in a bowl.

2 Make a well in the centre of the flour mixture, and add the egg, oil and a quarter of the milk. Mix well to incorporate, then gradually add the rest of the milk to make a thick batter. Leave to rest for 20 minutes in the refrigerator.

3 Heat a large, lightly oiled heavy frying pan. Using about 30ml/2 tbsp of batter for each pancake, cook two or three pancakes at a time. Drop the batter into the pan, and cook for

3 minutes on each side, until golden. Keep warm while you cook the remaining seven or eight pancakes.

4 To make the caramel bananas and pecan nuts, wipe out the frying pan and add the butter. Heat gently until the butter melts, then add the maple syrup and stir well. Add the bananas and pecan nuts to the pan.

5 Cook for about 4 minutes, turning once, until the bananas are just soft and the sauce has caramelized. To serve, place two pancakes on each of five warm serving plates. Top with the caramel bananas and pecan nuts. Serve immediately.

Nutritional information per portion: Energy 394kcal/1652kJ; Protein 8.1g; Carbohydrate 49.5g, of which sugars 23.2g; Fat 19.5g, of which saturates 7g; Cholesterol 62mg; Calcium 108mg; Fibre 2.9g; Sodium 109mg.

Chive scrambled eggs in brioches

An indulgent but truly delicious breakfast that should be reserved for lazy Sundays or special occasions. Eggs are a good source of protein, but are best eaten in moderation.

SERVES 4

115g/4oz/¹/₂ cup unsalted butter
75g/3oz/generous 1 cup brown cap
   (cremini) mushrooms, finely sliced
4 individual brioches

8 eggs
15ml/1 tbsp chopped fresh chives,
   plus extra to garnish
salt and ground black pepper

1 Preheat the oven to 180°C/350°F/Gas 4. Put a quarter of the butter in a frying pan, and heat until melted. Sauté the mushrooms for about 3 minutes or until soft, then set aside and keep warm.

2 Slice the tops off the brioches, then scoop out the soft centres and discard, leaving a 'shell' of bread and crust. Put the brioches and lids on a baking sheet and bake for 5 minutes until hot and slightly crisp.

3 Meanwhile, beat the eggs lightly and season to taste. Heat the remaining butter in a heavy pan over gentle heat. When the butter has melted and is foaming slightly, add the eggs. Using a wooden spoon, stir constantly, to ensure the egg does not stick to the bottom of the pan.

4 Continue to stir gently until about three-quarters of the egg is semi-solid and creamy – this should take 2–3 minutes. Remove the pan from the heat – the egg will continue to cook in the heat from the pan – then stir in the snipped chives.

5 To serve, spoon a little of the mushrooms into the bottom of each brioche, and top with the scrambled eggs. Sprinkle with extra chives, balance the brioche lids on top and serve immediately.

COOK'S TIP
Timing and temperature are crucial for perfect scrambled eggs. When cooked for too long over too high a heat, eggs become dry and crumbly; vice versa, and they are sloppy and unappealing.

Nutritional information per portion: Energy 533kcal/2218kJ; Protein 17.9g; Carbohydrate 31.9g, of which sugars 9.9g; Fat 38.2g, of which saturates 19.2g; Cholesterol 443mg; Calcium 137mg; Fibre 1.7g; Sodium 507mg.

Cannellini bean and rosemary bruschetta

More brunch than breakfast, this dish is a sophisticated version of beans on toast. Redolent with the flavours of the Mediterranean, it is satisfying, tasty and a good boost for energy levels.

SERVES 4

150g/5oz/²/₃ cup dried cannellini
  or flageolet beans
5 ripe tomatoes
45ml/3 tbsp olive oil, plus extra for drizzling
2 sun-dried tomatoes in oil, drained and
  finely chopped
1 garlic clove, crushed

30ml/2 tbsp chopped fresh rosemary
salt and ground black pepper
handful of fresh basil leaves, to garnish

TO SERVE
12 slices Italian-style bread, such as ciabatta
1 large garlic clove, halved

1 Put the beans in a large bowl, and cover with water. Leave to soak overnight. Drain and rinse the beans, then put in a pan and cover with fresh water. Bring to the boil, and boil rapidly for 10 minutes. Reduce the heat and simmer for 50–60 minutes until tender. Drain and set aside.

2 Meanwhile, put the tomatoes in a bowl, cover with boiling water and leave for 30 seconds, to loosen the skins. Peel, seed and chop the flesh.

3 Heat the oil in a frying pan. Add the fresh and sun-dried tomatoes, garlic and rosemary, and cook for 2 minutes until the tomatoes begin to break down and soften.

4 Add the tomato mixture to the cannellini beans, season to taste and mix well.

5 Rub the bread slices with the cut sides of the garlic clove, then toast lightly. Spoon the cannellini bean mixture on top. Sprinkle with basil leave and drizzle with a little extra olive oil before serving.

HEALTH BENEFITS
• *Cannellini beans are high in protein and low in fat. They are also a valuable source of B vitamins and minerals.*
• *Rosemary is reputed to have many healing qualities. It is said to alleviate headaches, to improve the circulation and to ease rheumatism. Use fresh rosemary if possible, as dried will have lost most of its beneficial oils.*

Nutritional information per portion: Energy 499kcal/2110kJ; Protein 20.2g; Carbohydrate 84.2g, of which sugars 8.5g; Fat 11.3g, of which saturates 1.7g; Cholesterol 0mg; Calcium 195mg; Fibre 8.1g; Sodium 749mg.

Griddled tomatoes on soda bread

Nothing could be simpler than this breakfast or brunch dish, yet a drizzle of olive oil and balsamic vinegar and shavings of Parmesan transform it into something really special.

SERVES 4

olive oil, for brushing and drizzling
6 ripe tomatoes, thickly sliced
4 thick slices soda bread
balsamic vinegar, for drizzling
salt and ground black pepper
shavings of Parmesan cheese, to serve

1 Brush a griddle pan with olive oil and heat. Add the tomato slices and cook for about 4 minutes, turning once, until softened and slightly blackened. Alternatively, heat a grill (broiler) to high, and line the rack with foil. Grill (broil) the tomato slices for 4–6 minutes, turning once, until softened.

2 Meanwhile, lightly toast the soda bread. Put the tomatoes on top of the toast, and drizzle each portion with a little olive oil and vinegar. Season to taste, and serve immediately with thin shavings of Parmesan.

HEALTH BENEFITS
Numerous studies have shown that tomatoes are effective in preventing many forms of cancer, including lung, stomach and prostate cancer. This is probably explained by their antioxidant content, notably beta carotene and vitamins C and E. Antioxidants are also believed to prevent appendicitis.

Nutritional information per portion: Energy 172kcal/724kJ; Protein 3.9g; Carbohydrate 25.1g, of which sugars 5.8g; Fat 6.9g, of which saturates 0.9g; Cholesterol 0mg; Calcium 63mg; Fibre 2.3g; Sodium 171mg.

Kedgeree

This spicy lentil and rice dish is a delicious variation of the original Indian version of kedgeree, kitchiri. Great served as it is, it is equally tempting served atop large field mushrooms.

SERVES 4

50g/2oz/¼ cup dried red lentils, rinsed
1 bay leaf
225g/8oz/1 cup basmati rice, rinsed
4 cloves
50g/2oz/4 tbsp butter
5ml/1 tsp curry powder
2.5ml/½ tsp mild chilli powder
30ml/2 tbsp chopped flat leaf parsley
salt and ground black pepper
4 hard-boiled eggs, quartered,
    to serve (optional)

1 Put the lentils in a pan, add the bay leaf and cover with cold water. Bring to the boil, skim off any foam, then reduce the heat. Cover and simmer for 25–30 minutes until tender. Drain, then discard the bay leaf.

2 Meanwhile, put the rice in a pan. Cover with 475ml/16fl oz/2 cups boiling water. Add the cloves and a generous pinch of salt. Cook, covered, for 10–15 minutes until all the water is absorbed and the rice is tender. Discard the cloves.

3 Melt the butter over gentle heat in a large frying pan, then add the curry and chilli powders, and cook for 1 minute.

4 Stir in the lentils and rice, and mix well until they are coated in the spiced butter. Season to taste and cook for 1–2 minutes until heated through. Stir in the parsley and serve with the hard-boiled eggs, if using.

Nutritional information per portion: Energy 320kcal/1336kJ; Protein 15.6g; Carbohydrate 46.6g, of which sugars 0g; Fat 7.6g, of which saturates 3.3g; Cholesterol 149mg; Calcium 39mg; Fibre 0g; Sodium 357mg.

Soups and Light Meals

Nutritious and sustaining, home-made soup is the perfect health food. There's nothing simpler to make, as quantities are seldom crucial and timing is flexible. Soup is a wonderful vehicle for vegetables, and this chapter introduces soups for all seasons. The selection of light meals is equally varied, ranging from Creamy Lemon Puy Lentils to the irresistible Thai Tempeh Cakes with Sweet Dipping Sauce.

Gazpacho with avocado salsa

Tomatoes, cucumber and peppers form the basis of this classic chilled soup. Add a spoonful of chunky avocado salsa and a scattering of croûtons, and serve for a light lunch on a warm day.

SERVES 4

2 slices day-old bread
1kg/2¼lb tomatoes
1 cucumber
1 red (bell) pepper, seeded and chopped
1 fresh green chilli, seeded and chopped
2 garlic cloves, chopped
30ml/2 tbsp extra virgin olive oil
juice of 1 lime and 1 lemon
a few drops of Tabasco sauce
salt and ground black pepper
handful of fresh basil leaves, to garnish
8 ice cubes, to serve

FOR THE CROÛTONS

2 slices day-old bread, crusts removed
1 garlic clove, halved
15ml/1 tbsp olive oil

FOR THE AVOCADO SALSA

1 ripe avocado
5ml/1 tsp lemon juice
2.5cm/1in piece of cucumber, diced
½ fresh red chilli, finely chopped

1 Soak the bread in 150ml/¼ pint/⅔ cup water for 5 minutes. Put the tomatoes in a bowl, cover with boiling water, and leave for 30 seconds. Peel, seed and chop the flesh. Thinly peel the cucumber, cut in half lengthways and scoop out the seeds with a teaspoon. Discard the seeds and chop the flesh.

2 Blend or process the bread, tomatoes, cucumber, red pepper, chilli, garlic, olive oil, citrus juices and Tabasco with 450ml/¾ pint/scant 2 cups chilled water until combined but still chunky. Season to taste and chill for 2–3 hours.

3 To make the croûtons, rub the bread slices with the garlic clove. Cube the bread, put in a sealable plastic bag with the olive oil, and shake until it is coated with oil. Fry in a large non-stick frying pan over medium heat until crisp and golden.

4 Just before serving, make the avocado salsa. Halve the avocado, remove the stone, then peel and dice. Toss the avocado in the lemon juice to prevent browning. Mix with the cucumber and chilli.

5 Ladle the soup into bowls, add the ice cubes, and top with a spoonful of avocado salsa. Garnish with the basil, and hand around the croûtons separately.

Nutritional information per portion: Energy 164kcal/685kJ; Protein 3.5g; Carbohydrate 16.6g, of which sugars 7.9g; Fat 9.7g, of which saturates 1.7g; Cholesterol 0mg; Calcium 40mg; Fibre 3.1g; Sodium 112mg.

Japanese-style noodle soup

This delicate, fragrant soup is flavoured with just a hint of chilli. It is best served as a light lunch or as a first course. According to Japanese etiquette, slurping while eating the soup is a sign of appreciation – so feel free to show your approval. Adding the vegetables very briefly at the end of cooking ensures they retain maximum nutrients.

SERVES 4

45ml/3 tbsp mugi miso powder

200g/7oz/scant 2 cups udon noodles,
   soba noodles or Chinese noodles

30ml/2 tbsp sake or dry sherry

15ml/1 tbsp rice or wine vinegar

45ml/3 tbsp Japanese soy sauce

115g/4oz asparagus tips or mangetouts
   (snow peas), thinly sliced diagonally

50g/2oz/scant 1 cup shiitake
   mushrooms, stalks removed
   and thinly sliced

1 carrot, sliced into julienne

3 spring onions (scallions), thinly
   sliced diagonally

salt and ground black pepper

5ml/1 tsp dried chilli flakes, to serve

1 Bring 1 litre/1³/₄ pints/4 cups water to the boil in a pan. Pour 150ml/¹/₄ pint/²/₃ cup of the boiling water over the miso powder, and stir until dissolved. Set aside.

2 Meanwhile, bring another large pan of lightly salted water to the boil, add the noodles and cook according to the packet instructions until just tender. Drain the noodles in a colander. Rinse under cold running water, then drain again.

3 Add the sake or sherry, rice or wine vinegar, and soy sauce to the pan of boiling water. Boil gently for 3 minutes or until the alcohol has evaporated, then reduce the heat and stir in the miso mixture.

4 Add the asparagus or mangetouts, mushrooms, carrot and spring onions, and simmer for about 2 minutes until the vegetables are just tender. Season to taste.

5 Divide the noodles among four warm bowls, and pour the soup over the top. Serve immediately, sprinkled with the chilli flakes.

Nutritional information per portion: Energy 223kcal/942kJ; Protein 7.5g; Carbohydrate 40.9g, of which sugars 3.8g; Fat 3.4g, of which saturates 0.1g; Cholesterol 0mg; Calcium 29mg; Fibre 2.5g; Sodium 807mg.

Italian pea and basil soup

Plenty of crusty country bread is a must with this fresh-tasting soup made with nutrient-rich green peas and fragrant basil.

SERVES 4

75ml/5 tbsp olive oil
2 large onions, chopped
1 celery stick, chopped
1 carrot, chopped
1 garlic clove, finely chopped
400g/14oz/3¹⁄₂ cups frozen petits pois (baby peas)
900ml/1¹⁄₂ pints/3³⁄₄ cups vegetable stock
25g/1oz/1 cup fresh basil leaves, roughly torn,
    plus extra to garnish
salt and ground black pepper
freshly grated Parmesan cheese, to serve

1 Heat the oil in a large pan and add the onions, celery, carrot and garlic. Cover and cook over low heat for 45 minutes or until the vegetables are soft, stirring occasionally to prevent the vegetables sticking.

2 Add the peas and stock to the pan, and bring to the boil. Reduce the heat, add the basil and season to taste, then simmer for 10 minutes.

3 Purée the soup in a food processor or blender until smooth. Ladle into warm bowls, sprinkle with grated Parmesan and garnish with basil. Serve immediately.

VARIATION
Use fresh mint leaves in place of the basil.

Nutritional information per portion: Energy 261kcal/1078kJ; Protein 8.7g; Carbohydrate 22.9g, of which sugars 10.9g; Fat 15.7g, of which saturates 2.3g; Cholesterol 0mg; Calcium 73mg; Fibre 7.3g; Sodium 16mg.

Spiced red lentil and coconut soup

Hot and spicy, this substantial soup is almost a meal in itself. Serve with chunks of warmed naan bread or thick slices of toast, if you like.

SERVES 4

30ml/2 tbsp sunflower oil
2 red onions, finely chopped
1 fresh bird's-eye chilli, seeded and finely sliced
2 garlic cloves, chopped
2.5cm/1in piece of lemon grass, outer layers removed
    and inside finely sliced
200g/7oz/scant 1 cup red lentils, rinsed
5ml/1 tsp ground coriander
5ml/1 tsp paprika
400ml/14fl oz/1²⁄₃ cups coconut milk
juice of 1 lime
3 spring onions (scallions), chopped
20g/³⁄₄oz/scant 1 cup fresh coriander (cilantro), finely chopped
salt and ground black pepper

1 Heat the oil in a large pan and add the onions, chilli, garlic and lemon grass. Cook for 5 minutes or until the onions are soft but not browned, stirring occasionally.

2 Add the lentils and spices. Pour in the coconut milk and 900ml/1¹⁄₂ pints/3³⁄₄ cups water, and stir. Bring to the boil, stir, then reduce the heat and simmer for 40–45 minutes until the lentils are soft and mushy.

3 Add the lime juice, then add the spring onions and coriander, reserving a little of each for the garnish. Season to taste, then ladle into warm bowls. Garnish with the reserved spring onions and coriander. Serve immediately.

Nutritional information per portion: Energy 245kcal/1034kJ; Protein 12.9g; Carbohydrate 35.8g, of which sugars 8.1g; Fat 6.6g, of which saturates 1g; Cholesterol 0mg; Calcium 75mg; Fibre 3.2g; Sodium 131mg.

Hot-and-sour soup

This light and invigorating soup originates from Thailand. It is best served at the beginning of a Thai meal, to stimulate the appetite for the dishes that follow.

SERVES 4

2 carrots
900ml/1¹/₂ pints/3³/₄ cups
    vegetable stock
2 fresh Thai chillies, seeded and
    finely sliced
2 lemon grass stalks, outer leaves
    removed and each stalk cut into
    3 pieces
4 kaffir lime leaves
2 garlic cloves, finely chopped
4 spring onions (scallions), finely sliced
5ml/1 tsp sugar
juice of 1 lime
45ml/3 tbsp chopped fresh
    coriander (cilantro)
salt
130g/4¹/₂oz/1 cup Japanese tofu, sliced

1 To make carrot flowers, cut each carrot in half crossways, Using a sharp knife, cut four V-shaped channels lengthways, then slice into thin rounds.

2 Pour the stock into a large pan. Reserve 2.5ml/¹/₂ tsp of the chillies and add the rest to the pan with the lemon grass, lime leaves, garlic and half the spring onions. Bring to the boil, then reduce the heat and simmer for 20 minutes. Strain the stock and discard the flavourings.

3 Return the stock to the pan and add the reserved chillies and spring onions together with the sugar, lime juice, coriander and salt to taste. Simmer for 5 minutes, then add the carrot flowers and tofu. Cook for a further 2 minutes until the carrot is just tender. Serve hot.

COOK'S TIP
Kaffir lime leaves have a distinctive citrus flavour. The fresh or frozen leaves can be bought from Asian shops, and some supermarkets now sell them dried.

Nutritional information per portion: Energy 102kcal/429kJ; Protein 7.3g; Carbohydrate 7.3g, of which sugars 0.3g; Fat 5.1g, of which saturates 1g; Cholesterol 44mg; Calcium 135mg; Fibre 0g; Sodium 208mg.

Roasted root vegetable soup

Roasting the vegetables gives this winter soup a wonderful depth of flavour. You can adapt the quantities, if you wish, or use other vegetables, depending on what's in season.

SERVES 6

50ml/2fl oz/¼ cup olive oil
1 small butternut squash, peeled,
    seeded and cubed
2 carrots, cut into thick rounds
1 large parsnip, cubed
1 small swede (rutabaga), cubed
2 leeks, thickly sliced
1 onion, quartered
3 bay leaves
4 fresh thyme sprigs, plus extra to garnish
3 fresh rosemary sprigs
1.2 litres/2 pints/5 cups vegetable stock
salt and ground black pepper
sour cream, to serve

1 Preheat the oven to 200°C/400°F/Gas 6. Put the olive oil in a large bowl. Add the prepared vegetables and toss until coated in the oil.

2 Spread out the vegetables in a single layer on one large or two small baking sheets. Tuck the bay leaves and thyme and rosemary sprigs among the vegetables. Roast the vegetables for about 50 minutes until tender, turning them occasionally to make sure that they brown evenly. Remove from the oven, discard the herbs and transfer the vegetables to a large pan.

3 Pour the stock into the pan with the vegetables and bring to the boil. Reduce the heat, season to taste, and simmer for 10 minutes. Transfer the soup to a food processor or blender (or use a hand-held blender), and purée for a few minutes until thick and smooth.

4 Return the soup to the pan to heat through. Check the seasoning and adjust if needed. Serve hot in warm bowls, with each serving topped with a swirl of sour cream and garnished with a sprig of thyme.

Nutritional information per portion: Energy 113kcal/473kJ; Protein 2.5g; Carbohydrate 12.4g, of which sugars 5.1g; Fat 6.3g, of which saturates 1g; Cholesterol 0mg; Calcium 50mg; Fibre 3.5g; Sodium 11mg.

Jerusalem artichoke soup with Gruyère toasts

Small, knobbly Jerusalem artichokes have a delicious mild nutty flavour. They make a remarkably good, creamy soup, which is great served with crunchy grilled Gruyère-topped toasts.

SERVES 4–6

30ml/2 tbsp olive oil
1 large onion, chopped
1 garlic clove, chopped
1 celery stick, chopped
675g/1½lb Jerusalem artichokes, peeled
    or scrubbed, and chopped
1.2 litres/2 pints/5 cups vegetable stock
300ml/½ pint/1¼ cups semi-skimmed
    (low-fat) milk
salt and ground black pepper

TO SERVE

8 slices French bread
115g/4oz/1 cup Gruyère cheese, grated

1 Heat the oil in a large pan. Add the onion, garlic and celery, and cook over medium heat for about 5 minutes until softened, stirring occasionally. Add the prepared Jerusalem artichokes, and cook for a further 5 minutes.

2 Add the stock, season to taste, and bring the soup to the boil. Reduce the heat and simmer for 20–25 minutes, stirring occasionally, until the artichokes are tender.

3 Blend or process the soup for a few minutes until smooth (or use a hand-held blender). Return the soup to the pan, stir in the milk and heat through gently for 2 minutes.

4 To make the Gruyère toasts, heat the grill (broiler) to high. Lightly toast the bread on one side. Sprinkle the other side with the Gruyère. Grill (broil) until the cheese melts and is golden. Ladle the soup into bowls and top with the Gruyère toasts.

Nutritional information per portion: Energy 340kcal/1427kJ; Protein 12.9g; Carbohydrate 46.5g, of which sugars 16g; Fat 12.3g, of which saturates 5.5g; Cholesterol 22mg; Calcium 313mg; Fibre 5g; Sodium 522mg.

Borlotti bean and pasta soup

A complete meal in a bowl, this is a version of the classic Italian soup pasta e fagioli. According to tradition, the person who finds the bay leaf is honoured with a kiss from the cook.

SERVES 4

1 onion, chopped
1 celery stick, chopped
2 carrots, chopped
75ml/5 tbsp olive oil
1 bay leaf
1 glass white wine (optional)
1.2 litres/2 pints/5 cups vegetable stock
400g/14oz/3 cups canned
   chopped tomatoes
175g/6oz/1¹/₂ cups pasta shapes, such as
   farfalle or conchiglie
400g/14oz/3 cups canned borlotti
   beans, drained
250g/9oz spinach, washed and thick
   stalks removed
salt and ground black pepper
50g/2oz/²/₃ cup freshly grated Parmesan
   cheese, to serve

1 Put the chopped onion, celery and carrots in a large pan with the olive oil. Cook over medium heat for 5 minutes or until the vegetables start to soften, stirring occasionally.

2 Add the bay leaf, wine (if using), stock and tomatoes to the pan. Bring to the boil, then reduce the heat and simmer the soup for 10 minutes until the vegetables are just tender.

3 Add the pasta and borlotti beans, and bring the soup back to the boil. Simmer for 8 minutes until the pasta is al dente, stirring frequently to prevent the pasta sticking.

4 Season to taste, add the spinach and cook for a further 2 minutes. Serve hot, sprinkled with the Parmesan.

Nutritional information per portion: Energy 321kcal/1363kJ; Protein 15g; Carbohydrate 57.8g, of which sugars 12.7g; Fat 5g, of which saturates 0.8g; Cholesterol 0mg; Calcium 166mg; Fibre 9.9g; Sodium 762mg.

Aubergine, smoked mozzarella and basil rolls

Grilled aubergine slices are stuffed with smoked mozzarella, tomato and fresh basil to make an attractive appetizer, or a light lunch if served with a green salad. These are also good barbecued.

SERVES 4

1 large aubergine (eggplant)
45ml/3 tbsp olive oil, plus extra for
    drizzling (optional)
165g/5½oz smoked mozzarella cheese,
    cut into 8 slices
2 ripe plum tomatoes, each cut into
    4 slices
8 large fresh basil leaves
balsamic vinegar, for drizzling (optional)
salt and ground black pepper

1 Cut the aubergine lengthways into 10 thin slices, discarding the two outermost slices. Sprinkle the other slices with salt, and leave for 20 minutes. Rinse well, then pat dry with kitchen paper.

2 Preheat the grill (broiler) and line the rack with foil. Place the dried aubergine slices on the grill rack, and brush liberally with oil. Grill (broil) for 8–10 minutes until tender and golden, turning once.

3 Remove the slices from the grill, then place a slice of mozzarella, a slice of tomato and a basil leaf in the centre of each one. Season to taste. Fold the aubergine over the filling, to form a parcel-like roll, and cook seam-side down under the grill until heated through and the mozzarella is starting to melt.

4 Serve the rolls drizzled with some extra olive oil and a little balsamic vinegar, if using.

Nutritional information per portion: Energy 196kcal/814kJ; Protein 8.5g; Carbohydrate 2.7g, of which sugars 2.6g; Fat 17g, of which saturates 7g; Cholesterol 24mg; Calcium 158mg; Fibre 1.5g; Sodium 169mg.

Creamy lemon Puy lentils

Tiny green Puy lentils have a good nutty flavour and, combined with lemon juice and crème fraîche, make a delicious, slightly tangy base for poached eggs.

SERVES 4

250g/9oz/generous 1 cup Puy lentils
1 bay leaf
30ml/2 tbsp olive oil
4 spring onions (scallions), sliced
2 large garlic cloves, chopped
15ml/1 tbsp Dijon mustard
finely grated rind and juice of
    1 large lemon
4 ripe plum tomatoes, seeded
    and diced
4 eggs
60ml/4 tbsp crème fraîche
salt and ground black pepper
30ml/2 tbsp chopped fresh flat leaf
    parsley, to garnish

1 Put the lentils and bay leaf in a pan, cover with cold water and bring to the boil. Reduce the heat and simmer, partially covered, for 25 minutes or until the lentils are tender. Stir occasionally, adding more water if necessary. Drain.

2 Heat the oil in a heavy pan and fry the spring onions and garlic for 1 minute or until softened. Add the mustard, lemon rind and juice, and mix well. Stir in the tomatoes and season to taste.

3 Cook gently for 1–2 minutes until the tomatoes are heated through, but still retain their shape. Add a little water if the mixture becomes too dry.

4 Meanwhile, poach the eggs in a pan of barely simmering salted water. Add the lentils and crème fraîche to the tomato mixture, remove the bay leaf, and heat through for 1 minute.

5 Divide the lentils among the plates, top each portion with a poached egg and sprinkle with parsley. Serve.

Nutritional information per portion: Energy 398kcal/1671kJ; Protein 22.4g; Carbohydrate 39g, of which sugars 5.2g; Fat 18.2g, of which saturates 6.6g; Cholesterol 207mg; Calcium 80mg; Fibre 4.2g; Sodium 106mg.

Courgette, mushroom and pesto muffuletta

Grilled courgettes are layered with garlic mushrooms, creamy Italian Taleggio cheese and pesto in this very tasty picnic loaf. Chilling the loaf overnight allows the flavours to mingle.

SERVES 6

1 medium country-style loaf of Italian
    or French bread
3 courgettes (zucchini), sliced lengthways
45ml/3 tbsp olive oil
250g/9oz/3²/₃ cups brown cap (cremini)
    mushrooms, thickly sliced
1 garlic clove, chopped
5ml/1 tsp dried oregano
45ml/3 tbsp pesto
250g/9oz Taleggio cheese, rind removed,
    and sliced
50g/2oz/2 cups green salad leaves
salt and ground black pepper

1 Slice off the top third of the loaf and remove the inside of both the lid and base, leaving a thickness of about 1cm/1/2in around the edge. (Use the inside of the loaf to make breadcrumbs for another dish.)

2 Preheat the grill (broiler) to high, and line the rack with foil. Brush the courgettes with 15ml/1 tbsp of the olive oil. Grill (broil) for 8–10 minutes, turning them occasionally, until tender and browned. Meanwhile, heat the remaining oil in a frying pan. Add the mushrooms, garlic and oregano, and sauté for 3 minutes.

3 Arrange half the courgettes in the bottom of the loaf, then spread with 25ml/1¹/₂ tbsp of the pesto. Top with half the cheese and salad leaves and all the mushroom mixture. Add one more layer each of the remaining cheese, salad leaves and courgettes. Spread the remaining pesto over the inside of the bread lid. Place the lid on top of the loaf and press down gently.

4 Wrap the loaf in clear film (plastic wrap) and leave to cool. Chill for at least a few hours, preferably overnight. Serve cut into wedges.

Nutritional information per portion: Energy 488kcal/2045kJ; Protein 21.5g; Carbohydrate 43.3g, of which sugars 4.2g; Fat 25.7g, of which saturates 11.2g; Cholesterol 43mg; Calcium 460mg; Fibre 2.7g; Sodium 765mg.

Courgette fritters with chilli jam

Chilli jam is hot, sweet and sticky – rather like a thick chutney. It adds a piquancy to these light courgette fritters but is also delicious with pies or a chunk of cheese.

MAKES 12

450g/1lb/3½ cups coarsely grated
    courgettes (zucchini)
50g/2oz/²⁄₃ cup freshly grated Parmesan
    cheese
2 eggs, beaten
60ml/4 tbsp unbleached plain
    (all-purpose) flour
vegetable oil, for frying
salt and ground black pepper

FOR THE CHILLI JAM

75ml/3fl oz/5 tbsp olive oil
4 large onions, diced
4 garlic cloves, chopped
1–2 fresh Thai chillies, seeded and sliced
25g/1oz/2 tbsp soft dark brown sugar

1 First, make the chilli jam. Heat the oil in a frying pan until hot, then add the onions and garlic. Reduce the heat to low, then cook for 20 minutes, stirring frequently, until the onions are very soft and caramelized.

2 Leave the onion mixture to cool, then transfer to a food processor or blender. Add the chillies and sugar, and blend until smooth, then return the mixture to the pan. Cook for 10 minutes, stirring frequently, until the liquid evaporates and the mixture has the consistency of jam. Cool slightly.

3 To make the fritters, squeeze the courgettes in a dish towel to remove any excess water. Combine with the Parmesan, eggs, flour, salt and pepper.

4 Heat enough oil to cover the base of a large frying pan. Cook three fritters at a time, using 30ml/2 tbsp of batter for each one. Cook for 2–3 minutes on each side until golden; keep warm while you cook the remaining fritters. Drain on kitchen paper and serve warm with a spoonful of the chilli jam.

Nutritional information per portion: Energy 218kcal/903kJ; Protein 6.6g; Carbohydrate 14.9g, of which sugars 8.8g; Fat 15.1g, of which saturates 3.2g; Cholesterol 69mg; Calcium 118mg; Fibre 1.7g; Sodium 87mg.

Coriander omelette parcels with oriental vegetables

Stir-fried vegetables in black bean sauce make a remarkably good omelette filling, one which is quick and easy to prepare, as well as tasty and full of various vitamins and minerals.

SERVES 4

130g/4¹/₂oz broccoli, cut into small florets
30ml/2 tbsp groundnut (peanut) oil
1cm/¹/₂in piece of fresh root ginger,
    finely grated
1 large garlic clove, crushed
2 fresh red chillies, seeded and finely sliced
4 spring onions (scallions), sliced diagonally
175g/6oz/3 cups pak choi
    (bok choy), shredded
50g/2oz/2 cups fresh coriander (cilantro)
    leaves, plus extra to garnish
115g/4oz/¹/₂ cup beansprouts
45ml/3 tbsp black bean sauce
4 eggs
salt and ground black pepper

1 Blanch the broccoli in boiling salted water for 2 minutes, drain, then refresh under cold running water. Leave to drain.

2 Heat 15ml/1 tbsp of the oil in a frying pan or wok. Add the ginger, garlic and half the chilli, and stir-fry for 1 minute. Add the spring onions, broccoli and pak choi, and stir-fry for 2 minutes more, tossing constantly.

3 Chop three-quarters of the coriander and add to the frying pan or wok. Add the beansprouts and stir-fry for 1 minute. Add the black bean sauce and heat through for another minute. Remove from the heat and keep warm.

4 Whisk the eggs lightly with a fork and season well. Heat a little of the remaining oil in a small frying pan and add a quarter of the beaten egg. Swirl the egg until it covers the bottom of the pan, then scatter over a quarter of the reserved coriander leaves. Cook until set, turn out on to a plate, and keep warm while you make three more omelettes, adding more oil to the pan when necessary.

5 Spoon the vegetable stir-fry on to the omelettes and roll up. Cut in half crossways and serve garnished with extra coriander leaves and the remaining chilli.

Nutritional information per portion: Energy 174kcal/722kJ; Protein 10.6g; Carbohydrate 6.4g, of which sugars 5.5g; Fat 12.1g, of which saturates 2.7g; Cholesterol 190mg; Calcium 158mg; Fibre 3.1g; Sodium 324mg.

Falafel with tahini yogurt dip

Sesame seeds are used to give a crunchy coating to these spicy bean patties. Serve with the tahini yogurt dip and warm pitta bread as a light lunch or dinner dish.

SERVES 4

250g/9oz/1¹/₃ cups dried chickpeas
2 garlic cloves, crushed
1 fresh red chilli, seeded and finely sliced
5ml/1 tsp ground coriander
5ml/1 tsp ground cumin
15ml/1 tbsp chopped fresh mint
15ml/1 tbsp chopped fresh parsley
2 spring onions (scallions), finely chopped
1 large (US extra large) egg, beaten
sesame seeds, for coating
sunflower oil, for frying
salt and ground black pepper

FOR THE TAHINI YOGURT DIP
30ml/2 tbsp light tahini
200g/7oz/scant 1 cup natural (plain)
   live yogurt
5ml/1 tsp cayenne pepper, plus extra
   for sprinkling
15ml/1 tbsp chopped fresh mint
1 spring onion (scallion), finely sliced

1 Put the chickpeas in a bowl, cover with cold water and leave to soak overnight. Drain and rinse the chickpeas, then put in a pan and cover with cold water. Bring to the boil and boil rapidly for 10 minutes, then reduce the heat and simmer for 1¹/₂–2 hours until tender.

2 Meanwhile, make the tahini yogurt dip. Mix together the tahini, yogurt, 5ml/1 tsp cayenne pepper and mint in a small bowl. Sprinkle the spring onion, chopped mint and extra cayenne pepper on top, and chill.

3 To make the falafel, combine the chickpeas with the garlic, chilli, ground spices, herbs, spring onions and seasoning, then mix in the egg. Blend in a food processor until the mixture forms a coarse paste. If the paste seems too soft, chill for 30 minutes.

4 Form the chilled chickpea paste into 12 patties with your hands, then roll each one in the sesame seeds to coat thoroughly. Heat enough oil to cover the base of a large frying pan. Fry the falafel, in batches if necessary, for 6 minutes until golden brown, turning once.

Nutritional information per portion: Energy 314kcal/1313kJ; Protein 14.3g; Carbohydrate 23.8g, of which sugars 3.8g; Fat 18.7g, of which saturates 2.6g; Cholesterol 32mg; Calcium 237mg; Fibre 5.8g; Sodium 63mg.

Tortilla wrap with tabbouleh and guacamole

To be successful, this classic Middle Eastern salad needs spring onions, lemon juice, plenty of fresh herbs and lots of ground black pepper. It is best served at room temperature.

SERVES 4–6

175g/6oz/1 cup bulgur wheat
30ml/2 tbsp chopped fresh mint
30ml/2 tbsp chopped fresh
    flat leaf parsley
1 bunch spring onions (scallions)
    (about 6), sliced
1/2 cucumber, diced
50ml/2fl oz/1/4 cup extra virgin
    olive oil
juice of 1 large lemon
salt and ground black pepper
4 wheat tortillas, to serve
flat leaf parsley, to garnish (optional)

FOR THE GUACAMOLE

1 ripe avocado
1/2 fresh red chilli, seeded and sliced
1 garlic clove, crushed
1/2 red (bell) pepper, seeded and
    finely diced

1 To make the tabbouleh, put the bulgur wheat in a large heatproof bowl, and pour over enough boiling water to cover. Leave for 30 minutes until the grains are tender but still retain a little resistance to the bite. Drain thoroughly in a strainer, then transfer back into the bowl.

2 Add the mint, parsley, spring onions and cucumber to the bulgur wheat and mix thoroughly.

3 Blend together the olive oil and lemon juice, and pour over the tabbouleh, season and toss to mix. Chill for 30 minutes to allow the flavours to mingle.

4 To make the guacamole, halve, stone (pit), and peel the avocado, and cut into cubes. Put in a bowl, and add the lemon juice, chilli and garlic. Season to taste and mash with a fork to form a smooth paste. Stir in the red pepper.

5 Warm the tortillas in a dry frying pan, and serve either flat, folded or rolled up with the tabbouleh and guacamole. Garnish with parsley, if using.

Nutritional information per portion: Energy 259kcal/1081kJ; Protein 5.1g; Carbohydrate 35g, of which sugars 1.9g; Fat 11.5g, of which saturates 1.9g; Cholesterol 0mg; Calcium 55mg; Fibre 1.7g; Sodium 52mg.

Thai tempeh cakes with sweet dipping sauce

Made from soya beans, tempeh is similar to tofu, but has a nuttier taste. Here, it is combined with a fragrant blend of lemon grass, coriander and ginger, and formed into small patties.

MAKES 8

1 lemon grass stalk, outer leaves removed
    and inside finely chopped
2 garlic cloves, chopped
2 spring onions (scallions), finely chopped
2 shallots, finely chopped
2 fresh red chillies, seeded and
    finely chopped
2.5cm/1in piece of fresh root ginger,
    finely chopped
60ml/4 tbsp chopped fresh coriander
    (cilantro), plus extra to garnish
250g/9oz/2¼ cups tempeh, defrosted
    if frozen, sliced
15ml/1 tbsp lime juice
5ml/1 tsp caster (superfine) sugar

45ml/3 tbsp plain (all-purpose) flour
1 large (US extra large) egg, lightly beaten
vegetable oil, for frying
salt and ground black pepper

FOR THE DIPPING SAUCE
45ml/3 tbsp mirin
45ml/3 tbsp white wine vinegar
2 spring onions (scallions), finely sliced
15ml/1 tbsp sugar
2 fresh red chillies, finely chopped
30ml/2 tbsp chopped fresh
    coriander (cilantro)
a large pinch of salt

1 To make the dipping sauce, mix together the mirin, vinegar, spring onions, sugar, chillies, coriander and salt in a small bowl, and set aside.

2 In a blender or food processor, process the lemon grass, garlic, spring onions, shallots, chillies, ginger and coriander to a coarse paste. Add the tempeh, lime juice and sugar, then blend until combined. Season to taste, and add the flour and egg. Process again until the mixture forms a coarse, sticky paste.

3 Take one-eighth of the tempeh mixture at a time, and form into rounds with your hands – the mixture will be quite sticky.

4 Heat enough oil to cover the base of a large frying pan. Fry the tempeh cakes for 5–6 minutes, turning once, until golden. Drain on kitchen paper, and serve warm with the dipping sauce, garnished with the extra coriander.

Nutritional information per portion: Energy 77kcal/322kJ; Protein 4.6g; Carbohydrate 8.4g, of which sugars 3.8g; Fat 2.3g, of which saturates 0.4g; Cholesterol 24mg; Calcium 204mg; Fibre 1.1g; Sodium 16mg.

Main Dishes

Most of the recipes in this chapter are

carbohydrate-based, putting the focus

firmly on pulses, pasta and rice. Not only

are these foods filling, but they are also

packed with fibre, vitamins and minerals,

and supply valuable low-fat protein.

The selection of innovative vegetarian main

courses on offer is a great way to increase

your repertoire of vegetarian dishes and

bring new tastes to your table.

Roasted vegetables with salsa verde

There are endless variations of the Italian salsa verde, which means 'green sauce'. It is usually a tongue-tingling blend of fresh chopped herbs, garlic, olive oil, anchovies and capers. The simplified version given here, still a refreshingly tasty blend of tart and sweet, is served with roasted vegetables and a traditional rice and vermicelli dish from the island of Cyprus.

SERVES 4

3 courgettes (zucchini),
   sliced lengthways
1 large fennel bulb, cut into wedges
450g/1lb butternut squash,
   cut into 2cm/¾in chunks
12 shallots
2 red (bell) peppers, seeded and cut
   lengthways into thick slices
4 plum tomatoes, halved and seeded
45ml/3 tbsp olive oil
2 garlic cloves, crushed
5ml/1 tsp balsamic vinegar
salt and ground black pepper

FOR THE SALSA VERDE

45ml/3 tbsp chopped fresh mint
90ml/6 tbsp chopped fresh flat leaf parsley
15ml/1 tbsp Dijon mustard
juice of ½ lemon
30ml/2 tbsp olive oil

FOR THE RICE

15ml/1 tbsp vegetable or olive oil
75g/3oz/¾ cup vermicelli,
   broken into short lengths
225g/8oz/generous 1 cup long grain rice
900ml/1½ pints/3¾ cups vegetable stock

1 Preheat the oven to 220°C/425°F/Gas 7. To make the salsa verde, put all the ingredients, with the exception of the olive oil, in a food processor or blender. Blend to a coarse paste, then add the oil, a little at a time, until the mixture forms a smooth purée. Season to taste.

2 To roast the vegetables, toss the courgettes, fennel, squash, shallots, peppers and tomatoes in the olive oil, garlic and balsamic vinegar. Leave to stand for 10 minutes to allow the flavours to mingle.

3 Place all the vegetables – apart from the squash and tomatoes – on a baking sheet, brush with half the oil and vinegar mixture, and season.

4 Roast for 25 minutes, then remove the tray from the oven. Turn the vegetables over, and brush with the rest of the oil and vinegar mixture. Add the squash and tomatoes, and cook for a further 20–25 minutes until all the vegetables are tender and lightly blackened around the edges.

5 Meanwhile, prepare the rice. Heat the oil in a heavy pan. Add the vermicelli and fry for about 3 minutes until golden and crisp. Season to taste.

6 Rinse the rice under cold running water, then drain well and add to the vermicelli. Cook for 1 minute, stirring to coat it in the oil.

7 Pour in the vegetable stock, then cover the pan and cook for about 12 minutes until the liquid is absorbed. Stir the rice, then cover and leave to stand for 10 minutes. Serve the warm rice with the roasted vegetables, accompanied by a bowl of the salsa verde for spooning over the top.

Nutritional information per portion: Energy 556kcal/2314kJ; Protein 13.3g; Carbohydrate 83.5g, of which sugars 20.5g; Fat 18.9g, of which saturates 2.8g; Cholesterol 0mg; Calcium 173mg; Fibre 9.3g; Sodium 34mg.

Potato rösti and tofu with fresh tomato and ginger sauce

Although this dish features various components, it is not difficult to make, and the finished result is well worth the effort. Make sure that you marinate the tofu for at least an hour to allow it to absorb the flavours of the ginger, garlic and tamari. Serve with a mixed leaf salad, dressed with a splash each of toasted sesame oil and lime juice.

SERVES 4

425g/15oz/3³/₄ cups tofu, cut into
   1cm/¹/₂in cubes
4 large potatoes, about 900g/2lb total
   weight, peeled
sunflower oil, for frying
salt and ground black pepper
30ml/2 tbsp sesame seeds, toasted

FOR THE MARINADE

30ml/2 tbsp tamari or dark soy sauce
15ml/1 tbsp clear honey
2 garlic cloves, crushed
4 cm/1¹/₂ in piece fresh root ginger, grated
5ml/1 tsp toasted sesame oil

FOR THE SAUCE

15ml/1 tbsp olive oil
8 tomatoes, halved, seeded and chopped

1 Mix together all the marinade ingredients in a shallow dish and add the tofu. Spoon the marinade over the tofu and leave to marinate in the refrigerator for at least 1 hour. Turn the tofu occasionally in the marinade to allow the flavours to infuse.

2 To make the rösti, parboil the potatoes for 10–15 minutes until almost tender. Leave to cool, then grate coarsely. Season well. Preheat the oven to 200°C/400°F/Gas 6.

3 Using a slotted spoon, remove the tofu from the marinade and reserve the marinade. Spread out the tofu on a baking tray and bake for 20 minutes, turning occasionally, until golden and crisp on all sides.

4 Take a quarter of the potato mixture in your hands at a time and form into rough cakes.

5 Heat a frying pan with just enough oil to cover the base. Put the cakes in the frying pan and flatten the mixture, using your hands or a spatula to form rounds about 1cm/¹/₂in thick. Cook for about 6 minutes until golden and crisp underneath. Carefully turn over the rösti and cook them for a further 6 minutes until golden.

6 Meanwhile, make the sauce. Heat the oil in a pan, add the reserved marinade and the tomatoes, and cook for 2 minutes, stirring. Reduce the heat and simmer, covered, for 10 minutes, stirring occasionally, until the tomatoes break down. Press through a sieve (strainer) to make a smooth sauce.

7 To serve, place a rösti on each of four warm serving plates. Scatter the tofu on top, spoon over the tomato sauce and sprinkle with sesame seeds.

COOK'S TIP
Tamari is a thick, mellow-flavoured Japanese soy sauce. It is sold in Japanese food shops and large health food stores.

Nutritional information per portion: Energy 433kcal/1811kJ; Protein 15g; Carbohydrate 42.3g, of which sugars 8.6g; Fat 23.7g, of which saturates 3.3g; Cholesterol 0mg; Calcium 618mg; Fibre 4.6g; Sodium 46mg.

Thai vegetable curry and lemon grass rice

Fragrant jasmine rice, subtly flavoured with lemon grass and cardamom, is the perfect accompaniment to this richly spiced vegetable curry. Don't be put off by the long list of ingredients, as this curry is very simple to make.

SERVES 4

10ml/2 tsp vegetable oil
400ml/14fl oz/1²/₃ cups coconut milk
300ml/¹/₂ pint/1¹/₄ cups vegetable stock
225g/8oz new potatoes, halved
   or quartered, if large
130g/4¹/₂oz baby corn cobs
5ml/1 tsp golden caster (superfine) sugar
185g/6¹/₂oz broccoli florets
1 red (bell) pepper, seeded and
   sliced lengthways
115g/4oz spinach, tough stalks removed
   and shredded
30ml/2 tbsp chopped fresh
   coriander (cilantro)
salt and ground black pepper

FOR THE SPICE PASTE
1 fresh red chilli, seeded and chopped
3 fresh green chillies, seeded and chopped

1 lemon grass stalk, outer leaves removed
   and lower 5cm/2in finely chopped
2 shallots, chopped
finely grated rind of 1 lime
2 garlic cloves, chopped
5ml/1 tsp ground coriander
2.5ml/¹/₂ tsp ground cumin
1cm/¹/₂in fresh galangal, finely chopped
   or 2.5ml/¹/₂ tsp dried (optional)
30ml/2 tbsp chopped fresh
   coriander (cilantro)
15ml/1 tbsp chopped fresh coriander
   (cilantro) roots and stems (optional)

FOR THE RICE
225g/8oz/generous 1 cup jasmine rice, rinsed
1 lemon grass stalk, outer leaves removed
   and cut into 3 pieces
6 cardamom pods, bruised

1 To make the spice paste, put all the ingredients in a food processor or blender and blend to a coarse paste.

2 Heat the oil in a large heavy pan and fry the spice paste for 1–2 minutes, stirring constantly. Add the coconut milk and stock, and bring to the boil.

3 Reduce the heat, add the potatoes and simmer for 15 minutes. Add the baby corn and seasoning, then cook for 2 minutes.

4 Stir in the sugar, broccoli and red pepper, and cook for 2 minutes more until the vegetables are tender. Stir in the shredded spinach and half the fresh coriander. Cook for a further 2 minutes.

5 Meanwhile, prepare the rice. Tip the rinsed rice into a large pan and add the lemon grass and cardamom pods. Pour over 475ml/16fl oz/2 cups water.

6 Bring to the boil, then reduce the heat, cover, and cook for 10–15 minutes until the water is absorbed and the rice is tender and slightly sticky. Season with salt, leave to stand for 10 minutes, then use a fork to fluff up the grains.

7 Remove the spices and serve the rice with the curry, sprinkled with the remaining fresh coriander.

Nutritional information per portion: Energy 328kcal/1375kJ; Protein 9.9g; Carbohydrate 64.9g, of which sugars 11.1g; Fat 3.3g, of which saturates 0.6g; Cholesterol 0mg; Calcium 142mg; Fibre 4g; Sodium 535mg.

Lemon, thyme and aduki bean stuffed mushrooms with pine nut tarator

Portobello mushrooms have a rich flavour and meaty texture that go well with this fragrant herb and lemon stuffing. The garlicky pine nut tarator is a traditional Middle Eastern sauce.

SERVES 4–6

45ml/3 tbsp olive oil, plus extra for brushing
1 onion, finely chopped
2 garlic cloves, crushed
30ml/2 tbsp fresh chopped or 5ml/1 tsp
   dried thyme
8 large field mushrooms, such as portabello
   mushrooms, stalks finely chopped
400g/14oz/2 cups drained canned aduki
   beans, rinsed well and drained
50g/2oz/1 cup fresh wholemeal
   (whole-wheat) breadcrumbs
juice of 1 lemon

185g/6¹/₂oz/³/₄ cup goat's cheese, crumbled
salt and ground black pepper

FOR THE PINE NUT TARATOR
50g/2oz/¹/₂ cup pine nuts toasted
50g/2oz/1 cup cubed white bread
2 garlic cloves, chopped
200ml/7fl oz/1 cup semi-skimmed
   (low-fat) milk
45ml/3 tbsp olive oil
15ml/1 tbsp chopped fresh parsley,
   to garnish (optional)

1 Preheat the oven to 200°C/400°F/Gas 6. Heat the oil in a large heavy frying pan. Sauté the onion and garlic for 5 minutes until soft. Add the thyme and mushroom stalks. Cook for 3 minutes, stirring occasionally, until tender.

2 Stir in the beans, breadcrumbs and lemon juice, season well, then cook for 2 minutes until heated through. Mash two-thirds of the beans with a fork or potato masher, leaving the remaining beans whole.

3 Brush a baking dish and the base and sides of the mushrooms with oil, then top each one with a spoonful of the bean mixture. Place the mushrooms in the dish, cover with foil and bake for 20 minutes. Remove the foil. Top each mushroom with some of the goat's cheese, and bake for a further 15 minutes or until the cheese is melted and bubbly, and the mushrooms are tender.

4 To make the pine nut tarator, put all the ingredients, except the parsley, in a food processor or blender. Purée until smooth and creamy. Add more milk if the mixture appears too thick. Sprinkle with parsley, if using, and serve with the stuffed mushrooms.

Nutritional information per portion: Energy 406kcal/1694kJ; Protein 17.5g; Carbohydrate 25.9g, of which sugars 5.9g; Fat 26.6g, of which saturates 8g; Cholesterol 31mg; Calcium 159mg; Fibre 6.1g; Sodium 573mg.

Potato, red onion and feta frittata

This Italian omelette is cooked with vegetables and cheese, and is served flat, like its Spanish equivalent, the tortilla. Cut it into wedges and serve with crusty bread and a tomato salad.

SERVES 2–4

25ml/1½ tbsp olive oil
1 red onion, sliced
350g/12oz cooked new potatoes,
   halved or quartered, if large
6 eggs, lightly beaten
115g/4oz/1 cup feta cheese, diced
salt and ground black pepper

1 Heat the oil in a large heavy flameproof frying pan. Add the onion and sauté for 5 minutes until softened, stirring occasionally.

2 Add the potatoes and cook for a further 5 minutes until golden, stirring to prevent them sticking. Spread the mixture evenly over the base of the pan.

3 Preheat the grill (broiler) to high. Season the eggs, then pour the mixture over the onion and potatoes. Sprinkle the cheese on top. Cook over medium heat for 5–6 minutes until the eggs are just set and the bottom of the frittata is golden.

4 Place the pan under the preheated grill (protect the pan handle with a double layer of foil if it is not flameproof), and cook the top of the omelette for about 3 minutes until it is set and lightly golden. Serve warm or cold, cut into wedges.

HEALTH BENEFIT
Eggs are a source of vitamin B12, which is vital for the nervous system and red blood cells.

Nutritional information per portion: Energy 289kcal/1207kJ; Protein 15.5g; Carbohydrate 15.7g, of which sugars 2.4g; Fat 18.9g, of which saturates 7g; Cholesterol 306mg; Calcium 155mg; Fibre 1.1g; Sodium 529mg.

Teriyaki soba noodles with tofu and asparagus

You can, of course, buy ready-made teriyaki sauce, but it is easy to prepare at home. Japanese soba noodles are made from buckwheat flour, which gives them a unique texture and colour.

SERVES 4

350g/12oz soba noodles
30ml/2 tbsp toasted sesame oil
200g/7oz/1/2 bunch fresh asparagus tips
30ml/2 tbsp groundnut (peanut)
   or vegetable oil
225g/8oz block of firm tofu
2 spring onions (scallions), cut diagonally
1 carrot, cut into matchsticks
2.5ml/1/2 tsp chilli flakes
15ml/1 tbsp sesame seeds
salt and ground black pepper

FOR THE TERIYAKI SAUCE

60ml/4 tbsp dark soy sauce
60ml/4 tbsp Japanese sake or dry sherry
60ml/4 tbsp mirin
5ml/1 tsp caster (superfine) sugar

1 Cook the noodles according to the instructions on the packet, then drain and rinse under cold running water. Set aside.

2 Heat the sesame oil in a griddle pan or a baking tray placed under the grill (broiler) until very hot. Reduce the heat to medium, then cook the asparagus for 8–10 minutes, turning frequently, until tender and browned. Set aside.

3 Meanwhile, heat the groundnut or vegetable oil in a wok or large frying pan until very hot. Add the tofu and fry for 8–10 minutes until golden, turning occasionally to crisp all sides. Carefully remove from the wok or pan and leave to drain on kitchen paper. Cut the tofu into 1cm/1/2 in slices.

4 To prepare the teriyaki sauce, mix all the ingredients together, then heat the sauce in the wok or frying pan. Toss in the noodles and stir to coat them well. Heat through for 1–2 minutes, then spoon into warmed individual serving bowls with the tofu and asparagus. Sprinkle the spring onions and carrot on top, then sprinkle with the chilli flakes and sesame seeds. Serve immediately.

Nutritional information per portion: Energy 476kcal/2007kJ; Protein 17g; Carbohydrate 71.6g, of which sugars 6.5g; Fat 13.7g, of which saturates 1g; Cholesterol 0mg; Calcium 332mg; Fibre 4.1g; Sodium 1081mg.

Broccoli, chilli and artichoke pasta

Chilli flakes add a fiery touch to this southern Italian dish that is simplicity itself. The two staples, pasta and fresh vegetables, provide a balance of carbohydrates, vitamins and minerals.

SERVES 4–6

350g/12oz/3 cups dried gnocchi pasta
300g/11oz broccoli florets
90ml/6 tbsp olive oil
1 large garlic clove, crushed
2.5–5ml/1/2–1 tsp dried chilli flakes
185g/61/2oz/11/2 cups artichoke hearts
    in oil, drained
salt and ground black pepper
15ml/1 tbsp chopped fresh flat leaf
    parsley, to garnish
freshly grated Pecorino cheese,
    to garnish (optional)

1 Cook the pasta in a large pan of boiling salted water, according to the instructions on the packet, until al dente. Add the broccoli for the last 3 minutes of cooking time. Drain, reserving a little of the cooking water.

2 Meanwhile, heat the olive oil in a large heavy pan and sauté the garlic and chilli flakes for 1 minute.

3 Add the pasta, broccoli and artichoke hearts, and cook for 2 minutes until hot. Add a little of the reserved pasta water if the mixture seems a little dry. Season, and sprinkle with the parsley and Pecorino, if using. Serve hot.

HEALTH BENEFITS
• *Broccoli provides valuable amounts of calcium, vitamin C, folic acid, zinc and iron.*
• *The heart, blood and immune system will all benefit from the combination of garlic, chilli and broccoli in this dish.*

Nutritional information per portion: Energy 317kcal/1334kJ; Protein 9.4g; Carbohydrate 44.4g, of which sugars 3g; Fat 12.6g, of which saturates 1.8g; Cholesterol 0mg; Calcium 55mg; Fibre 3.3g; Sodium 24mg.

Rustic buckwheat pasta and Fontina cheese bake

Characteristic of the mountain regions of northern Italy, this bake is a spicy combination of nutty-flavoured buckwheat pasta, vegetables and Fontina cheese.

SERVES 6

2 potatoes, cubed
225g/8oz/2 cups buckwheat pasta
    shapes, such as spirals
275g/10oz/2¹/₂ cups Savoy
    cabbage, shredded
45ml/3 tbsp olive oil, plus extra
    for greasing
1 onion, chopped
2 leeks, sliced
2 garlic cloves, chopped
175g/6oz/2¹/₂ cups brown cap
    (cremini) mushrooms, sliced
5ml/1 tsp caraway seeds
5ml/1 tsp cumin seeds
150ml/¹/₄ pint/²/₃ cup vegetable stock
150g/5oz/1¹/₄ cups Fontina
    cheese, diced
25g/1oz/¹/₄ cup walnuts,
    roughly chopped
salt and ground black pepper

1 Preheat the oven to 200°C/400°F/Gas 6, and grease a deep baking dish. Cook the potatoes in boiling, salted water for 8–10 minutes until tender, then drain and set aside.

2 Meanwhile, cook the pasta in boiling, salted water according to the packet instructions until it is only just cooked and very al dente. Add the cabbage in the last minute of cooking time. Drain, then rinse under cold running water.

3 Heat the olive oil in a large heavy pan and fry the onion and leeks for 5 minutes until softened. Add the garlic and mushrooms, and cook for a further 3 minutes until tender, stirring occasionally. Stir in the spices and cook for 1 minute, stirring.

4 Add the cooked potatoes, pasta and cabbage, and stir to combine, then season well. Spoon the mixture into the baking dish. Pour the stock over the vegetables, then sprinkle with the cheese and walnuts. Bake for 15 minutes or until the cheese is melted and bubbling.

Nutritional information per portion: Energy 328kcal/1379kJ; Protein 11.5g; Carbohydrate 40.1g, of which sugars 6.1g; Fat 14.6g, of which saturates 4.6g; Cholesterol 18mg; Calcium 141mg; Fibre 3.9g; Sodium 374mg.

Cheat's lasagne with mixed mushrooms

This simple-to-assemble vegetarian version of lasagne requires neither baking nor the lengthy preparation of various sauces and fillings, but is no less delicious.

SERVES 4

40g/1¹/₂oz/²/₃ cup dried porcini mushrooms
50ml/2fl oz/¹/₄ cup olive oil
1 large garlic clove, chopped
375g/13oz/5 cups mixed mushrooms,
    including brown cap, field (portabello),
    shiitake and wild varieties, roughly sliced
175ml/6fl oz/³/₄ cup dry white wine

90ml/6 tbsp canned chopped tomatoes
2.5ml/¹/₂ tsp sugar
8 fresh lasagne sheets
40g/1¹/₂oz/¹/₂ cup freshly grated
    Parmesan cheese
salt and ground black pepper
fresh basil leaves, to garnish

1 Put the porcini mushrooms in a bowl and cover with boiling water. Leave to soak for 15 minutes, then drain and rinse.

2 Heat the olive oil in a large heavy frying pan and sauté the soaked mushrooms over high heat for 5 minutes until the edges are slightly crisp. Reduce the heat, then add the garlic and fresh mushrooms, and sauté for a further 5 minutes until tender, stirring occasionally.

3 Add the wine and cook for 5–7 minutes until reduced. Stir in the tomatoes and sugar, and season to taste. Cook over medium heat for about 5 minutes until thickened.

4 Meanwhile, cook the lasagne according to the instructions on the packet until al dente. Drain lightly – the pasta should still be moist.

5 To serve, spoon a little of the sauce on to each of four warm serving plates. Place a sheet of lasagne on top, and spoon a quarter of the remaining mushroom sauce over each serving. Sprinkle with some Parmesan and top with another pasta sheet. Sprinkle with black pepper and more Parmesan, and garnish with basil leaves. Serve immediately.

HEALTH BENEFIT
Shiitake mushrooms contain zinc, iron and potassium, and are reputed to help reduce the risk of heart disease.

Nutritional information per portion: Energy 331kcal/1397kJ; Protein 13.3g; Carbohydrate 47.7g, of which sugars 3.2g; Fat 7.9g, of which saturates 2.7g; Cholesterol 10mg; Calcium 147mg; Fibre 3.1g; Sodium 119mg.

Fresh herb risotto

Distinctive, nutty-flavoured wild rice is combined with arborio rice to create this creamy, comforting risotto. An aromatic blend of fresh herbs adds a light summery flavour.

SERVES 4

90g/3¹/₂oz/¹/₂ cup wild rice
15ml/1 tbsp butter
15ml/1 tbsp olive oil
1 small onion, finely chopped
450g/1lb/2¹/₂ cups arborio rice
300ml/¹/₂ pint/1¹/₄ cups dry white wine
1.2 litres/2 pints/5 cups vegetable stock
45ml/3 tbsp chopped fresh oregano
45ml/3 tbsp chopped fresh chives
60ml/4 tbsp chopped fresh flat
    leaf parsley
60ml/4 tbsp chopped fresh basil
75g/3oz/1 cup freshly grated
    Parmesan cheese
salt and ground black pepper

1 Cook the wild rice in boiling salted water according to the instructions on the packet.

2 Heat the butter and oil in a large heavy pan. When the butter has melted, add the onion and cook for 3 minutes. Add the arborio rice and cook for 2 minutes, stirring to coat the grains in the oil mixture.

3 Pour in the wine and bring to the boil. Reduce the heat and cook for 10 minutes until the wine is absorbed. Add the stock, a little at a time, and simmer, stirring, for 20–25 minutes until the liquid is absorbed and the rice is creamy. Season well.

4 Add the herbs and wild rice; heat for 2 minutes, stirring frequently. Stir in two-thirds of the Parmesan and continue to cook until melted. Serve the risotto sprinkled with the remaining Parmesan.

Nutritional information per portion: Energy 632kcal/2637kJ; Protein 18g; Carbohydrate 109.3g, of which sugars 1.2g; Fat 12.8g, of which saturates 6.2g; Cholesterol 27mg; Calcium 280mg; Fibre 0.8g; Sodium 232mg.

Rice and beans with avocado salsa

Mexican-style rice and beans make a delicious supper dish. Spoon on to tortillas and serve with a tangy salsa. Alternatively, serve as an accompaniment to a spicy stew.

SERVES 4

4 tomatoes, halved and seeded
2 garlic cloves, chopped
1 onion, sliced
45ml/3 tbsp olive oil
225g/8oz/generous 1 cup long grain
   brown rice, rinsed
600ml/1 pint/2¹/₂ cups vegetable stock
75g/3oz/¹/₂ cup canned kidney beans,
   rinsed and drained
2 carrots, diced
75g/3oz/³/₄ cup green beans
salt and ground black pepper
4 wheat tortillas and sour cream, to serve

FOR THE AVOCADO SALSA

1 avocado
juice of 1 lime
1 small red onion, diced
1 small red chilli, seeded and chopped
15ml/1 tbsp chopped fresh
   coriander (cilantro)

1 Heat the grill (broiler) to high. Put the tomatoes, garlic and onion on a baking tray. Toss in 15ml/1 tbsp of the olive oil. Grill (broil) for 10 minutes or until the tomatoes and onions are softened, turning once. Set aside to cool.

2 Heat the remaining oil in a pan. Add the rice and cook for 2 minutes, stirring, until light golden. Blend or process the cooled tomatoes and onion to a purée. Add to the rice and cook for 2 minutes more, stirring frequently. Pour in the stock, cover and cook gently, for 20 minutes, stirring occasionally.

3 Reserve 30ml/2 tbsp of the kidney beans for the salsa. Add the rest to the stock mixture with the carrots and green beans, and cook for 10 minutes until the vegetables are tender. Season well. Remove the pan from the heat and leave to stand, covered, for 15 minutes.

4 To make the salsa, cut the avocado in half and remove the stone (pit). Peel and dice the flesh, then toss in the lime juice. Add the onion, chilli, coriander and reserved kidney beans, and season with salt. To serve, spoon the hot rice and beans on to warm tortillas. Hand around the salsa and sour cream.

Nutritional information per portion: Energy 390kcal/1642kJ; Protein 8g; Carbohydrate 58.4g, of which sugars 9g; Fat 15.4g, of which saturates 2.8g; Cholesterol 0mg; Calcium 49mg; Fibre 5.8g; Sodium 24mg.

Jamaican black bean pot

Molasses imparts the rich flavour of treacle to the spicy sauce, which incorporates a stunning mix of black beans, vibrant red and yellow peppers and orange butternut squash. This dish is delicious served with cornbread or plain rice to make a substantial, nutritionally balanced meal.

SERVES 4

225g/8oz/1¼ cups dried black beans
1 bay leaf
30ml/2 tbsp vegetable oil
1 large onion, chopped
1 garlic clove, chopped
5ml/1 tsp English mustard powder
15ml/1 tbsp blackstrap molasses
30ml/2 tbsp soft dark brown sugar
5ml/1 tsp dried thyme

2.5ml/½ tsp dried chilli flakes
5ml/1 tsp vegetable bouillon powder
1 red (bell) pepper, seeded and diced
1 yellow (bell) pepper, seeded and diced
675g/1½lb/5¼ cups butternut squash
    or pumpkin, seeded and cut into
    1cm/½in dice
salt and ground black pepper
sprigs of thyme, to garnish

1 Soak the dried black beans overnight in plenty of water, then drain and rinse well.

2 Put the soaked beans in a large pan, cover with fresh water and add the bay leaf. Bring to the boil, then boil rapidly for 10 minutes. Reduce the heat, cover, and simmer for 30 minutes until tender. Drain, reserving the cooking water. Preheat the oven to 180°C/350°F/Gas 4.

3 Heat the oil in the pan and sauté the onion and garlic for about 5 minutes until softened, stirring occasionally.

4 Add the mustard powder, molasses, sugar, thyme and chilli, and cook for 1 minute, stirring. Stir in the black beans and spoon the mixture into a flameproof casserole.

5 Add enough water to the reserved cooking liquid to make 400ml/14fl oz/1⅔ cups, then mix in the bouillon powder and pour into the casserole. Bake for 25 minutes.

6 Add the peppers and squash or pumpkin, and mix well. Cover, and bake for a further 45 minutes until the vegetables are tender. Serve garnished with thyme.

Nutritional information per portion: Energy 297kcal/1252kJ; Protein 15.1g; Carbohydrate 45.9g, of which sugars 20.3g; Fat 7.1g, of which saturates 1g; Cholesterol 0mg; Calcium 129mg; Fibre 12.6g; Sodium 16mg.

Aubergine and chickpea tagine

Spiced with coriander, cumin, cinnamon, turmeric and a dash of chilli sauce, this Moroccan-style stew makes a filling main course dish when served with couscous.

SERVES 4

1 small aubergine (eggplant)
2 courgettes (zucchini), thickly sliced
60ml/4 tbsp olive oil
1 large onion, sliced
2 garlic cloves, chopped
150g/5oz/2 cups brown cap (cremini)
    mushrooms, halved
15ml/1 tbsp ground coriander
10ml/2 tsp cumin seeds
15ml/1 tbsp ground cinnamon
10ml/2 tsp ground turmeric
225g/8oz new potatoes, quartered
600ml/1 pint/2¹/₂ cups passata
    (bottled strained tomatoes)
15ml/1 tbsp tomato purée (paste)
15ml/1 tbsp chilli sauce
75g/3oz/¹/₃ cup unsulphured
    ready-to-eat dried apricots
400g/14oz/3 cups canned chickpeas,
    drained and rinsed
salt and ground black pepper
15ml/1 tbsp chopped fresh coriander
    (cilantro), to garnish

1 Cut the aubergine into 1cm/¹/₂in dice. Sprinkle salt over the aubergine and courgettes. Leave for 30 minutes. Rinse and pat dry with a dish towel. Heat the grill (broiler) to high. Arrange the aubergine and courgettes on a baking sheet. Toss in 30ml/2 tbsp of the olive oil. Grill (broil) for 20 minutes, turning occasionally, until tender and golden.

2 Meanwhile, heat the remaining oil in a large heavy pan and cook the onion and garlic for about 5 minutes until softened, stirring occasionally. Add the mushrooms and sauté for 3 minutes until tender. Add the spices and cook for 1 minute more, stirring, to allow the flavours to mingle.

3 Add the potatoes and cook for about 3 minutes, stirring. Pour in the passata, tomato purée and 150ml/¹/₄ pint/²/₃ cup water. Cover, and cook for 10 minutes or until the sauce begins to thicken.

4 Add the aubergine, courgettes, chilli sauce, apricots and chickpeas. Season to taste, and cook, partially covered, for 10–15 minutes until the potatoes are tender. Add a little extra water if the tagine becomes too dry. To serve, sprinkle with the chopped fresh coriander and serve hot.

Nutritional information per portion: Energy 359kcal/1509kJ; Protein 13.9g; Carbohydrate 45g, of which sugars 19.3g; Fat 15g, of which saturates 2.1g; Cholesterol 0mg; Calcium 123mg; Fibre 9.7g; Sodium 597mg.

Tomato and lentil dhal with toasted almonds

Richly flavoured with spices, coconut milk and tomatoes, this lentil dish makes a filling main course. Warm naan bread and natural yogurt are all that are needed as accompaniments.

SERVES 4

30ml/2 tbsp vegetable oil

1 large onion, finely chopped

3 garlic cloves, chopped

1 carrot, diced

10ml/2 tsp cumin seeds

10ml/2 tsp yellow mustard seeds

2.5cm/1in piece of fresh root
   ginger, grated

10ml/2 tsp ground turmeric

5ml/1 tsp mild chilli powder

5ml/1 tsp garam masala

225g/8oz/1 cup split red lentils

400ml/14fl oz/1²/₃ cups coconut milk

5 tomatoes, peeled, seeded and chopped

juice of 2 limes

60ml/4 tbsp chopped fresh
   coriander (cilantro)

salt and ground black pepper

25g/1oz/¹/₄ cup flaked (sliced) almonds,
   toasted, to serve

1 Heat the oil in a large heavy pan. Sauté the onion for 5 minutes until softened, stirring occasionally. Add the garlic, carrot, cumin and mustard seeds, and ginger. Cook for 5 minutes, stirring, until the seeds begin to pop and the carrot softens slightly.

2 Stir in the ground turmeric, chilli powder and garam masala, and cook for 1 minute or until the flavours begin to mingle and become aromatic, stirring to prevent the spices burning.

3 Add the lentils and 400ml/14fl oz/1²/₃ cups water. Tip in the coconut milk and tomatoes, and season well. Bring to the boil, then reduce the heat and simmer, covered, for about 45 minutes, stirring occasionally to prevent the lentils sticking.

4 Stir in the lime juice and 45ml/3 tbsp of the fresh coriander, then check the seasoning. Cook for a further 15 minutes until the lentils soften and become tender. To serve, sprinkle with the remaining coriander and the flaked almonds, and serve hot.

Nutritional information per portion: Energy 326kcal/1372kJ; Protein 16.9g; Carbohydrate 43.8g, of which sugars 11.5g; Fat 10.5g, of which saturates 1.2g; Cholesterol 0mg; Calcium 102mg; Fibre 6.6g; Sodium 44mg.

Tarts, Pies and Pizzas

Whether you are looking for a hearty winter pie or a light summer tart, you'll find a slice of something special in this chapter. Try treats such as Wild Mushroom and Fontina Tarts or a Summer Herb Ricotta Flan with a spoonful of tapenade. Fed up with vegetarian lasagne? Here you'll find a tasty alternative. Or if pizza's on your mind, try a yeast-free polenta pan pizza topped with garlicky mushrooms.

Caramelized onion tart

Served warm with a mixed-leaf salad, this classic and elegant French tart makes a perfect light summer lunch. Caramelizing the onions before baking brings out their natural sweetness.

SERVES 6

15ml/1 tbsp unsalted butter
15ml/1 tbsp olive oil
500g/1¼lb onions, sliced
large pinch of ground nutmeg
5ml/1 tsp soft dark brown sugar
2 eggs
150ml/¼ pint/⅔ cup single
   (light) cream
50g/2oz/½ cup Gruyère cheese, grated
salt and ground black pepper

FOR THE PASTRY

75g/3oz/⅔ cup unbleached plain
   (all-purpose) flour
75g/3oz/⅔ cup wholemeal
   (whole-wheat) flour
75g/3oz/6 tbsp unsalted butter
1 egg yolk

1 To make the pastry, rub together the plain and wholemeal flours and butter until the mixture resembles fine breadcrumbs. Mix in the egg yolk and enough cold water to form a dough. Turn out the dough on to a lightly floured work surface, and form into a smooth ball, then wrap in clear film (plastic wrap) and chill for about 30 minutes.

2 Meanwhile, make the filling. Heat the butter and oil in a large heavy frying pan. Cook the onions over low heat for 30 minutes, stirring often, until very soft and translucent. Stir in the nutmeg, sugar and seasoning. Cook for a further 5 minutes until golden and caramelized. Set aside to cool slightly.

3 Preheat the oven to 220°C/425°F/Gas 7. Lightly grease a loose-based 35 x 12cm/14 x 4½in fluted baking tin (pan). Roll out the pastry and use to line the prepared tin. Trim the top, then chill for 20 minutes.

4 Prick the pastry base with a fork, then line with baking parchment and baking beans. Bake blind for 10 minutes until lightly golden. Remove the paper and beans, then spoon the onions into the pie shells. Beat the eggs with the cream, then add the cheese and season to taste. Pour the mixture over the onions and bake for 30 minutes until set and golden. Serve warm.

Nutritional information per portion: Energy 905kcal/3748kJ; Protein 15g; Carbohydrate 36.7g, of which sugars 3g; Fat 78.2g, of which saturates 47.1g; Cholesterol 384mg; Calcium 272mg; Fibre 1.6g; Sodium 383mg.

Wild mushroom and Fontina tarts

Italian Fontina cheese gives these tarts a creamy, nutty flavour. Serve them warm with a simple salad of peppery rocket leaves, the ideal complement to the richness of the cheese.

SERVES 4

25g/1oz/¹⁄₂ cup dried wild mushrooms
30ml/2 tbsp olive oil
1 red onion, chopped
2 garlic cloves, chopped
30ml/2 tbsp medium-dry sherry
1 egg
120ml/4fl oz/¹⁄₂ cup single (light) cream
25g/1oz Fontina cheese, thinly sliced
salt and ground black pepper
rocket (arugula) leaves, to serve

FOR THE PASTRY

115g/4oz/1 cup wholemeal
   (whole-wheat) flour
50g/2oz/4 tbsp unsalted butter
25g/1oz/¹⁄₄ cup walnuts, roasted
   and ground
1 egg, lightly beaten

1 To make the pastry, rub the flour and butter together until the mixture resembles fine breadcrumbs. Stir in the walnuts, add the egg and mix to form a soft dough. Wrap in clear film (plastic wrap) and chill for about 30 minutes. Meanwhile, soak the dried mushrooms in 300ml/¹⁄₂ pint/1¹⁄₄ cups boiling water for 30 minutes. Drain and reserve the liquid.

2 Heat the oil in a frying pan. Fry the onion for 5 minutes. Add the garlic and fry for 2 minutes, stirring. Add the soaked mushrooms. Cook for 7 minutes over high heat until the edges are crisp. Add the sherry and reserved liquid. Cook for about 10 minutes until the liquid evaporates. Season. Leave to cool.

3 Preheat the oven to 200°C/400°F/Gas 6. Lightly grease four 10cm/4in tart tins (pans). Roll out the pastry on a lightly floured work surface and use to line the tart tins. Prick the pastry, line with baking parchment and baking beans, and bake blind for 10 minutes. Remove the beans and parchment.

4 Whisk the egg and cream to mix, add to the mushroom mixture, then season to taste. Spoon into the pie shells, top with cheese slices and bake for 18 minutes until the filling is set. Serve warm with rocket.

Nutritional information per portion: Energy 409kcal/1701kJ; Protein 10.2g; Carbohydrate 21.9g, of which sugars 2.3g; Fat 31g, of which saturates 13.4g; Cholesterol 143mg; Calcium 121mg; Fibre 2.3g; Sodium 199mg.

Red onion and goat's cheese pastries

These attractive little pastries couldn't be easier to make. Ring the changes by spreading the pastry base with pesto or tapenade before you add the filling.

SERVES 4

15ml/1 tbsp olive oil
450g/1lb/1½ cups red onions, sliced
30ml/2 tbsp fresh thyme or
    10ml/2 tsp dried
15ml/1 tbsp balsamic vinegar
425g/15oz packet ready-rolled
    puff pastry
115g/4oz/½ cup goat's cheese, cubed
1 egg, beaten
salt and ground black pepper
fresh thyme sprigs, to garnish (optional)
mixed green salad leaves, to serve

1 Heat the oil in a large heavy frying pan, add the onions and fry over a gentle heat for 10 minutes or until softened, stirring occasionally to prevent them browning. Add the thyme, seasoning and balsamic vinegar, and cook for a further 5 minutes. Remove the pan from the heat and leave to cool.

2 Preheat the oven to 220°C/425°F/Gas 7. Unroll the pastry and, using a 15cm/6in plate as a guide, cut four rounds. Place the pastry rounds on a dampened baking sheet and, using the point of a knife, score a border, 2cm/¾in inside the edge of each round.

3 Divide the onions among the pastry rounds and top with the goat's cheese. Brush the edge of each round with a little beaten egg and bake for 25–30 minutes until golden. Garnish with thyme sprigs, if using, before serving warm with mixed salad leaves.

Nutritional information per portion: Energy 554kcal/2308kJ; Protein 13.5g; Carbohydrate 48.5g, of which sugars 8g; Fat 36.4g, of which saturates 5.6g; Cholesterol 27mg; Calcium 128mg; Fibre 1.6g; Sodium 506mg.

Summer herb ricotta flan

Simple to make and infused with aromatic herbs, this delicate flan with its robust tapenade accompaniment makes a delightful lunch dish – particularly served alfresco.

SERVES 4

olive oil, for greasing and glazing
800g/1lb 11oz/3¹/₂ cups ricotta cheese
75g/3oz/1 cup finely grated
    Parmesan cheese
3 eggs, separated
60ml/4 tbsp torn fresh basil leaves
60ml/4 tbsp snipped fresh chives
45ml/3 tbsp fresh oregano leaves
2.5ml/¹/₂ tsp salt
2.5ml/¹/₂ tsp paprika, plus extra
    for sprinkling
ground black pepper
fresh herb leaves, to garnish

FOR THE TAPENADE

400g/14oz/3¹/₂ cups pitted black olives,
    rinsed and halved, reserving a few
    whole to garnish (optional)
5 garlic cloves, crushed
75ml/5 tbsp/¹/₃ cup olive oil

1 Preheat the oven to 180°C/350°F/Gas 4 and lightly grease a 23cm/9in springform cake tin (pan) with oil. Mix together the ricotta, Parmesan and egg yolks in a food processor or blender. Add the herbs, salt and paprika, and season with black pepper. Blend until smooth and creamy.

2 Whisk the egg whites in a large bowl until they form soft peaks. Gently fold the egg whites into the ricotta mixture, taking care not to knock out too much air. Transfer the ricotta mixture into the tin and smooth the top.

3 Bake for 1 hour 20 minutes or until the flan is risen and the top golden. Remove from the oven and brush lightly with olive oil, then sprinkle with paprika. Leave the flan to cool before removing from the tin.

4 Make the tapenade. Put the olives and garlic in a food processor or blender, and process until finely chopped. Gradually add the olive oil and blend to a coarse paste, then transfer to a serving bowl. Garnish the flan with fresh herb leaves and serve with the tapenade.

Nutritional information per portion: Energy 730kcal/3021kJ; Protein 32.7g; Carbohydrate 8.6g, of which sugars 6.7g; Fat 63g, of which saturates 26.7g; Cholesterol 245mg; Calcium 335mg; Fibre 4g; Sodium 2512mg.

Mediterranean one-crust pie

This free-form pie encases a rich tomato, aubergine and kidney bean filling. If your pastry cracks as you form the casing, just patch it up – it adds to the pie's rustic character.

SERVES 4

500g/1¹/₄lb aubergine
   (eggplant), cubed
1 red (bell) pepper
30ml/2 tbsp olive oil
1 large onion, finely chopped
1 courgette (zucchini), sliced
2 garlic cloves, crushed
15ml/1 tbsp fresh oregano or 5ml/1 tsp
   dried, plus extra fresh oregano
   to garnish
200g/7oz/1¹/₂ cups canned red
   kidney beans, drained and rinsed
115g/4oz/1 cup pitted black
   olives, rinsed

375g/13oz/²/₃ cup passata
   (bottled strained tomatoes)
1 egg, beaten, or a little milk
30ml/2 tbsp semolina
salt and ground black pepper

FOR THE PASTRY

75g/3oz/²/₃ cup unbleached plain
   (all-purpose) flour
75g/3oz/²/₃ cup wholemeal
   (whole-wheat) flour
75g/3oz/6 tbsp vegetable margarine
50g/2oz/²/₃ cup freshly grated
   Parmesan cheese

1 Preheat the oven to 220°C/425°F/Gas 7. To make the pastry, sift the plain and wholemeal flours into a large bowl. Rub in the vegetable margarine until the mixture resembles fine breadcrumbs, then stir in the grated Parmesan. Mix in enough cold water to form a firm dough.

2 Turn out the dough on to a lightly floured work surface and form into a smooth ball. Wrap the dough in clear film (plastic wrap) or a plastic bag and chill for about 30 minutes.

3 To make the filling, put the aubergine in a colander, sprinkle with salt, and leave for about 30 minutes. Rinse and pat dry with kitchen paper.

4 Meanwhile, put the whole pepper on a baking tray and roast in the oven for 20 minutes until the flesh is soft and the skin is blistered. Put the pepper in a plastic bag and leave to sweat.

5 When the pepper is cool enough to handle, peel and seed it, then dice the flesh. Set aside.

6 Heat the oil in a large heavy frying pan. Fry the onion for 5 minutes until softened, stirring from time to time.

7 Add the rinsed and dried aubergine and fry for a further 5 minutes until tender. Add the courgette, garlic and oregano, and cook for 5 minutes more, stirring frequently.

8 Finally, add the kidney beans and olives, stir through, then add the passata and diced pepper. Cook until heated through and set aside to cool.

9 Roll out the pastry on a lightly floured board or work surface to form a rough 30cm/12in round. Place on a lightly oiled baking sheet. Brush with a little of the beaten egg or milk. Sprinkle over the semolina, leaving a 4cm/1½in border around the edge, then spoon over the filling.

10 Gather up the edges of the pastry to partly cover the filling, roughly fluting the edge so that it forms a casing – it should be open in the middle. Brush with the remaining egg or milk and bake for 30–35 minutes until golden. Garnish with the extra oregano.

Nutritional information per portion: Energy 554kcal/2318kJ; Protein 17.7g; Carbohydrate 56.6g, of which sugars 15.7g; Fat 30.2g, of which saturates 4.2g; Cholesterol 13mg; Calcium 295mg; Fibre 11.6g; Sodium 1353mg.

Chestnut, Stilton and ale pie

This hearty winter dish has a rich Guinness gravy and a herb pastry top. The Stilton adds a mouth-watering creaminess, but can be left out to make a less rich version of the pie.

SERVES 4

30ml/2 tbsp sunflower oil
2 large onions, chopped
500g/1¼lb/8 cups button (white) mushrooms
3 carrots, sliced
1 parsnip, cut into thick slices
15ml/1 tbsp fresh thyme or 5ml/1 tsp dried
2 bay leaves
250ml/8fl oz/1 cup Guinness
120ml/4fl oz/½ cup vegetable stock
5ml/1 tsp vegetarian Worcestershire sauce
5ml/1 tsp soft dark brown sugar
350g/12oz/3 cups canned chestnuts, halved

30ml/2 tbsp unbleached plain
   (all-purpose) flour
150g/5oz/1¼ cups Stilton cheese, cubed
1 egg, beaten, or milk, to glaze
salt and ground black pepper

FOR THE PASTRY
115g/4oz/1 cup wholemeal (whole-wheat) flour
a pinch of salt
50g/2oz/4 tbsp unsalted butter
   or vegetable margarine
15ml/1 tbsp fresh thyme or 5ml/1 tsp dried

1 To make the pastry, rub together the flour, salt and butter or margarine. Add the thyme and enough water to form a soft dough. Knead for 1 minute to form a smooth dough. Wrap in clear film (plastic wrap). Chill for 30 minutes.

2 Meanwhile, heat the oil in a heavy pan and fry the onions for 5 minutes until softened, stirring. Halve the mushrooms, add to the pan and cook for 3 minutes. Add the carrots, parsnip and herbs. Stir, cover and cook for 3 minutes.

3 Add the Guinness, stock, Worcestershire sauce, sugar and seasoning. Simmer, covered, for 5 minutes, stirring. Add the chestnuts. Mix the flour to a paste with 30ml/2 tbsp water. Add to the Guinness mixture and cook, uncovered, for 5 minutes, stirring. Add the cheese and heat until melted, stirring.

4 Preheat the oven to 220°C/425°F/Gas 7. Roll out the pastry to fit the top of a 1.5 litre/2½ pint/ 6¼ cup deep pie dish. Spoon the chestnut mixture into the dish. Dampen the edges of the dish and cover with the pastry. Seal, trim and crimp the edges. Cut a small slit in the top of the pie. Use any extra pastry to make decorative leaves. Brush with egg or milk. Bake for 30 minutes until golden.

Nutritional information per portion: Energy 666kcal/2782kJ; Protein 18.9g; Carbohydrate 70.3g, of which sugars 22.6g; Fat 32.7g, of which saturates 16.6g; Cholesterol 62mg; Calcium 238mg; Fibre 11g; Sodium 415mg.

Layered polenta bake

Baked polenta, a rich tomato sauce and the classy combination of spinach, cream and Gorgonzola cheese make a tasty main course dish – and a great alternative to vegetarian lasagne.

SERVES 6

5ml/1 tsp salt
375g/13oz/3 cups fine polenta
olive oil, for greasing and brushing
25g/1oz/¹⁄₃ cup freshly grated
   Parmesan cheese
salt and ground black pepper

FOR THE TOMATO SAUCE

15ml/1 tbsp olive oil
2 garlic cloves, chopped
400g/14oz/3 cups chopped tomatoes

15ml/1 tbsp chopped fresh sage
2.5ml/¹⁄₂ tsp soft brown sugar
200g/7oz/1¹⁄₂ cups canned cannellini
   beans, rinsed and drained

FOR THE SPINACH SAUCE

250g/9oz spinach, tough stalks removed
150ml/¹⁄₄ pint/²⁄₃ cup single
   (light) cream
115g/4oz/1 cup Gorgonzola cheese, cubed
large pinch of ground nutmeg

1 Make the polenta. Bring 2 litres/3¹⁄₂ pints/8 cups water to the boil in a large heavy pan and add the salt. Remove the pan from the heat. Gradually pour in the polenta, whisking constantly.

2 Return the pan to the heat, and stir constantly for 15–20 minutes until the polenta is thick and creamy and comes away from the side of the pan. Remove the pan from the heat.

3 Season well with pepper, then spoon the polenta on to a wet work surface or piece of marble. Using a wet spatula, spread out the polenta until it is 1cm/¹⁄₂ in thick. Leave to cool for about 1 hour.

4 Preheat the oven to 190°C/375°F/Gas 5. To make the tomato sauce, heat the oil in a pan, then fry the garlic for 1 minute. Add the tomatoes and sage, and bring to the boil. Reduce the heat, add the sugar and seasoning, and simmer for 10 minutes until the sauce is slightly reduced, stirring occasionally. Stir in the drained cannellini beans and cook for a further 2 minutes.

5 Meanwhile, to make the spinach sauce, wash the spinach thoroughly and put in a large pan with only the water that clings to the leaves. Cover the pan tightly and cook over medium heat for about 3 minutes until the spinach is tender and just wilted, stirring occasionally. Transfer the spinach into a colander and allow to drain, then squeeze out as much excess water as possible using the back of a wooden spoon.

6 Heat the cream, cheese and nutmeg in a small pan. Bring to the boil, then reduce the heat. Stir in the spinach and seasoning, then cook gently until slightly thickened, stirring frequently.

7 Cut the polenta into triangles, then place a layer of polenta in an oiled deep baking dish. Spoon over the tomato sauce, then top with another polenta layer. Top with the spinach sauce and cover with the remaining polenta triangles. Brush with olive oil, sprinkle with Parmesan and bake for 35–40 minutes. Heat the grill (broiler) to high, and grill (broil) until the top is golden before serving.

Nutritional information per portion: Energy 436kcal/1820kJ; Protein 16.2g; Carbohydrate 55.4g, of which sugars 4.9g; Fat 16.3g, of which saturates 8g; Cholesterol 32mg; Calcium 267mg; Fibre 5g; Sodium 481mg.

Rocket and tomato pizza

Peppery rocket and aromatic fresh basil add both colour and flavour to this crisp pizza with its tangy tomato and mozzarella topping. Sometimes simple really is the best.

SERVES 2

10ml/2 tsp olive oil, plus extra
    for drizzling
1 garlic clove, crushed
150g/5oz/1 cup canned
    chopped tomatoes
2.5ml/¹⁄₂ tsp sugar
30ml/2 tbsp torn fresh basil leaves
2 tomatoes, seeded and chopped
150g/5oz/²⁄₃ cup mozzarella
    cheese, sliced
20g/³⁄₄oz/1 cup rocket (arugula) leaves
rock salt and ground black pepper

FOR THE PIZZA BASE

225g/8oz/2 cups strong white bread
    flour, sifted
5ml/1 tsp salt
2.5ml/¹⁄₂ tsp easy-blend (rapid-rise)
    dried yeast
15ml/1 tbsp olive oil

1 To make the pizza base, put the flour, salt and yeast in a bowl. Make a well in the centre and add the oil and 150ml/¹⁄₄ pint/²⁄₃ cup warm water. Mix with a round-bladed knife to form a soft dough.

2 Turn out the dough on to a lightly floured work surface and knead for 5 minutes. Cover with the upturned bowl or a dish towel and leave to rest for about 5 minutes.

3 Knead for 5 minutes more until the dough is smooth. Place in a lightly oiled bowl and cover with clear film (plastic wrap). Leave in a warm place for 45 minutes until doubled in bulk.

4 Preheat the oven to 220°C/425°F/ Gas 7. Heat the oil in a frying pan and fry the garlic for 1 minute. Add the tomatoes and sugar, and cook for 5–7 minutes until thickened. Stir in the basil and seasoning. Set aside.

5 Lightly knead the dough. Roll out to form a 30cm/12in round. Place on a lightly oiled baking sheet; push up the edges to form a shallow rim. Spoon over the tomato mixture, top with the fresh tomatoes and arrange the mozzarella on top. Season to taste, then drizzle with a little olive oil. Bake in the top of the oven for 10–12 minutes until crisp. Scatter over the rocket and serve.

Nutritional information per portion: Energy 683kcal/2874kJ; Protein 26.1g; Carbohydrate 92.3g, of which sugars 6.5g; Fat 25.8g, of which saturates 11.9g; Cholesterol 44mg; Calcium 494mg; Fibre 5.7g; Sodium 1312mg.

Polenta pan pizza with red onions and mushrooms

This yeast-free pizza is cooked in a frying pan rather than the oven. The slightly cakey base is complemented by the garlicky red onions and mushrooms. Serve with a tomato and basil salad.

SERVES 2

30ml/2 tbsp olive oil
1 large red onion, sliced
3 garlic cloves, crushed
115g/4oz/1¹/₂ cups brown cap (cremini)
mushrooms, sliced
5ml/1 tsp dried oregano
115g/4oz mozzarella cheese, crumbled
15ml/1 tbsp pine nuts (optional)

FOR THE PIZZA BASE
50g/2oz/¹/₂ cup unbleached plain
(all-purpose) flour, sifted
2.5ml/¹/₂ tsp salt
115g/4oz/1 cup fine polenta
5ml/1 tsp baking powder
1 egg, beaten
150ml/¹/₄ pint/²/₃ cup milk
25g/1oz/¹/₃ cup freshly grated
Parmesan cheese
2.5ml/¹/₂ tsp dried chilli flakes
15ml/1 tbsp olive oil

1 Heat half the olive oil in a heavy frying pan, add the onion and fry for 10 minutes until tender, stirring occasionally. Remove and set aside.

2 Add the remaining oil to the pan and fry the garlic for 1 minute until just coloured. Add the mushrooms and oregano, and cook for 5 minutes until the mushrooms are tender.

3 To make the pizza base, combine the flour, salt, polenta and baking powder in a bowl. Make a well in the centre and add the egg. Gradually add the milk and mix with a fork to make into a thick, smooth batter. Stir in the Parmesan and chilli flakes.

4 Heat the oil in a 25cm/10in heavy flameproof frying pan until very hot. Spoon in the batter and spread evenly. Cook over medium heat for about 3 minutes until the base is set. Remove from the heat. Run a knife around the edge of the pizza base. Carefully invert on to a plate. Slide back into the pan on its uncooked side. Cook for 2 minutes until golden.

5 Preheat the grill (broiler) to high. Spoon the onions over the base. Top with the mushrooms and mozzarella, then grill (broil) for about 6 minutes until the cheese has melted. Sprinkle over the pine nuts, if using, and grill until golden. Serve cut into wedges.

Nutritional information per portion: Energy 782kcal/3262kJ; Protein 31.9g; Carbohydrate 77.1g, of which sugars 12.4g; Fat 39.1g, of which saturates 14.5g; Cholesterol 145mg; Calcium 540mg; Fibre 4.8g; Sodium 439mg.

Salads

Salads have been growing in both popularity and variety in recent years. As well as numerous different types of lettuce, shoppers can now choose chicory, baby spinach and fresh herbs, as well as an astonishing array of additional ingredients. Rice, noodles, pulses, nuts, seeds, couscous and seaweed can be added for bulk and extra nutrition. Try buying salad ingredients from local growers for the freshest produce.

Feta and mint potato salad

Sharp feta cheese, creamy yogurt and fragrant fresh mint combine perfectly with warm new potatoes in this salad.

SERVES 4

500g/1¼lb salad potatoes
90g/3½oz feta cheese, crumbled

FOR THE DRESSING
225g/8oz/1 cup natural (plain) live yogurt
15g/½oz/½ cup fresh mint leaves
30ml/2 tbsp mayonnaise
salt and ground black pepper

1 Steam the potatoes over a pan of boiling water for about 20 minutes until tender, then drain well and transfer into a large bowl.

2 Meanwhile, make the dressing. Blend the yogurt and mint in a food processor for a few minutes until the mint leaves are finely chopped. Transfer the dressing to a small bowl. Stir in the mayonnaise and season to taste.

3 Spoon the dressing over the warm potatoes and scatter with the feta cheese. Serve immediately.

COOK'S TIP
Pink fir apple potatoes have a smooth waxy texture, and they retain their shape when cooked, making them an ideal choice for salads. Charlotte and other special salad potatoes could be used instead, if you wish.

Nutritional information per portion: Energy 229kcal/959kJ; Protein 8.7g; Carbohydrate 25g, of which sugars 6.3g; Fat 11.2g, of which saturates 4.4g; Cholesterol 22mg; Calcium 204mg; Fibre 1.3g; Sodium 419mg.

Apple and beetroot salad with red leaves

Bitter salad leaves are complemented by sweet-flavoured apples and beetroot in this refreshing summer salad.

SERVES 4

50g/2oz/⅓ cup whole unblanched almonds
2 red apples, cored and diced
juice of ½ lemon
115g/4oz/4 cups red salad leaves, such as
     lollo rosso, oak leaf and radicchio
200g/7oz cooked beetroot (beets) in natural juice, sliced

FOR THE DRESSING
30ml/2 tbsp olive oil
15ml/1 tbsp walnut oil
15ml/1 tbsp red or white wine vinegar
salt and ground black pepper

1 Toast the almonds in a dry frying pan over medium heat for 2–3 minutes until golden brown, tossing frequently to prevent them burning.

2 Meanwhile, make the dressing. Put the olive and walnut oils, vinegar and seasoning in a bowl or screw-top jar. Stir or shake thoroughly to combine.

3 Toss the apples in the lemon juice to prevent them browning, then put in a large bowl. Add the salad leaves, beetroot and toasted almonds.

4 Pour over the dressing and toss the salad together gently. Serve immediately.

Nutritional information per portion: Energy 216kcal/895kJ; Protein 4.1g; Carbohydrate 9.5g, of which sugars 8.8g; Fat 18.2g, of which saturates 1.9g; Cholesterol 0mg; Calcium 54mg; Fibre 2.7g; Sodium 58mg.

Avocado, red onion and spinach salad with polenta croûtons

The simple lemon dressing gives a sharp tang to the creamy avocado, sweet red onions and crisp spinach leaves. Crunchy golden polenta croûtons, with their soft centre, add a delicious contrast.

SERVES 4

1 large red onion, cut into wedges
300g/11oz ready-made polenta,
  cut into 1cm/1/2in cubes
olive oil, for brushing
225g/8oz baby spinach leaves
1 avocado
5ml/1 tsp lemon juice

FOR THE DRESSING

60ml/4 tbsp extra virgin olive oil
juice of 1/2 lemon
salt and ground black pepper

1 Preheat the oven to 200°C/400°F/Gas 6. Place the onion wedges and polenta cubes on a lightly oiled baking sheet and bake for 25 minutes or until the onion is tender and the polenta is crisp and golden, turning them regularly to prevent them sticking. Leave to cool slightly.

2 Meanwhile, make the dressing. Put the olive oil, lemon juice and seasoning to taste in a bowl or screw-top jar. Stir or shake thoroughly to combine.

3 Put the baby spinach leaves in a serving bowl. Peel, stone (pit) and slice the avocado, and toss the slices in the lemon juice to prevent them browning, Add to the spinach with the roasted onions.

4 Pour the dressing over the salad and toss gently to combine. Sprinkle the polenta croûtons on top or hand them around separately, and serve immediately.

HEALTH BENEFITS

Spinach contains many valuable nutrients and is rich in folates, vitamin C, beta carotene, zinc, potassium and iron. Spinach, like rhubarb, contains oxalic acid, which limits the body's absorption of iron and calcium. However, the vitamin C content found in spinach and other vegetables may temper the effects of the oxalic acid to some extent. In natural medicine, spinach is often prescribed to treat constipation, arthritis and high blood pressure.

Nutritional information per portion: Energy 445kcal/1849kJ; Protein 8.1g; Carbohydrate 48.3g, of which sugars 1.8g; Fat 23.9g, of which saturates 3.5g; Cholesterol 0mg; Calcium 104mg; Fibre 3.6g; Sodium 81mg.

Watercress, Roquefort, pear and walnut salad

Sharp-tasting blue Roquefort and peppery watercress leaves are complemented in this salad by sweet pears and crunchy walnuts.

SERVES 4

75g/3oz/¹/₂ cup shelled walnuts, halved
2 red Williams pears
15ml/1 tbsp lemon juice
150g/5oz/1 large bunch watercress, tough stalks removed
200g/7oz/scant 2 cups Roquefort cheese, cut into chunks

FOR THE DRESSING
45ml/3 tbsp extra virgin olive oil
30ml/2 tbsp lemon juice
2.5ml/¹/₂ tsp clear honey
5ml/1 tsp Dijon mustard
salt and ground black pepper

1 Toast the walnuts in a dry frying pan for 2 minutes until golden, tossing frequently to prevent them burning.

2 Meanwhile, make the dressing. Put the olive oil, lemon juice, honey, mustard and seasoning in a bowl or screw-top jar. Stir or shake thoroughly to combine.

3 Core and slice the pears, and toss the slices in the lemon juice. Put them in a bowl and add the watercress, walnuts and Roquefort. Pour the dressing over the salad, toss well and serve immediately.

Nutritional information per portion: Energy 414kcal/1716kJ; Protein 14.4g; Carbohydrate 8.8g, of which sugars 8.6g; Fat 36g, of which saturates 11.9g; Cholesterol 38mg; Calcium 334mg; Fibre 2.9g; Sodium 632mg.

Tuscan-style panzanella

Open-textured, Italian-style bread is essential for this colourful classic Tuscan salad. Use the choicest fresh produce you can find.

SERVES 6

275g/10oz/10 slices day-old Italian-style bread, thickly sliced
1 cucumber, peeled and cut into chunks
5 tomatoes, seeded and diced
1 large red onion, chopped
200g/7oz/1¹/₃ cups good-quality olives
20 basil leaves, torn

FOR THE DRESSING
60ml/4 tbsp extra virgin olive oil
15ml/1 tbsp red or white wine vinegar
salt and ground black pepper

1 Soak the bread in water for about 2 minutes, then lift out and squeeze gently, first with your hands, then in a dish towel, to remove any excess water. Chill for 1 hour.

2 Meanwhile, to make the dressing, put the oil, vinegar and seasoning to taste in a bowl or screw-top jar. Stir or shake to combine. Put the cucumber, tomatoes, onion and olives in a serving bowl.

3 Break the chilled bread into chunks and add to the bowl with the basil. Pour the dressing over the salad and toss before serving.

Nutritional information per portion: Energy 239kcal/1003kJ; Protein 5.5g; Carbohydrate 29.6g, of which sugars 7.1g; Fat 11.8g, of which saturates 1.6g; Cholesterol 0mg; Calcium 93mg; Fibre 3.3g; Sodium 905mg.

Roasted tomato and mozzarella salad

Roasting the tomatoes adds a new dimension to this traditional salad. Make the basil oil just before serving to retain its fresh flavour and vivid colour.

SERVES 4

**6 large plum tomatoes, halved
    lengthways and seeded**
olive oil, for brushing
**2 balls fresh mozzarella cheese,
    cut into 8–12 slices**
salt and ground black pepper
fresh basil leaves, to garnish

FOR THE BASIL OIL

25 fresh basil leaves
60ml/4 tbsp extra virgin olive oil
1 garlic clove, crushed

1 Preheat the oven to 200°C/ 400°F/Gas 6, and oil a baking sheet. Put the tomato halves skin-side down on the baking sheet. Roast for 20 minutes or until they are tender, but still retain their shape.

2 Meanwhile, make the basil oil. Put the basil leaves, olive oil and garlic in a food processor or blender, and process until smooth. Transfer to a bowl, and chill until required.

3 For each serving, place three tomato halves on top of two or three slices of mozzarella, and drizzle over the oil. Season well. Garnish with basil leaves, and serve immediately.

HEALTH BENEFITS

Basil is a natural relaxant and calms the nervous system. It also stimulates the appetite and aids digestion, easing cramps and nausea.

Nutritional information per portion: Energy 525kcal/2175kJ; Protein 20.2g; Carbohydrate 7g, of which sugars 4.8g; Fat 46.4g, of which saturates 15.9g; Cholesterol 51mg; Calcium 371mg; Fibre 2.8g; Sodium 381mg.

Mixed herb salad with toasted mixed seeds

This simple salad is the perfect antidote to a rich, heavy meal because it contains fresh herbs that can ease the digestion. Balsamic vinegar adds a rich, sweet taste to the dressing.

SERVES 4

90g/3¹/₂oz/4 cups mixed salad leaves
50g/2oz/2 cups mixed salad herbs,
    such as coriander, parsley, basil and
    rocket (arugula)
25g/1oz/3 tbsp pumpkin seeds
25g/1oz/3 tbsp sunflower seeds

FOR THE DRESSING

60ml/4 tbsp extra virgin olive oil
15ml/1 tbsp balsamic vinegar
2.5 ml/¹/₂ tsp Dijon mustard
salt and ground black pepper

1 To make the dressing, combine the ingredients in a bowl or screw-top jar. Shake or mix with a small whisk or fork until combined.

2 Toast the pumpkin and sunflower seeds in a dry frying pan over medium heat for 2 minutes until golden, tossing frequently to prevent them burning. Allow to cool slightly while you prepare the leaves.

3 Put the salad and herb leaves in a large bowl. Sprinkle over the seeds.

4 Pour the dressing over the salad and toss with your hands until the leaves are well coated, then serve.

HEALTH BENEFIT
Parsley contains useful amounts of vitamin C and iron.

Nutritional information per portion: Energy 179kcal/738kJ; Protein 2.9g; Carbohydrate 3.1g, of which sugars 1g; Fat 17.2g, of which saturates 2.2g; Cholesterol 0mg; Calcium 26mg; Fibre 1.1g; Sodium 20mg.

Warm vegetable salad with peanut sauce

Based on the classic Indonesian salad gado-gado, this salad features raw red pepper and sprouted beans, which make a crunchy contrast to the warm steamed broccoli, green beans and carrots. Topped with slices of hard-boiled egg, this salad is substantial enough to serve as a main course.

SERVES 2–4

8 new potatoes
225g/8oz broccoli, cut into small florets
200g/7oz/1¹/₂ cups fine green beans
2 carrots, cut into thin ribbons with
    a vegetable peeler
1 red (bell) pepper, seeded and cut into strips
50g/2oz/¹/₂ cup beansprouts
sprigs of watercress, to garnish

FOR THE PEANUT SAUCE
15ml/1 tbsp sunflower oil
1 bird's-eye chilli, seeded and sliced

1 garlic clove, crushed
5ml/1 tsp ground coriander
5ml/1 tsp ground cumin
60ml/4 tbsp crunchy peanut butter
15ml/1 tbsp dark soy sauce
1cm/¹/₂in piece fresh root ginger,
    finely grated
5ml/1 tsp soft dark brown sugar
15ml/1 tbsp lime juice
60ml/4 tbsp coconut milk

1 To make the peanut sauce, heat the oil in a pan. Add the chilli and garlic, and cook for 1 minute or until softened. Add the spices and cook for a further 1 minute. Stir in the peanut butter and 75ml/5 tbsp water, then cook for 2 minutes until combined, stirring constantly.

2 Add the soy sauce, ginger, sugar, lime juice and coconut milk, then cook over low heat until smooth and heated through, stirring frequently. Transfer to a bowl.

3 Bring a pan of lightly salted water to the boil, add the potatoes and cook for 10–15 minutes, until tender. Drain, then halve or thickly slice the potatoes, depending on their size. Meanwhile, steam the broccoli and green beans for 4–5 minutes until tender but still crisp. Add the carrots 2 minutes before the end of the cooking time.

4 Arrange the cooked vegetables on a serving platter with the red pepper and beansprouts. Garnish with watercress and serve immediately with the peanut sauce.

Nutritional information per portion: Energy 253kcal/1057kJ; Protein 9.6g; Carbohydrate 28.3g, of which sugars 11.4g; Fat 11.9g, of which saturates 2.6g; Cholesterol 0mg; Calcium 79mg; Fibre 5.9g; Sodium 360mg.

White bean salad with roasted red pepper dressing

The speckled herb and red pepper dressing adds a wonderful colour contrast to this salad, which is best served warm. Canned beans are used for convenience – substitute cooked dried beans, if you prefer, remembering to allow the time to soak them first.

SERVES 4

1 large red (bell) pepper
60ml/4 tbsp olive oil
1 large garlic clove, crushed
25g/1oz/1 cup fresh oregano leaves
    or flat leaf parsley
15ml/1 tbsp balsamic vinegar

400g/14oz/3 cups canned flageolet (small
    cannellini) beans, drained and rinsed
200g/7oz/1½ cups canned cannellini
    beans, drained and rinsed
salt and ground black pepper

1 Preheat the oven to 200°C/400°F/Gas 6. Place the red pepper on a baking sheet, brush with oil and roast for 30 minutes or until the skin wrinkles and the flesh is soft. Remove the pepper from the oven and put in a plastic bag. Seal and leave to cool. (This makes the skin easier to remove.)

2 When the pepper is cool enough to handle, remove it from the bag and peel off the skin. Gently rinse under cold running water. Slice the pepper in half, remove and discard the seeds, and dice the flesh. Set aside.

3 Heat the remaining oil in a pan and cook the garlic for 1 minute until softened. Remove from the heat, then add the oregano or parsley, the diced red pepper and any juices, and the balsamic vinegar.

4 Put the beans in a large bowl and pour over the warm dressing. Season to taste, then stir gently until combined. Serve warm.

HEALTH BENEFITS

Low in fat and high in fibre and protein, pulses (legumes) such as cannellini beans should be a regular part of a healthy balanced diet. They are also a good source of many minerals, including iron, potassium, phosphorus and magnesium, as well as B complex vitamins.

Nutritional information per portion: Energy 267kcal/1117kJ; Protein 11.1g; Carbohydrate 29.8g, of which sugars 8.3g; Fat 12.2g, of which saturates 1.8g; Cholesterol 0mg; Calcium 133mg; Fibre 10.6g; Sodium 591mg.

Roasted beetroot with tangy horseradish dressing

Fresh beetroot is enjoying a well-deserved renaissance. Roasting gives it a delicious sweet flavour, which contrasts wonderfully with this sharp, piquant dressing.

SERVES 4

450g/1lb baby beetroot (beets),
    preferably with leaves
15ml/1 tbsp olive oil

FOR THE DRESSING
30ml/2 tbsp lemon juice
30ml/2 tbsp mirin
120ml/8 tbsp olive oil
30ml/2 tbsp creamed horseradish
salt and ground black pepper

1 Cook the beetroot in boiling salted water for 30 minutes. Drain, add the olive oil and toss gently. Preheat the oven to 200°C/400°F/Gas 6.

2 Place the beetroot on a baking sheet and roast for 40 minutes or until tender when pierced with a knife.

3 Meanwhile, make the dressing. Whisk together the ingredients until smooth and creamy. Season to taste.

4 Cut the beetroot in half, put in a bowl and add the dressing. Toss gently and serve immediately.

COOK'S TIP
This salad is probably at its best served warm, but you can make it in advance, if you wish, and serve it at room temperature. Add the dressing to the beetroot just before serving.

HEALTH BENEFITS
Beetroot has a reputation for containing cancer-fighting compounds and enhancing the immune system. It is a powerful blood-purifier and rich in iron, vitamins C and A, and folates, which are essential for healthy cells.

Nutritional information per portion: Energy 254kcal/1052kJ; Protein 2.1g; Carbohydrate 10g, of which sugars 9.1g; Fat 22.2g, of which saturates 3.2g; Cholesterol 1mg; Calcium 26mg; Fibre 2.3g; Sodium 143mg.

Sesame noodle salad

Toasted sesame oil adds a nutty flavour to this Asian-style noodle salad. Best served warm, it is substantial enough to serve as a main meal.

SERVES 2–4

250g/9oz medium egg noodles
200g/7oz/1 cup mangetouts (snow peas) or sugar snap peas, sliced diagonally
2 carrots, cut into julienne
2 tomatoes, seeded and diced
30ml/2 tbsp chopped fresh coriander (cilantro)
15ml/1 tbsp sesame seeds
3 spring onions (scallions), shredded
fresh coriander (cilantro), to garnish

FOR THE DRESSING

10ml/2 tsp light soy sauce
30ml/2 tbsp toasted sesame seed oil
15ml/1 tbsp sunflower oil
4cm/1½ in piece of fresh root ginger, finely grated
1 garlic clove, crushed

1 Put the noodles in a pan of lightly salted boiling water and bring back to the boil. Cook for 2 minutes. Add the sugar snap peas or mangetout and cook for a further 2 minutes. Drain in a colander and rinse under cold running water.

2 Meanwhile, make the dressing. Combine the soy sauce, sesame and sunflower oils, ginger and garlic in a screw-top jar or a small bowl. Cover the jar and shake well, or mix with a small whisk to combine thoroughly.

3 Tip the noodles and peas or mangetouts into a large bowl, and add the carrots, tomatoes and coriander. Pour the dressing over the top and toss with your hands to combine. Sprinkle with the sesame seeds and top with the spring onions and coriander.

HEALTH BENEFIT

Garlic is highly antiseptic, particularly in its raw form, and can help to ward off colds and flu and stimulate circulation.

Nutritional information per portion: Energy 386kcal/1622kJ; Protein 10.9g; Carbohydrate 52.9g, of which sugars 8.6g; Fat 16g, of which saturates 3g; Cholesterol 19mg; Calcium 85mg; Fibre 5.1g; Sodium 310mg.

Japanese salad

Hijiki is a mild-tasting seaweed that is a rich source of minerals. When combined with radishes, cucumber and beansprouts, it makes a delicate, refreshing salad.

SERVES 4

15g/¹/₂oz/¹/₂ cup hijiki
250g/9oz/1¹/₄ cups radishes,
    sliced into very thin rounds
1 small cucumber, cut into thin sticks
75g/3oz/¹/₂ cup beansprouts

FOR THE DRESSING

15ml/1 tbsp sunflower oil
15ml/1 tbsp toasted sesame oil
5ml/1 tsp light soy sauce
30ml/2 tbsp rice vinegar or
    15ml/1 tbsp wine vinegar
15ml/1 tbsp mirin

1 Soak the hijiki in a bowl of cold water for 10–15 minutes until it is rehydrated, then drain, rinse under cold running water and drain again. It should almost triple in volume.

2 Put the hijiki in a pan of water. Bring to the boil, then reduce the heat and simmer for 30 minutes or until tender. Drain.

3 Meanwhile, make the dressing. Put the sunflower and sesame oils, soy sauce, vinegar and mirin in a bowl or screw-top jar. Stir or shake thoroughly to combine.

4 Arrange the hijiki in a shallow bowl or platter with the radishes, cucumber and beansprouts. Pour over the dressing and toss lightly.

Nutritional information per portion: Energy 68kcal/280kJ; Protein 1.4g; Carbohydrate 2.8g, of which sugars 2.4g; Fat 5.8g, of which saturates 0.8g; Cholesterol 0mg; Calcium 23mg; Fibre 1.1g; Sodium 276mg.

Side Dishes

Put as much thought into your selection of side dishes as you do when choosing your main course, and you'll find it easy to create healthy, well-balanced meals. This eclectic selection of recipes is based largely on vegetables, which are valued for the cancer-thwarting phytochemicals, vitamins, minerals, antioxidants and fibre they provide. Brightly coloured orange and green vegetables are particularly rich in nutrients.

Root vegetable gratin with Indian spices

Subtly spiced with curry powder, turmeric, coriander and mild chilli powder, this rich gratin is substantial enough to serve on its own for lunch or dinner, perhaps with a green salad. It also makes a good accompaniment to a vegetable or bean curry.

SERVES 4

2 large potatoes, total weight about 450g/1lb
2 sweet potatoes, total weight about 275g/10oz
175g/6oz celeriac
15ml/1 tbsp unsalted butter
5ml/1 tsp curry powder
5ml/1 tsp ground turmeric

2.5ml/1/2 tsp ground coriander
5ml/1 tsp mild chilli powder
3 shallots, chopped
150ml/1/4 pint/2/3 cup single (light) cream
150ml/1/4 pint/2/3 cup semi-skimmed (low-fat) milk
salt and ground black pepper
chopped fresh flat leaf parsley, to garnish

1 Thinly slice the potatoes, sweet potatoes and celeriac, using a sharp knife or the slicing attachment on a food processor. Immediately put the vegetables in a bowl of cold water to prevent them discolouring.

2 Preheat the oven to 180°C/350°F/Gas 4. Heat half the butter in a heavy pan, add the curry powder, turmeric and coriander, and half the chilli powder. Cook for 2 minutes, then leave to cool slightly. Drain the vegetables, then pat dry with kitchen paper. Put in a bowl, add the spice mixture and the shallots, and mix well.

3 Arrange the vegetables in a gratin dish, seasoning between the layers. Mix together the cream and milk, and pour the mixture over the vegetables. Sprinkle the remaining chilli powder on top.

4 Cover with baking parchment, and bake for about 45 minutes. Remove the baking parchment, dot with the remaining butter and bake for a further 50 minutes until the top is golden. Serve hot, garnished with chopped fresh parsley.

COOK'S TIP
The cream adds richness to this gratin; replace with semi-skimmed (low-fat) milk, if you prefer.

Nutritional information per portion: Energy 268kcal/1129kJ; Protein 5.8g; Carbohydrate 37.7g, of which sugars 9.8g; Fat 11.6g, of which saturates 7.1g; Cholesterol 31mg; Calcium 127mg; Fibre 3.6g; Sodium 117mg.

Potato pan gratin

Potatoes, layered with mustard butter and baked until golden, are perfect to serve with a green salad for dinner, or as an accompaniment to a vegetable or nut roast.

SERVES 4

4 large potatoes, total weight
    about 900g/2lb
25g/1oz/2 tbsp butter
15ml/1 tbsp olive oil
2 large garlic cloves, crushed
30ml/2 tbsp Dijon mustard
15ml/1 tbsp lemon juice
15ml/1 tbsp fresh thyme leaves, plus
    extra to garnish
50ml/2fl oz/¼ cup vegetable stock
salt and ground black pepper

1 Thinly slice the potatoes using a knife or a slicing attachment on a food processor. Put in a bowl of cold water to prevent them discolouring.

2 Preheat the oven to 200°C/400°F/Gas 6. Heat the butter and oil in a deep ovenproof frying pan or skillet. Add the garlic and cook gently for 3 minutes until light golden, stirring constantly. Stir in the mustard, lemon juice and thyme. Remove from the heat and pour the mixture into a jug (pitcher).

3 Drain the potatoes and pat dry with kitchen paper. Arrange a layer of potatoes in the frying pan or skillet, season and pour over one-third of the butter mixture. Put another layer of potatoes on top, season, and pour over another third of the butter mixture. Arrange a final layer of potatoes on top, and first pour over the rest of the butter mixture, then the stock. Season to taste and sprinkle with the extra thyme leaves.

4 Cover the top with baking parchment, and bake for 1 hour. Remove the paper and cook the gratin for a further 15 minutes or until golden.

Nutritional information per portion: Energy 238kcal/1002kJ; Protein 3.9g; Carbohydrate 36.3g, of which sugars 3g; Fat 9.6g, of which saturates 4.5g; Cholesterol 16mg; Calcium 15mg; Fibre 2.3g; Sodium 70mg.

Garlic sweet potato mash

Delicious mashed with garlicky butter, orange-fleshed sweet potatoes not only look good, with their vivid colour, but are also packed with valuable vitamins.

SERVES 4

4 large sweet potatoes, total weight
  about 900g/2lb, cubed
40g/1¹/₂oz/3 tbsp unsalted butter
3 garlic cloves, crushed
salt and ground black pepper

1 Cook the sweet potatoes in a large pan of boiling salted water for about 15 minutes until tender, then drain and return to the pan.

2 Melt the butter in a heavy pan over a low to medium heat. Sauté the garlic for 1–2 minutes until light golden, stirring to prevent the garlic burning.

3 Pour the garlic butter over the sweet potatoes, season with salt and plenty of black pepper, and mash thoroughly until the potatoes are smooth and creamy. Serve immediately.

COOK'S TIPS

• If the sweet potatoes seem to be on the dry side when you are mashing them, simply add a little milk.
• You can add some chopped fresh herbs, if you wish.

Nutritional information per portion: Energy 586kcal/2477kJ; Protein 16.3g; Carbohydrate 101.4g, of which sugars 52.1g; Fat 15.8g, of which saturates 7.1g; Cholesterol 240mg; Calcium 182mg; Fibre 2.8g; Sodium 968mg.

Rosemary and garlic roasted new potatoes

These crisp-roasted new potatoes, flavoured with fresh rosemary and lots of garlic, are good with vegetable stews.

SERVES 4

800g/1³/₄lb small new potatoes
5 garlic cloves, peeled and bruised
3 sprigs of rosemary
30ml/2 tbsp olive oil
sea salt and ground black pepper

1 Preheat the oven to 200°C/400°F/Gas 6. Put the potatoes, garlic and rosemary in a roasting tin (pan). Add the oil and toss to coat. Season well.

2 Bake for 40–45 minutes until the potatoes are crisp on the outside and soft in the centre. Remove the tin from the oven halfway through cooking and shake the tin to turn the potatoes and coat them in oil.

3 Discard the rosemary and garlic, if you wish, and serve the potatoes piping hot.

VARIATION
Shallots can be roasted in the same way. Roast for 35 minutes or until tender.

HEALTH BENEFITS
Garlic is valued for its ability to boost the immune system; it has been found to be helpful in treating people with HIV.

Nutritional information per portion: Energy 691kcal/2900kJ; Protein 24.9g; Carbohydrate 85.3g, of which sugars 6.4g; Fat 30.2g, of which saturates 10.6g; Cholesterol 39mg; Calcium 410mg; Fibre 4.2g; Sodium 620mg.

Honey-glazed carrots with rosemary

Naturally sweet carrots, sautéed in a glossy honey and mustard glaze, are delicious with all sorts of vegetarian main courses.

SERVES 4

450g/1lb/2¹/₂ cups carrots, cut into thick matchsticks
25g/1oz/2 tbsp butter
15ml/1 tbsp olive oil
1 garlic clove, crushed
15ml/1 tbsp chopped fresh rosemary leaves
5ml/1 tsp Dijon mustard
10ml/2 tsp clear honey

1 Steam the carrots over a pan of boiling water for 2–4 minutes until just tender.

2 Heat the butter and oil in a heavy pan, add the garlic and rosemary, and cook, stirring, for 1 minute or until the garlic is golden brown.

3 Add the carrots, mustard and honey to the pan, and cook, stirring constantly, for 2 minutes or until the carrots are only just tender. Serve immediately.

COOK'S TIP
Other root vegetables, such as parsnips, celeriac, baby turnips and swede (rutabaga) can be cooked in this glaze. Buy organic vegetables when possible, and simply scrub or peel very thinly.

Nutritional information per portion: Energy 118kcal/488kJ; Protein 0.7g; Carbohydrate 10.8g, of which sugars 10.3g; Fat 8.2g, of which saturates 3.8g; Cholesterol 13mg; Calcium 30mg; Fibre 2.7g; Sodium 66mg.

Split pea and shallot mash

Greatly underrated, split peas are delicious when puréed with shallots and enlivened with cumin seeds and fresh herbs. The purée makes an excellent alternative to mashed potatoes, and is particularly good with winter pies and nut roasts. It can also be served with warmed pitta bread, accompanied by diced tomatoes and a splash of olive oil.

SERVES 4–6

225g/8oz/1 cup yellow split peas
1 bay leaf
8 sage leaves, roughly chopped
15ml/1 tbsp olive oil
3 shallots, finely chopped

8ml/heaped 1 tsp cumin seeds
1 large garlic clove, chopped
50g/2oz/4 tbsp butter, softened
salt and ground black pepper

1 Put the split peas in a bowl and cover with cold water. Leave to soak overnight, then rinse and drain.

2 Transfer the peas to a pan, cover with fresh cold water and bring to the boil. Skim off any foam that rises to the surface, then reduce the heat. Add the bay leaf and sage, and simmer for 30–40 minutes until the peas are tender. Add more water during cooking, if necessary.

3 Meanwhile, heat the oil in a frying pan, and cook the shallots, cumin seeds and garlic for 3 minutes or until the shallots soften, stirring occasionally. Add the mixture to the split peas while they are still cooking.

4 Drain the split peas, reserving the cooking water. Remove the bay leaf, then put the split peas in a food processor or blender with the butter and season well.

5 Add 105ml/7 tbsp of the reserved cooking water and blend until the mixture forms a coarse purée. Add more water if the purée seems to be too dry. Adjust the seasoning and serve warm.

Nutritional information per portion: Energy 156kcal/658kJ; Protein 9.1g; Carbohydrate 21.9g, of which sugars 1.5g; Fat 4.2g, of which saturates 0.6g; Cholesterol 0mg; Calcium 22mg; Fibre 2g; Sodium 14mg.

Courgettes in rich tomato sauce

This rich-flavoured Mediterranean dish can be served hot or cold, either as a side dish or as part of a tapas meal. Cut the courgettes into fairly thick slices, so that they stay slightly crunchy.

SERVES 4

15ml/1 tbsp olive oil
1 onion, chopped
1 garlic clove, chopped
4 courgettes (zucchini), thickly sliced
400g/14oz/3 cups canned
   tomatoes, strained
2 tomatoes, peeled, seeded and chopped
5ml/1 tsp vegetable bouillon powder
15ml/1 tbsp tomato purée (paste)
salt and ground black pepper

1 Heat the oil in a heavy pan, add the onion and garlic, and sauté for 5 minutes or until the onion is softened, stirring occasionally. Add the courgettes and cook for a further 5 minutes.

2 Add the canned and fresh tomatoes, bouillon powder and tomato purée. Stir well, then simmer for 10–15 minutes until the sauce is thickened and the courgettes are just tender. Season to taste and serve hot.

VARIATION
Add 1 or 2 sliced and seeded red (bell) peppers with the courgettes (zucchini) in step 1.

Nutritional information per portion: Energy 89kcal/370kJ; Protein 4.3g; Carbohydrate 9.2g, of which sugars 8.6g; Fat 4.1g, of which saturates 0.7g; Cholesterol 0mg; Calcium 54mg; Fibre 3.2g; Sodium 235mg.

Baked fennel with a crumb crust

The delicate aniseed flavour of baked fennel coated in a crispy wholemeal crust makes it a very good accompaniment to all sorts of pasta dishes and risottos.

SERVES 4

3 fennel bulbs, cut lengthways
    into quarters
30ml/2 tbsp olive oil
1 garlic clove, chopped
50g/2oz/1 cup day-old wholemeal
    (whole-wheat) breadcrumbs
30ml/2 tbsp chopped fresh
    flat leaf parsley
salt and ground black pepper
fennel leaves, to garnish (optional)

1 Preheat the oven to 190°C/375°F/Gas 5.

2 Cook the fennel in a pan of boiling salted water for 10 minutes or until just tender. Drain, and put the fennel in a baking dish or roasting tin (pan). Brush with half the olive oil.

3 In a small bowl, mix together the garlic, breadcrumbs and parsley with the rest of the oil. Sprinkle the mixture evenly over the fennel, then season well.

4 Bake for 30 minutes or until the fennel is tender and the breadcrumbs are crisp and golden. Serve hot, garnished with a few fennel leaves (if using).

Nutritional information per portion: Energy 114kcal/477kJ; Protein 3g; Carbohydrate 12.6g, of which sugars 3.1g; Fat 6.1g, of which saturates 0.8g; Cholesterol 0mg; Calcium 67mg; Fibre 4.3g; Sodium 114mg.

Spring vegetable stir-fry

Fast to the table, filled with fresh flavour and packed with healthy spring vegetables, this stir-fry is delicious served with marinated tofu and rice or noodles.

SERVES 4

15ml/1 tbsp groundnut (peanut)
   or vegetable oil
5ml/1 tsp toasted sesame oil
1 garlic clove, chopped
2.5cm/1in piece of fresh root ginger,
   finely chopped
225g/8oz baby carrots
350g/12oz/3 cups broccoli florets
175g/6oz/^{1}/3 cup fresh asparagus tips
2 spring onions (scallions),
   cut on the diagonal
175g/6oz/1^1/2 cups spring greens
   (collards), finely shredded
30ml/2 tbsp light soy sauce
15ml/1 tbsp apple juice
15ml/1 tbsp sesame seeds, toasted

1 Heat a frying pan or wok over high heat. Add the groundnut or vegetable oil and the sesame oil, reduce the heat and add the garlic. Sauté for 2 minutes.

2 Add the ginger, carrots, broccoli and asparagus tips to the pan, and stir-fry for 4 minutes.

3 Next, add the spring onions and spring greens, and stir-fry for a further 2 minutes.

4 Add the soy sauce and apple juice and cook for 1–2 minutes until the vegetables are tender; add a little water if they appear dry. Sprinkle the sesame seeds on top and serve.

HEALTH BENEFITS
Green and orange vegetables are excellent sources of beta carotene, the plant form of vitamin A, as well as vitamins C and E.

Nutritional information per portion: Energy 134kcal/554kJ; Protein 7.8g; Carbohydrate 9.4g, of which sugars 8.6g; Fat 7.4g, of which saturates 1.1g; Cholesterol 0mg; Calcium 195mg; Fibre 6.2g; Sodium 566mg.

Oriental green beans

This is a simple and delicious way of enlivening green beans. The dish can be served hot or cold, and, accompanied by an omelette and some crusty bread, makes a perfect light lunch or dinner.

SERVES 4

450g/1lb/3 cups fresh green beans
15ml/1 tbsp olive oil
5ml/1 tsp sesame oil
2 garlic cloves, crushed
2.5cm/1in piece of fresh root ginger, finely chopped
30ml/2 tbsp dark soy sauce

1 Steam the beans over a pan of boiling salted water for 4 minutes or until just tender.

2 Meanwhile, heat the olive and sesame oils in a heavy pan, add the garlic and sauté for 2 minutes.

3 Stir in the ginger and soy sauce, and cook, stirring constantly, for a further 2–3 minutes until the liquid has reduced, then pour this mixture over the warm beans. Leave for a few minutes to allow all the flavours to mingle before serving.

Nutritional information per portion: Energy 62kcal/254kJ; Protein 2.4g; Carbohydrate 4.2g, of which sugars 3.1g; Fat 4.1g, of which saturates 0.6g; Cholesterol 0mg; Calcium 42mg; Fibre 2.5g; Sodium 534mg.

Desserts

Sumptuous sweets do not have to be laden

with fat and sugar. Many of the recipes in

this chapter, such as delicately flavoured

Mango and Orange Sorbet, are as luscious

as you like, but won't add to your waistline.

Date, Fig and Orange Pudding and Winter

Fruit Poached in Mulled Wine make the most

of dried fruit. You'll also find inspiring rice

pudding variations, such as the saffron- and

cardamom-scented Indian Rice Pudding.

Mango and orange sorbet

Fresh and tangy, and gloriously vibrant in colour, this sorbet is the perfect finale to a spicy meal, with its delicate balance of sweet tropical flavour and icy freshness.

SERVES 2–4

115g/4oz/¹/₂ cup golden caster
    (superfine) sugar
2 large mangoes
juice of 1 orange
1 egg white (optional)
thinly pared strips of fresh unwaxed
    orange rind, to decorate

1 Gently heat the sugar and 300ml/
¹/₂ pint/1¹/₄ cups water in a pan until
the sugar has dissolved. Bring to the
boil, reduce the heat and simmer for
5 minutes. Leave the syrup to cool.

2 Cut away the two sides of the
mangoes as close to the stones
(pits) as possible. Peel, then cut the
flesh from the stones. Dice the fruit
and discard the stones.

3 Process the mango flesh and orange
juice in a food processor or blender
with the syrup to a smooth purée.

4 Pour the mixture into a
freezerproof container and freeze
for 2 hours until semi-frozen.

5 Whisk the egg white, if using,
until it forms stiff peaks, then stir
it into the sorbet. Whisk well to
remove any ice crystals and freeze
until solid.

6 Transfer the frozen sorbet to the
refrigerator 10 minutes before
serving to allow it to soften a little.

7 Serve decorated with orange rind.

Nutritional information per portion: Energy 161kcal/686kJ; Protein 0.7g; Carbohydrate 41.7g, of which sugars 41.5g; Fat 0.2g, of which saturates 0.1g; Cholesterol 0mg; Calcium 26mg; Fibre 2g; Sodium 5mg.

Rhubarb and ginger yogurt ice

This delicate pink yogurt ice is subtly flavoured with honey and ginger, combined with the tangy flavour of rhubarb. The fromage frais adds an extra layer of smoothness.

SERVES 6

300g/11oz/scant 1¹/₂ cups set natural (plain) live yogurt
200g/7oz/scant 1 cup fromage frais (low-fat cream cheese)
375g/13oz/3 cups rhubarb, trimmed and chopped
45ml/3 tbsp preserved stem ginger syrup
30ml/2 tbsp clear honey
3 pieces of preserved stem ginger, finely chopped

1 In a bowl, whisk together the yogurt and fromage frais.

2 Pour the yogurt mixture into a shallow freezerproof container and freeze for 1 hour.

3 Meanwhile, put the rhubarb, stem ginger syrup and honey in a large pan and cook over low heat for 15 minutes or until the rhubarb is soft. Leave to cool, then purée in a food processor or blender.

4 Remove the semi-frozen yogurt mixture from the freezer and fold in the rhubarb and stem ginger purée. Beat well until smooth. Add the chopped stem ginger.

5 Return to the freezer and freeze for a further 2 hours. Remove from the freezer and beat again, then freeze until solid. Transfer the yogurt ice to the refrigerator 10 minutes before serving. Serve in scoops on individual plates or in bowls.

Nutritional information per portion: Energy 106kcal/446kJ; Protein 6.2g; Carbohydrate 9.1g, of which sugars 9.1g; Fat 5.4g, of which saturates 3.3g; Cholesterol 15mg; Calcium 150mg; Fibre 0.8g; Sodium 44mg.

Raspberry fromage frais and amaretti scrunch

This pudding looks stunning when it comes to the table, but it is actually very simple to make. The raspberries provide a luscious swirl of vibrant colour, while the melt-in-the-mouth amaretti biscuits make a crunchy contrast to the creamy fromage frais or yogurt.

SERVES 4–6

250g/9oz/1¹/₂ cups frozen or
    fresh raspberries
500g/1¹/₄lb/2¹/₂ cups fromage frais
    (low-fat cream cheese) or thick
    natural (plain) live yogurt
30ml/2 tbsp clear honey
finely grated rind of 1 small lemon
75g/3oz/1¹/₂ cups amaretti, broken
    into pieces
crystallized rose petals, to
    decorate (optional)

1 If using frozen raspberries, allow them to partly defrost. If using fresh ones, partly freeze them.

2 Put the fromage frais or yogurt in a large bowl and stir in the honey and lemon rind. Gently fold in the raspberries, being careful not to overmix. Chill for 1 hour.

3 Stir in the amaretti just before serving. Decorate with crystallized rose petals, if you wish.

HEALTH BENEFITS
Raspberries are extremely cleansing for the body and can relieve menstrual cramps and cystitis.

Nutritional information per portion: Energy 183kcal/771kJ; Protein 5.7g; Carbohydrate 27.2g, of which sugars 21.3g; Fat 6.4g, of which saturates 3.7g; Cholesterol 17mg; Calcium 99mg; Fibre 1.2g; Sodium 72mg.

Tropical fruit with hot rum and cinnamon sauce

Dark rum and cinnamon give this hot fruit dessert a distinctly Caribbean flavour. It is best eaten as soon as it is ready, so prepare the fruit ahead of time (except for the banana), and keep covered until needed. All that's left is to poach the fruit between courses – this takes only a few minutes.

SERVES 4

25g/1oz/2 tbsp unsalted butter

1 medium pineapple, peeled,
    cored and sliced

1 mango, peeled, stoned (pitted) and
    cut into 1cm/1/2in cubes

1 papaya, peeled, halved,
    seeded and sliced

2 bananas, thickly sliced

30ml/2 tbsp clear honey or maple syrup

5ml/1 tsp ground cinnamon

60ml/4 tbsp dark rum

natural (plain) live yogurt
    or yogurt ice, to serve

1 Melt the butter in a large heavy frying pan. Add the pineapple and cook for 3 minutes or until starting to brown, turning occasionally.

2 Add the prepared mango, papaya and bananas to the pan, and cook for 1 minute, turning occasionally.

3 Stir in the honey or maple syrup, cinnamon and rum, and cook for a further 2 minutes or until the sauce thickens and the fruit is tender. Be careful not to overcook.

4 Serve immediately with a dollop of yogurt or a scoop of yogurt ice.

Nutritional information per portion: Energy 413kcal/1765kJ; Protein 1.8g; Carbohydrate 107.5g, of which sugars 107.1g; Fat 0.4g, of which saturates 0.1g; Cholesterol 0mg; Calcium 81mg; Fibre 6g; Sodium 13mg.

Lemon and almond tart

This refreshing, tangy tart has a rich, creamy lemon filling set off by a caramelized sugar top. Serve warm or cold with a dollop of crème fraîche or natural yogurt.

SERVES 8–10

2 eggs
50g/2oz/¹/₄ cup golden caster
   (superfine) sugar
finely grated rind and juice of
   4 unwaxed lemons
2.5ml/¹/₂ tsp vanilla extract
50g/2oz/¹/₂ cup ground almonds
120ml/4fl oz/¹/₂ cup single (light) cream

FOR THE PASTRY

225g/8oz/2 cups unbleached
   spelt flour
75g/3oz/³/₄ cup icing (confectioners')
   sugar, plus extra for dusting
130g/4¹/₂oz/9 tbsp butter
1 egg, beaten
pinch of salt

1 Preheat the oven to 180°C/350°F/Gas 4. To make the pastry, sift together the flour and sugar in a bowl. Rub in the butter until the mixture resembles fine breadcrumbs. Add the egg and salt, and mix to a smooth dough. Knead lightly on a floured work surface. Form into a smooth flat round. Wrap in clear film (plastic wrap) and chill for 15 minutes.

2 Roll out the dough on a floured surface and use to line a 23cm/9 in loose-bottomed flan tin (pan). Prick the pastry base and chill for 15 minutes.

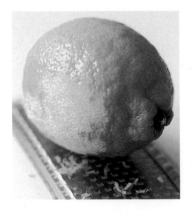

3 Line the pastry case with non-stick baking parchment. Add enough baking beans to cover the base of the pastry case and bake blind for about 10 minutes. Remove the paper and beans and return the pastry case to the oven for a further 10 minutes or until light golden.

4 Meanwhile, make the filling. Beat the eggs with the sugar until the mixture leaves a thin ribbon trail. Gently stir in the lemon rind and juice, vanilla extract, almonds and cream. Carefully pour the filling into the pastry case and level the surface. Bake for about 25 minutes until the filling is set.

5 Heat the grill (broiler) to high. Sift a thick layer of icing sugar over the tart. Grill until the sugar caramelizes. Dust with a little extra sifted icing sugar before serving warm or cold with crème fraîche or yogurt.

Nutritional information per portion: Energy 292kcal/1219kJ; Protein 6.3g; Carbohydrate 28.1g, of which sugars 14.1g; Fat 17.9g, of which saturates 8.9g; Cholesterol 91mg; Calcium 49mg; Fibre 2.4g; Sodium 105mg.

Pan-fried apple slices with walnut shortbread

Soft, caramelized apples and crisp nutty shortbread make a perfect combination. Serve warm with a spoonful of yogurt or fromage frais, or a scoop of vanilla ice cream.

SERVES 4

25g/1oz/2 tbsp unsalted butter
4 dessert apples, cored and thinly sliced
30ml/2 tbsp soft light brown sugar
10ml/2 tsp ground ginger
5ml/1 tsp ground cinnamon
2.5ml/¹/₂ tsp ground nutmeg

FOR THE WALNUT SHORTBREAD
75g/3oz/²/₃ cup wholemeal
   (whole-wheat) flour

75g/3oz/²/₃ cup unbleached plain
   (all-purpose) flour
25g/1oz/¹/₄ cup oatmeal
5ml/1 tsp baking powder
1.5ml/¹/₄ tsp salt
50g/2oz/¹/₄ cup golden caster
   (superfine) sugar
115g/4oz/8 tbsp unsalted butter
40g/1¹/₂oz/¹/₄ cup walnuts, finely chopped
15ml/1 tbsp milk, plus extra for brushing
demerara (raw) sugar, for sprinkling

1 Preheat the oven to 180°C/350°F/Gas 4 and lightly grease one or two baking sheets.

2 To make the walnut shortbread, sift together the wholemeal and plain flours, adding any bran left in the sieve (strainer). Mix with the oatmeal, baking powder, salt and sugar. Rub in the butter with your fingertips until the mixture resembles fine breadcrumbs. Add the chopped walnuts, then stir in enough of the milk to form a soft dough.

3 Gently knead the dough on a floured work surface. Form into a round, then roll out to a 5mm/¹/₄in thickness. Using a 7.5cm/3in fluted cutter, stamp out eight rounds – you may have some dough left over.

4 Place the shortbread rounds on the prepared baking sheets. Brush the tops with milk and sprinkle with sugar. Bake for 12–15 minutes until golden, then transfer to a wire rack and leave to cool.

5 To prepare the apple slices, melt the butter in a heavy frying pan. Add the apples and cook for 3–4 minutes over gentle heat until softened. Increase the heat to medium, add the sugar and spices, and stir well. Cook for a few minutes, stirring frequently so that the sauce doesn't burn, until it turns golden brown and caramelizes.

6 Place two shortbread rounds on each of four individual serving plates and spoon over the warm apple slices and sauce. Serve immediately.

COOK'S TIP
To prevent the apples browning after they are sliced, put them in a large bowl of water mixed with about 15ml/1 tbsp freshly squeezed lemon juice.

Nutritional information per portion: Energy 583kcal/2436kJ; Protein 6.5g; Carbohydrate 60.3g, of which sugars 27.1g; Fat 36.8g, of which saturates 18.9g; Cholesterol 75mg; Calcium 89mg; Fibre 3.6g; Sodium 221mg.

Coconut rice puddings with grilled oranges

Sticky rice pudding is a speciality of many South-east Asian countries. In these little desserts, Thai jasmine rice is cooked with rich and creamy coconut milk.

SERVES 4

175g/6oz/scant 1 cup jasmine rice, rinsed
    and drained
400ml/14fl oz/1²/₃ cup coconut milk
2.5ml/¹/₂ tsp grated nutmeg, plus extra
    for sprinkling
large pinch of salt
60ml/4 tbsp golden caster
    (superfine) sugar
oil, for greasing
2 oranges, skin and pith removed and cut
    into thin rounds
orange peel twists, to decorate

1 Put the rice in a pan, cover with water and bring to the boil. Cook for 5 minutes until the grains are just beginning to soften. Drain well. Put in a steamer lined with muslin (cheesecloth). Make a few holes in the muslin to allow steam to get through. Steam the rice for 15 minutes or until tender.

2 Put the steamed rice in a heavy pan with the coconut milk, nutmeg, salt and sugar, and cook over gentle heat until the mixture begins to simmer. Simmer for about 5 minutes until the mixture is thick and creamy, stirring frequently to prevent the rice sticking. Spoon the rice mixture into four lightly oiled 175ml/6fl oz/³/₄ cup moulds or ramekins, and leave to cool.

3 When ready to serve, heat the grill (broiler) to high. Line a baking sheet or the grill (broiler) rack with foil and place the orange slices on top. Sprinkle the oranges with a little grated nutmeg, then grill (broil) for 6 minutes until lightly golden, turning the slices halfway through cooking.

4 When the rice mixture is completely cold, run a knife around the edge of the moulds or ramekins and turn out the rice. Decorate with orange peel twists and serve with the warm orange slices.

Nutritional information per portion: Energy 261kcal/1103kJ; Protein 4.3g; Carbohydrate 60.8g, of which sugars 25.9g; Fat 0.6g, of which saturates 0.2g; Cholesterol 0mg; Calcium 75mg; Fibre 1.1g; Sodium 114mg.

Indian rice pudding

This creamy pudding is scented with saffron, cardamom and freshly grated nutmeg. Shelled pistachio nuts provide a subtle contrast in colour and add a delicious crunch.

SERVES 4

115g/4oz/³/₄ cup short grain brown rice
350ml/12fl oz/1¹/₂ cups boiling water
600ml/1 pint/2¹/₂ cups semi-skimmed (low-fat) milk
6 cardamom pods, bruised
2.5ml/¹/₂ tsp freshly grated nutmeg
pinch of saffron strands
60ml/4 tbsp maize (corn) malt syrup
15ml/1 tbsp clear honey
50g/2oz/¹/₂ cup pistachio nuts, chopped

1 Wash the rice under cold running water and place in a pan with the boiling water. Return to the boil and boil, uncovered, for 15 minutes.

2 Pour the milk over the rice, then reduce the heat and simmer, partially covered, for 15 minutes.

3 Add the cardamom pods, grated nutmeg, saffron, maize malt syrup and honey, and cook for a further 15 minutes or until the rice is tender, stirring occasionally.

4 Spoon the rice into small serving bowls and sprinkle with pistachio nuts before serving hot or cold.

HEALTH BENEFITS
Brown rice is unrefined and therefore, unlike white polished rice, retains most of its fibre and nutrients. It is a source of some B complex vitamins and vitamin E.

Nutritional information per portion: Energy 228kcal/961kJ; Protein 7.3g; Carbohydrate 44.7g, of which sugars 21.8g; Fat 2.7g, of which saturates 1.6g; Cholesterol 9mg; Calcium 188mg; Fibre 0g; Sodium 106mg.

Date, fig and orange pudding

This light steamed pudding avoids the use of suet, which is usually made from hydrogenated fat, often animal in origin. The addition of fresh orange juice and rind, and orange liqueur, gives the pudding an intense citrus tang, contrasting beautifully with the sweet dates and figs.

SERVES 6

juice and rind of 2 oranges
115g/4oz/²/₃ cup stoned (pitted), ready-to-eat dried dates, chopped
115g/4oz/²/₃ cup ready-to-eat dried figs, chopped
30ml/2 tbsp orange liqueur (optional)
175g/6oz/³/₄ cup unsalted butter, plus extra for greasing

175g/6oz/³/₄ cup soft light brown sugar
3 eggs
75g/3oz/²/₃ cup self-raising wholemeal (self-rising whole-wheat) flour
115g/4oz/1 cup unbleached self-raising (self-rising) flour
30ml/2 tbsp golden (light corn) syrup (optional)

1 Reserve a few strips of orange rind for decorating the pudding, and put the rest in a pan with the orange juice. Add the chopped dates and figs, and orange liqueur, if using. Cook, covered, over gentle heat for 8–10 minutes, until the fruit is soft.

2 Leave the fruit mixture to cool, then transfer to a food processor or blender and purée until smooth. Press the fig purée through a sieve (strainer) to remove the fig seeds, if you wish.

3 Cream the butter and sugar until pale and fluffy, then beat in the fig purée. Beat in the eggs, then fold in the flours and mix until combined.

4 Grease a 1.5 litre/2¹/₂ pint/6 cup pudding basin and pour in the golden syrup, if using. Tilt the bowl to coat the inside with a layer of syrup. Spoon in the pudding mixture. Cover the top with baking parchment, with a pleat down the centre, then with pleated foil. Tie down with string.

5 Sit the bowl in a large pan and pour in enough water to come halfway up the sides of the bowl. Cover with a tight-fitting lid and steam for 2 hours. Check the water level occasionally and top up if necessary. Turn out and decorate with the reserved orange rind.

Nutritional information per portion: Energy 583kcal/2447kJ; Protein 7.7g; Carbohydrate 81.4g, of which sugars 57.6g; Fat 27.5g, of which saturates 16.1g; Cholesterol 157mg; Calcium 177mg; Fibre 3.1g; Sodium 312mg.

Baked ricotta cakes with red sauce

These honey and vanilla-flavoured desserts take only minutes to make. The fragrant fruity sauce provides a contrast of both colour and flavour.

SERVES 4

250g/9oz/generous 1 cup ricotta cheese
2 egg whites, beaten
60ml/4 tbsp clear honey, plus extra
    to taste
5ml/1 tsp vanilla extract
450g/1lb/4 cups mixed fresh or frozen
    fruit, such as strawberries, raspberries,
    blackberries and cherries
fresh mint leaves, to decorate (optional)

1 Preheat the oven to 180°C/ 350°F/Gas 4.

2 Put the ricotta cheese in a bowl and break it up with a wooden spoon. Add the beaten egg whites, honey and vanilla extract, and mix thoroughly until the mixture is smooth and well combined.

3 Lightly grease four ramekins. Spoon the ricotta mixture into the prepared ramekins and level the tops. Bake for 20 minutes or until the cakes are risen and golden.

4 Meanwhile, make the fruit sauce. Reserve about a quarter of the fruit for decoration. Put the rest of the fruit in a pan, with a little water if the fruit is fresh, and heat gently until softened. Leave to cool slightly, and remove any cherry stones (pits), if using cherries.

5 Press the fruit through a sieve (strainer), then taste and sweeten with more honey if it is too tart. Serve the sauce, warm or cold, with the ricotta cakes. Decorate with the reserved fruit and mint leaves, if using.

Nutritional information per portion: Energy 161kcal/674kJ; Protein 8.1g; Carbohydrate 11.5g, of which sugars 11.5g; Fat 9.6g, of which saturates 5.9g; Cholesterol 26mg; Calcium 23mg; Fibre 0.6g; Sodium 63mg.

Apricot panettone bread and butter pudding

Panettone makes a rich addition to this traditional pudding, taking the place of the more usual white bread. Plump dried apricots add their own characteristic tang.

SERVES 6

unsalted butter, for greasing
350g/12oz panettone, sliced
    into triangles
25g/1oz/¼ cup pecan nuts
75g/3oz/⅓ cup ready-to-eat
    unsulphured dried apricots, chopped
500ml/17fl oz/2¼ cups semi-skimmed
    (low-fat) milk
5ml/1 tsp vanilla extract
1 large (US extra large) egg, beaten
30ml/2 tbsp maple syrup
freshly grated nutmeg
demerara (raw) sugar, for sprinkling

1 Butter a 1 litre/1¾ pint/4 cup baking dish. Arrange half the panettone triangles in the dish, scatter over half the pecan nuts and all the apricots, then add another layer of panettone on top.

2 Heat the milk and vanilla extract in a small pan until it just simmers. Put the egg and maple syrup in a large bowl, grate in 2.5ml/½ tsp nutmeg, then whisk in the hot milk.

3 Preheat the oven to 200°C/400°F/Gas 6. Pour the egg mixture over the panettone, lightly pressing down on the bread so that it is submerged. Leave the pudding to stand for 10 minutes.

4 Sprinkle over the reserved pecan nuts with a little freshly grated nutmeg and demerara sugar. Bake for 40–45 minutes until risen and golden. Serve hot.

Nutritional information per portion: Energy 972kcal/4068kJ; Protein 19.1g; Carbohydrate 105.8g, of which sugars 69.2g; Fat 55.6g, of which saturates 31.5g; Cholesterol 262mg; Calcium 332mg; Fibre 5g; Sodium 510mg.

Winter fruit poached in mulled wine

In this warming winter dessert, fresh apples and pears are combined with dried apricots and figs, and cooked in a fragrant, spicy wine until tender and intensely flavoured.

SERVES 4

300ml/¹/₂ pint/1¹/₄ cups red wine

300ml/¹/₂ pint/1¹/₄ cups fresh orange juice

finely grated rind and juice of 1 orange

45ml/3 tbsp clear honey or barley malt syrup

1 cinnamon stick, broken in half

4 cloves

4 cardamom pods, split

2 pears, such as Comice or William, peeled, cored and halved

8 ready-to-eat dried figs

12 ready-to-eat unsulphured dried apricots

2 eating apples, peeled, cored and thickly sliced

1 Put the wine, the fresh and squeezed orange juice and half the orange rind in a pan with the honey or syrup and spices. Bring to the boil, then reduce the heat and simmer for 2 minutes, stirring occasionally.

2 Add the pears, figs and apricots to the pan. Cook, covered, for 25 minutes, occasionally turning the fruit in the wine mixture. Add the sliced apples and cook for a further 12–15 minutes until the fruit is tender.

3 Remove the fruit from the pan and discard the spices. Cook the wine mixture over high heat until reduced and syrupy, then pour over the fruit. Serve decorated with the remaining orange rind, if you wish.

HEALTH BENEFITS

• *The combination of fresh and dried fruit ensures a healthy amount of vitamins and minerals, particularly vitamin C, beta carotene, potassium and iron. The fruit is also rich in fibre.*

• *Cardamom and cinnamon soothe indigestion and, along with cloves, can offer relief from colds and coughs.*

Nutritional information per portion: Energy 494kcal/2100kJ; Protein 7.3g; Carbohydrate 105.5g, of which sugars 105.5g; Fat 2.2g, of which saturates 0g; Cholesterol 0mg; Calcium 309mg; Fibre 14.6g; Sodium 85mg.

Cakes, Bakes and Bread

There is nothing more inviting than the

aroma of freshly baked bread and cakes.

Fresh and dried fruits are included in many

of the cakes, lending a natural sweetness.

Equally tempting are the vitamins, fibre and

minerals that high-carbohydrate breads can

provide, especially when made with

wholemeal flour. Flavourful extras, such as

herbs, garlic, vegetables and spices, boost

the nutritional and therapeutic benefits.

Plum crumble pie

Polenta adds a wonderful golden hue and crunchiness to the crumble topping for this fruit-filled pie. A spoonful of warm custard or fresh cream on top completes the indulgence.

SERVES 6–8

115g/4oz/1 cup unbleached plain
    (all-purpose) flour, sifted
115g/4oz/1 cup wholemeal
    (whole-wheat) flour
150g/5oz/³⁄₄ cup golden caster
    (superfine) sugar
115g/4oz/1 cup polenta
5ml/1 tsp baking powder
pinch of salt
150g/5oz unsalted butter,
    plus extra for greasing

1 egg
15ml/1 tbsp olive oil
25g/1oz/¹⁄₄ cup rolled oats
15ml/1 tbsp demerara (raw) sugar
custard or cream, to serve

FOR THE FILLING
10ml/2 tsp caster (superfine) sugar
15ml/1 tbsp polenta
450g/1lb dark plums

1 Mix together the flours, sugar, polenta, baking powder and salt in a large bowl. Rub in the butter with your fingertips until the mixture resembles fine breadcrumbs. Stir in the egg and olive oil, and enough cold water to form a smooth dough.

2 Grease a 23cm/9in spring-form cake tin (pan). Press two-thirds of the dough evenly over the bottom and up the sides of the tin. Wrap the remaining dough in clear film (plastic wrap) and chill while you make the filling.

3 Preheat the oven to 180°C/350°F/Gas 4. Sprinkle the sugar and polenta into the pastry case. Cut the plums in half and remove the stones (pits), then put the plums, cut-side down, on top of the polenta.

4 Remove the remaining dough from the refrigerator and crumble it between your fingers, then combine with the oats. Sprinkle evenly over the plums, then sprinkle the demerara sugar on top.

5 Bake for 50 minutes or until golden. Leave for 15 minutes before removing the pie from the tin. Leave to cool on a wire rack. Serve with custard or cream.

Nutritional information per portion: Energy 426kcal/1787kJ; Protein 6.4g; Carbohydrate 60.5g, of which sugars 26.5g; Fat 18.9g, of which saturates 10.2g; Cholesterol 64mg; Calcium 53mg; Fibre 3.2g; Sodium 127mg.

Courgette and double-ginger cake

Both fresh and preserved ginger are used to flavour this unusual tea bread. It is delicious served warm, cut into thick slices and spread with butter or margarine.

SERVES 8–10

3 eggs
225g/8oz/generous 1 cup caster
    (superfine) sugar
250ml/8fl oz/1 cup sunflower oil
5ml/1 tsp vanilla extract
15ml/1 tbsp syrup from a jar of
    preserved stem ginger
225g/8oz courgettes (zucchini), grated
2.5cm/1in piece of fresh root
    ginger, grated
350g/12oz/3 cups unbleached plain
    (all-purpose) flour
5ml/1 tsp baking powder
pinch of salt
5ml/1 tsp ground cinnamon
2 pieces of preserved stem
    ginger, chopped
15ml/1 tbsp demerara (raw) sugar

1 Preheat the oven to 190°C/325°F/Gas 5. Beat together the eggs and sugar until light and fluffy. Slowly beat in the oil until the mixture forms a batter. Mix in the vanilla extract and ginger syrup, then stir in the courgettes and fresh ginger.

2 Sift together the flour, baking powder and salt into a large bowl. Add the cinnamon and mix well, then quickly but gently stir the dried ingredients into the courgette mixture.

3 Lightly grease a 900g/2lb loaf tin (pan), and pour in the courgette mixture. Smooth and level the top, then sprinkle the chopped ginger and demerara sugar over the surface.

4 Bake for 1 hour or until a skewer inserted into the centre of the cake comes out clean. Leave the cake in the tin to cool for about 20 minutes, then turn out on to a wire rack.

Nutritional information per portion: Energy 252kcal/1060kJ; Protein 5.6g; Carbohydrate 35.6g, of which sugars 8.8g; Fat 10.7g, of which saturates 1.6g; Cholesterol 57mg; Calcium 73mg; Fibre 1.3g; Sodium 82mg.

Rich lemon poppy seed cake

The classic combination of poppy seeds and lemon is used for this cake, which has a wonderful lemon curd and fromage frais filling.

SERVES 8

350g/12oz/1¹/₂ cups unsalted butter,
  plus extra for greasing
350g/12oz/1³/₄ cups golden caster
  (superfine) sugar
45ml/3 tbsp poppy seeds
20ml/4 tsp finely grated lemon rind
70ml/4 heaped tbsp luxury lemon curd
6 eggs, separated
120ml/4fl oz/¹/₂ cup semi-skimmed
  (low-fat) milk
350g/12oz/3 cups unbleached
  self-raising (self-rising) flour, plus
  extra for flouring
icing (confectioners') sugar, to decorate

FOR THE FILLING

150g/5oz/¹/₂ cup luxury lemon curd
150ml/5fl oz/²/₃ cup fromage frais
  or mascarpone

1 Butter and lightly flour two 23cm/9in springform cake tins (pans). Preheat the oven to 180°C/350°F/Gas 4.

2 Cream together the butter and sugar with a wooden spoon until light and fluffy. Add the poppy seeds, lemon rind, lemon curd and egg yolks, and beat well, then add the milk and mix well. Gently fold in the flour until combined.

3 Whisk the egg whites using a hand-held electric mixer until they form soft peaks. Carefully fold the egg whites into the cake mixture until just combined. Divide the cake mixture between the prepared tins.

4 Bake for 40–45 minutes, until a skewer inserted into the centre of the cakes comes out clean and the tops are golden. Leave to cool in the tins for 5 minutes, then remove from the tins and leave to cool completely on wire racks. To finish, spread one cake with the lemon curd and spoon the fromage frais or mascarpone evenly over the lemon curd. Put the second cake on top, press down gently, then dust with icing sugar before serving.

Nutritional information per portion: Energy 805kcal/3374kJ; Protein 10.7g; Carbohydrate 99.6g, of which sugars 60.9g; Fat 43.3g, of which saturates 25.3g; Cholesterol 246mg; Calcium 242mg; Fibre 1.4g; Sodium 509mg.

Date and walnut spice cake

This deliciously moist and richly spiced cake is topped with a sticky honey and orange glaze.
You can serve it as a dessert if you like. Simply cut into wedges, and serve with a generous
spoonful of natural yogurt or crème fraîche, flavoured with grated orange rind.

SERVES 8

115g/4oz/^{1}/$_2$ cup unsalted butter,
   plus extra for greasing
175g/6oz/^{3}/$_4$ cup soft dark brown sugar
2 eggs
175g/6oz/1^1/$_2$ cups unbleached self-raising
   (self-rising) flour, plus extra for dusting
5ml/1 tsp bicarbonate of soda (baking soda)
2.5ml/^{1}/$_2$ tsp freshly grated nutmeg
5ml/1 tsp mixed (apple pie) spice
pinch of salt

175ml/6fl oz/^{3}/$_4$ cup buttermilk
50g/2oz/^{1}/$_3$ cup ready-to-eat stoned (pitted)
   dates, chopped
25g/1oz/^{1}/$_4$ cup walnuts, chopped

FOR THE TOPPING

60ml/4 tbsp clear honey
45ml/3 tbsp fresh orange juice
15ml/1 tbsp coarsely grated orange rind, plus
   extra to decorate

1 Grease and lightly flour a 23cm/9in springform cake tin
(pan). Preheat the oven to 180°C/350°F/Gas 4.

2 Cream together the butter and sugar with a wooden
spoon until fluffy and creamy. Add the eggs, one at a time,
and beat well to combine.

3 Sift together the flour, bicarbonate of soda, spices and
salt. Gradually add this to the creamed mixture, alternating
with the buttermilk. Add the dates and walnuts, and stir
well to combine evenly.

4 Spoon the mixture into the prepared cake tin and level the top. Bake for 50 minutes or until a
skewer inserted into the centre of the cake comes out clean. Leave to cool for 5 minutes, then turn
out on to a wire rack to cool completely.

5 To make the topping, heat the honey, orange juice and rind in a small heavy pan. Bring to the boil
and boil rapidly for 3 minutes, without stirring, until syrupy. Make small holes over the top of the
warm cake using the skewer, and pour over the hot syrup. Decorate with the extra orange rind.

Nutritional information per portion: Energy 350kcal/1472kJ; Protein 5.1g; Carbohydrate 50.3g, of which sugars 34.1g; Fat 15.7g, of which saturates 8.1g;
Cholesterol 79mg; Calcium 131mg; Fibre 1g; Sodium 196mg.

Chunky chocolate and banana muffins

Luxurious but not overly sweet, these muffins are simple and quick to make – and practically impossible to resist. Serve warm while the chocolate is still gooey.

MAKES 12

**90ml/6 tbsp semi-skimmed
    (low-fat) milk**
2 eggs
**150g/5oz/10 tbsp unsalted
    butter, melted**
**225g/8oz/2 cups unbleached plain
    (all-purpose) flour**
pinch of salt
5ml/1 tsp baking powder
**150g/5oz/³/₄ cup golden caster
    (superfine) sugar**
**150g/5oz plain (semisweet) chocolate,
    cut into large chunks**
2 small bananas, mashed

1 Place 12 large paper cases in a deep patty tins (muffin pans). Preheat the oven to 200°C/400°F/Gas 6.

2 In a bowl, whisk together the milk, eggs and butter until combined. Sift together the flour, salt and baking powder into a separate bowl. Add the sugar and chocolate to the flour mixture, then stir to combine. Slowly stir in the milk mixture, but do not beat. Fold in the mashed bananas.

3 Spoon the mixture into the paper cases. Bake for 20 minutes until golden. Cool on a wire rack.

HEALTH BENEFITS
Bananas are rich in potassium, which is vital for muscle and nerve function.

Nutritional information per portion: Energy 240kcal/1003kJ; Protein 3.7g; Carbohydrate 26.3g, of which sugars 11.6g; Fat 14.1g, of which saturates 8.4g; Cholesterol 59mg; Calcium 47mg; Fibre 1g; Sodium 92mg.

Apricot and hazelnut oat cookies

These cookie-cum-flapjacks have a chewy, crumbly texture. They are sprinkled with apricots and toasted hazelnuts, but any combination of dried fruit and nuts can be used.

MAKES 9

115g/4oz/½ cup unsalted butter,
    plus extra for greasing
75g/3oz/scant ½ cup golden caster
    (superfine) sugar
15ml/1 tbsp clear honey
115g/4oz/1 cup self-raising (self-rising)
    flour, sifted
115g/4oz/1 cup rolled oats
75g/3oz/scant ½ cup unsulphured
    ready-to-eat dried apricots, chopped

FOR THE TOPPING

25g/1oz/2 tbsp unsulphured ready-to-
    eat dried apricots, chopped
25g/1oz/¼ cup hazelnuts, toasted
    and chopped

1 Preheat the oven to 170°C/325°F/Gas 3. Lightly grease a large baking sheet. Put the butter, sugar and honey in a small heavy pan, and cook over a gentle heat, stirring occasionally, until the butter melts and the sugar dissolves. Remove the pan from the heat.

2 Put the flour, oats and apricots in a bowl, add the honey mixture and mix with a wooden spoon to form a sticky dough.

3 Divide the dough into nine pieces and place on the baking sheet. Press into 1cm/½in thick rounds. Scatter over the apricots and hazelnuts, and press into the dough.

4 Bake for 15 minutes until golden and slightly crisp. Leave to cool on the baking sheet for 5 minutes, then transfer to a wire rack.

Nutritional information per portion: Energy 262kcal/1098kJ; Protein 3.7g; Carbohydrate 33.2g, of which sugars 14.4g; Fat 13.6g, of which saturates 6.8g; Cholesterol 27mg; Calcium 71mg; Fibre 2.1g; Sodium 130mg.

Cheese and potato scones

The unusual addition of creamy mashed potato gives these wholemeal scones a light moist crumb and a crisp crust. A sprinkling of mature Cheddar and sesame seeds adds the finishing touch.

MAKES 9

115g/4oz/1 cup wholemeal
   (whole-wheat) flour
2.5ml/¹/₂ tsp salt
20ml/4 tsp baking powder
40g/1¹/₂oz/3 tbsp unsalted butter,
   plus extra for greasing
2 free-range (farm fresh) eggs, beaten

50ml/2fl oz/¹/₄ cup semi-skimmed (low-fat)
   milk or buttermilk
115g/4oz/1¹/₃ cups cooked mashed potato
45ml/3 tbsp chopped fresh sage
50g/2oz/¹/₂ cup grated mature (sharp)
   vegetarian Cheddar cheese
sesame seeds, for sprinkling

1 Preheat the oven to 220°C/425°F/Gas 7. Grease a baking sheet.

2 Sift the flour, salt and baking powder into a bowl. Rub in the butter using your fingertips until the mixture resembles fine breadcrumbs, then mix in half the beaten eggs and all the milk or buttermilk. Add the mashed potato, sage and half the Cheddar, and mix to a soft dough with your hands.

3 Turn out the dough on to a floured surface and knead lightly until smooth. Roll out the dough to 2cm/³/₄in thick, then stamp out nine scones using a 6cm/2¹/₂in fluted cutter.

4 Place the scones on the prepared baking sheet and brush the tops with the remaining beaten egg. Sprinkle the rest of the cheese and the sesame seeds on top and bake for 15 minutes until golden. Transfer to a wire rack. Leave to cool.

VARIATIONS
• *Use unbleached self-raising (self-rising) flour instead of wholemeal (whole-wheat) flour and baking powder, if you wish.*
• *Fresh rosemary, basil or thyme can be used in place of the sage.*

Nutritional information per portion: Energy 124kcal/517kJ; Protein 4.9g; Carbohydrate 10.5g, of which sugars 0.7g; Fat 7.1g, of which saturates 4g; Cholesterol 57mg; Calcium 60mg; Fibre 1.3g; Sodium 87mg.

Spicy millet bread

This is a delicious spicy bread with a golden crust and flecked with nutritious millet grains.
Cut into wedges, as you would a cake, and serve warm with a thick vegetable soup.

MAKES 1 LOAF

90g/3¹/₂oz/¹/₂ cup millet
550g/1lb 6oz/5¹/₂ cups strong unbleached
   plain (all-purpose) flour
10ml/2 tsp salt
5ml/1 tsp sugar
5ml/1 tsp dried chilli flakes (optional)

7g/¹/₄oz sachet easy-blend (rapid-rise)
   dried yeast
25g/1oz/2 tbsp unsalted butter
1 onion, roughly chopped
15ml/1 tbsp cumin seeds
5ml/1 tsp ground turmeric

1 Bring 200ml/7fl oz/scant 1 cup water to the boil, add the
millet, cover and simmer gently for 20 minutes until the
grains are soft and the water is absorbed. Remove from
the heat and leave to cool until just warm.

2 Mix together the flour, salt, sugar, chilli flakes, if using, and
yeast in a large bowl. Stir in the millet, then add 350ml/
12fl oz/1¹/₂ cups warm water and mix to form a soft
dough. Turn out on to a floured work surface. Knead well for
10 minutes or until smooth and elastic. Place in an oiled
bowl, cover with oiled clear film (plastic wrap) and leave
to rise in a warm place for 1 hour until doubled in bulk.

3 Meanwhile, to make the onion filling, melt the butter in a heavy frying pan, add the onion and fry
for 10 minutes until softened, stirring occasionally. Add the cumin seeds and turmeric, and fry for a
further 5–8 minutes, stirring constantly, until the cumin seeds begin to pop. Set aside.

4 Knock back (punch down) the dough by pressing down with your knuckles to deflate the dough,
then shape into a round. Place the onion mixture in the middle of the dough and bring the sides
over the filling to make a parcel. Seal well. Place the loaf on an oiled baking sheet, seam-side down,
cover with oiled clear film and leave in a warm place for 45 minutes until doubled in bulk.

5 Preheat the oven to 220°C/425°F/Gas 7. Bake the bread for 30 minutes until golden. It should
sound hollow when tapped underneath. Leave to cool on a wire rack.

Nutritional information per loaf: Energy 2464kcal/10426kJ; Protein 59.7g; Carbohydrate 509.5g, of which sugars 15.9g; Fat 31.5g, of which saturates 14.1g;
Cholesterol 53mg; Calcium 957mg; Fibre 22.5g; Sodium 4209mg.

Wholemeal sunflower bread

Sunflower seeds, which are rich in vitamin E, give a nutty crunchiness to this wholemeal loaf.
Serve with a chunk of cheese and a slathering of rich tomato chutney.

MAKES 1 LOAF

450g/1lb/4 cups strong wholemeal
   (whole-wheat) bread flour
2.5ml/¹⁄₂ tsp easy-blend (rapid-rise)
   dried yeast
2.5ml/¹⁄₂ tsp salt
50g/2oz/¹⁄₂ cup sunflower seeds, plus
   extra for sprinkling

1 Grease and lightly flour a 450g/
1lb loaf tin (pan).

2 In a large bowl, mix together the
flour, yeast, salt and sunflower
seeds. Make a well in the centre and
gradually stir in 300ml/¹⁄₂ pint/
1¹⁄₄ cups warm water. Using a
wooden spoon, mix vigorously to
form a soft, sticky dough. The dough
should be quite sticky, so don't be
tempted to add any extra flour.

3 Cover the bowl with a damp dish
towel and leave the dough to rise in
a warm place for 45–50 minutes or
until doubled in bulk.

4 Preheat the oven to 200°C/
400°F/Gas 6. Turn out the dough on
to a floured work surface and knead
for 10 minutes – the dough will still
be quite sticky.

5 Form the dough into a rectangle
and place it in the prepared loaf tin.
Sprinkle the top with sunflower
seeds. Cover with a damp dish
towel, and leave to rise again for
another 15 minutes.

6 Bake for 40–45 minutes until
golden. Leave in the tin for
5 minutes, then turn out and
cool on a wire rack.

Nutritional information per loaf: Energy 1686kcal/7136kJ; Protein 67g; Carbohydrate 296.9g, of which sugars 10.3g;
Fat 33.6g, of which saturates 3.6g; Cholesterol 0mg; Calcium 226mg; Fibre 43.5g; Sodium 998mg.

Polenta and red pepper bread

Full of Mediterranean flavour, this satisfying sunshine-coloured bread is best eaten while still warm, drizzled with a little olive oil and served with soup.

MAKES 2 LOAVES

175g/6oz/1¹⁄₂ cups polenta

5ml/1 tsp salt

350g/12oz/3 cups unbleached strong white bread flour, plus extra for dusting

5ml/1 tsp sugar

7g/¹⁄₄oz sachet easy-blend (rapid-rise) dried yeast

1 red (bell) pepper, roasted, peeled and diced

15ml/1 tbsp olive oil

1 Mix together the polenta, salt, flour, sugar and yeast in a large bowl. Stir in the diced red pepper until evenly distributed, then make a well in the centre. Grease two loaf tins (pans).

2 Add 300ml/¹⁄₂ pint/1¹⁄₄ cups warm water and the oil, and mix to a soft dough. Knead for 10 minutes until smooth and elastic. Place in an oiled bowl and cover with oiled clear film (plastic wrap). Leave to rise in a warm place for 1 hour until doubled in bulk.

3 Knock back (punch down) the dough, knead lightly, then divide in half. Shape each piece of dough into an oblong and place in the tins. Cover each one with oiled clear film (plastic wrap) and leave to rise in a warm place for 45 minutes.

4 Preheat the oven to 220°C/425°F/Gas 7. Bake the loaves for 30 minutes until golden. Leave in the tins for 5 minutes, then turn out and cool on a wire rack.

Nutritional information per loaf: Energy 985kcal/4164kJ; Protein 24.7g; Carbohydrate 204g, of which sugars 9.7g; Fat 10.9g, of which saturates 1.2g; Cholesterol 0mg; Calcium 623mg; Fibre 8.8g; Sodium 634mg.

Fruit soda bread

This traditional Irish bread is quick to make because it does not require prolonged kneading or rising. It is best eaten while still warm, on the day of baking.

SERVES 4

225g/8oz/2 cups unbleached plain
   (all-purpose) flour
225g/8oz/2 cups wholemeal
   (whole-wheat) flour
5ml/1 tsp salt
5ml/1 tsp bicarbonate of soda (baking soda)

20ml/heaped 1 tbsp sugar
75g/3oz/³/₄ cup raisins
50g/2oz/¹/₄ cup ready-to-eat stoned
   (pitted) prunes, chopped
1 egg, lightly beaten
300ml/¹/₂ pint/1¹/₄ cups buttermilk

1 Preheat the oven to 200°C/400°F/Gas 6. Sift together the plain and wholemeal flours, salt and bicarbonate of soda into a large bowl, adding any bran left in the sieve (strainer). Add the sugar and dried fruit, and mix well to combine.

2 Make a well in the centre. Add the egg and buttermilk. Mix first with a wooden spoon, then with your hands, until it forms a soft, slightly sticky dough. If the dough is too dry, add a little more buttermilk.

3 Turn out the dough on to a lightly floured work surface and knead lightly until smooth. Form into a flat round, about 4cm/1¹/₂ in thick.

4 Place on a greased baking sheet and dust the loaf with plain flour. Cut a large deep cross in the top of the loaf, slicing almost through to the bottom of the dough round.

5 Bake for 30–35 minutes until risen and golden. The bread should sound hollow when tapped underneath. Transfer to a wire rack and leave to cool.

HEALTH BENEFITS
Dried fruit is recognized as a good source of fibre, as well as minerals such as potassium and iron.

Nutritional information per portion: Energy 497kcal/2112kJ; Protein 17.3g; Carbohydrate 105.4g, of which sugars 27.8g; Fat 3.7g, of which saturates 0.8g; Cholesterol 50mg; Calcium 214mg; Fibre 7.9g; Sodium 67mg.

Rosemary and rock salt focaccia

Enriched with olive oil and flavoured with rosemary, garlic and black olives, this popular Italian bread takes its name from the Italian word for hearth – which is where it was traditionally baked.

MAKES 1 LOAF

225g/8oz/2 cups unbleached plain
   (all-purpose) flour, sifted
2.5ml/$^1/_2$ tsp salt
7g/$^1/_4$oz sachet easy-blend (rapid-rise)
   dried yeast
4 garlic cloves, finely chopped
2 sprigs of fresh rosemary, leaves removed
   and chopped

10 black olives, pitted and roughly
   chopped (optional)
15ml/1 tbsp olive oil

FOR THE TOPPING
90ml/6 tbsp olive oil
10ml/2 tsp rock salt
sprig of fresh rosemary, leaves removed

1 Mix together the flour, salt, yeast, garlic, rosemary and olives, if using, in a large bowl. Make a well in the centre and add the olive oil and 150ml/$^1/_4$ pint/$^2/_3$ cup warm water. Mix thoroughly to form a soft dough.

2 Turn out the dough on to a floured work surface. Knead for 10–15 minutes. Put in an oiled bowl and cover with oiled clear film (plastic wrap) or a dish towel. Leave to rise in a warm place for 45 minutes until doubled in bulk.

3 Turn out the dough and knead lightly again. Roll out to a longish oval shape, about 1cm/$^1/_2$in thick. Place the dough on a greased baking sheet, cover loosely with oiled clear film or a dish towel, and leave in a warm place for 25–30 minutes to rise again.

4 Preheat the oven to 200°C/400°F/Gas 6. Make indentations with your fingertips all over the top of the bread. Drizzle two-thirds of the olive oil over the top, then sprinkle with the rock salt and rosemary. Bake for 25 minutes until golden. When ready, the bread will sound hollow when tapped underneath. Transfer to a wire rack and spoon the remaining olive oil over the top.

HEALTH BENEFITS
The oil in olives is monounsaturated, and this type of oil is believed to reduce blood cholesterol levels. Olives also provide good amounts of iron and the antioxidant vitamin E.

Nutritional information per loaf: Energy 1699kcal/7177kJ; Protein 37.8g; Carbohydrate 311g, of which sugars 9.7g; Fat 42.3g, of which saturates 6.1g; Cholesterol 0mg; Calcium 568mg; Fibre 13.1g; Sodium 14mg.

The Wholefood Kitchen

*This informative guide includes every kind
of natural food, from fruit and vegetables
to grains, and from dairy products to herbs
and spices. There are essential facts about
the key health benefits and traditional
healing qualities of each food, as well as
useful advice on buying, storing, preparing
and cooking wholefoods. It is an inspiration
to anyone interested in learning about foods
that can make you live, look and feel better.*

The basic vegetarian wholefood diet

We are often told to eat a balanced diet, but what does this mean in the context of a vegetarian diet? The key to good health is to eat a variety of foods that provide you with the right proportion of protein, carbohydrates, fibre, fat, vitamins and minerals, as well as water.

The ideal diet features enough calories to provide the body with vital energy but not an excess, which leads to weight gain. Getting this balance right is crucial to health.

When people opt for a vegetarian diet, it is not simply a matter of swapping meat and fish for cheese and eggs. Vegetarians need to ensure that they eat plenty of fruit and vegetables, legumes, nuts, seeds, rice, bread, pasta and potatoes and some dairy foods. They should aim to eat

nutrient-rich foods, rather than those that provide plenty of calories but few nutrients, such as cakes and crisps (potato chips). The following may be a useful guide:

WHOLE GRAINS AND POTATOES
Aim for 6–11 servings a day
This group includes cereals, such as oats, wheat, corn, millet, barley, bread, rice and pasta, as well as potatoes. Whole grains and potatoes should form the main part of every meal.

ABOVE: *Include breads made with whole grains and wholemeal flour in your diet.*

Wholemeal (whole-wheat) bread and pasta, brown rice, and potatoes with their skins on contain the most nutrients and provide starchy carbohydrates, fibre, protein, B complex vitamins and minerals.

A serving equals: 1 slice of bread, 1/2 cup of cooked cereal, rice or pasta or 1 medium potato.

FRUIT AND VEGETABLES
Aim for at least 5 servings a day
Fruit and vegetables provide significant amounts of vitamins, minerals and fibre, and are low in fat and calories. Cruciferous vegetables such as broccoli, cabbage, sprouts, cauliflower and chard provide a powerful combination of antioxidants, which are believed to provide protection

BELOW: *Potatoes in their skins provide more nutrients than if peeled.*

against certain cancers. Bright orange, yellow and red fruit and vegetables are rich in the antioxidant beta carotene and vitamin C.

A serving equals: 1 medium apple, banana or orange, a handful of cherry tomatoes, a glass of fresh fruit juice, 2 or more heaped serving spoonfuls of cooked vegetables or a bowl of salad.

LEGUMES, NUTS AND SEEDS
Aim for 2–3 servings a day
Legumes, including beans, peas and lentils, tofu and tempeh, and nuts and seeds provide valuable protein, fibre, iron, calcium, zinc and vitamins B and E. Legumes are low in fat and provide plenty of fibre. Nuts and seeds are very nutritious, but are high in fat and should be eaten in moderation.

A serving equals: a small handful of nuts and seeds, $1/2$ cup cooked beans or 115g/4oz tofu or tempeh.

DAIRY FOODS AND NON-DAIRY ALTERNATIVES
Aim for 2–3 servings a day
This group includes milk, cheese and yogurt from both dairy and non-dairy

sources, such as soya products, and provides valuable amounts of protein, calcium, vitamin B12, A and D. These foods can be high in fat, so should be consumed in moderation. Eggs are also included in this group; a maximum of 3–4 eggs a week is recommended.

A serving equals: 1 egg, a small slice of cheese, a small glass of milk, or a small pot of yogurt.

ABOVE: Fresh peas, beans and corn provide an abundance of nutrients.

FATS, SWEETS AND SNACKS
Eat sparingly
This diverse group includes chocolate, crisps, cakes and biscuits (cookies), as well as butter, margarine and cooking oils. These foods provide the body with few nutrients, but are high in calories and, if eaten to excess, will lead to weight gain. Sugary foods can cause tooth decay.

BELOW: Butter and margarine provide few nutrients and are laden with calories.

RIGHT: Tofu and beancurd are made from soya beans.

The essentials for good health

Along with water, there are six essential components for good health, which if consumed in the correct proportions will provide the body with both sustained energy and the correct balance of nutrients required.

CARBOHYDRATES

At one time carbohydrates, which are made up of starches, fibre and sugars, were considered to be fattening and less valuable than protein-rich foods. However, they are now recognized as the body's major source of energy, and they supply a substantial amount of protein, vitamins, minerals and fibre, with very little fat. About half the food we eat should be unrefined complex carbohydrates such as wholegrain cereals, wholemeal (whole-wheat) bread and pasta, and brown rice. These high-fibre foods are broken down slowly by the body and provide a steady supply of energy. They are preferable to sugars, or simple carbohydrates, because the energy supply is slowly released and has long term benefits, whereas sugars are quickly absorbed into the bloodstream and give only a short-term energy boost.

ABOVE: *Plantains, yams and potatoes provide us with a steady supply of energy.*

When feasible, opt for unrefined carbohydrates, as the refined versions such as white flour, rice and sugar are stripped of nutrients, including vitamins, minerals and fibre. It's important to remember that the more carbohydrates you eat, the more you depend on them for supplying essential nutrients.

FIBRE

Fruits, vegetables, grains, legumes, nuts and seeds are our main source of fibre, of which there are two types: insoluble and soluble. Insoluble fibre, which is found in wholegrain wheat, brown rice, bran and nuts, provides bulk to the diet and helps to combat constipation. Soluble fibre, found in

RIGHT: *Soluble fibre found in oats helps reduce blood cholesterol.*

legumes, vegetables and oats, binds with toxins in the gut and promotes their excretion, and also helps to reduce blood cholesterol. Both types of fibre reduce the risk of bowel disorders, including diverticulitis, colon and rectal cancer, and irritable bowel syndrome (although bran has been found to aggravate symptoms of IBS). Few people get enough fibre. On average we eat about 12g/¹⁄₂oz of fibre a day, but we should be consuming about 18g/³⁄₄oz. People who wish to lose weight will find that a high-fibre diet is beneficial because it provides bulk and naturally limits the amount of food eaten.

PROTEIN

This macro-nutrient is essential for the maintenance and repair of every cell in the body, and also ensures that enzymes, hormones and antibodies function properly. Protein is made up of amino acids, of which there are 20,

BELOW: *Remember that nuts contain fat as well as valuable protein.*

and eight of these need to be supplied by diet. A food that contains all eight amino acids is known as a 'complete' or high-quality protein. For vegetarians, these include eggs, dairy products and soya beans. Protein from plant sources such as nuts, pasta, potatoes, legumes, cereals and rice do not usually contain all eight amino acids and are known as 'incomplete' or low-quality protein. We should aim to get 10–15 per cent of our calories from protein.

Vegetarians are often asked where they get their protein, and lack of this nutrient can be a concern for those cutting out meat and fish from their diet. Yet in reality most people eat too much protein and deficiency is virtually unheard of. In fact, an excess of protein can be detrimental rather than beneficial to health. High-protein foods such as dairy products and nuts are a source of fat, and have been found to leach calcium from the body, which increases the risk of osteoporosis. It is also a common misconception that vegetarians have to meticulously combine protein foods in every meal to achieve the correct balance of amino acids. Nutritionists now believe that intentionally combining proteins is unnecessary, as long as a varied diet of grains, legumes, dairy produce, eggs and vegetables is eaten daily.

ABOVE: *Buckwheat pasta is 'complete' protein containing essential amino acids.*

How to increase your fibre intake
• Base your diet on wholegrain bread and pasta, brown rice and fruit and vegetables. Refined and processed foods contain less fibre and nutrients.
• Start the day with a wholegrain cereal, such as porridge or bran flakes.
• Eat plenty of dried fruit – add it to breakfast cereals, natural yogurt or use to make a compote.
• Add beans and lentils to salads and soups to boost their fibre content.
• Avoid peeling fruits and vegetables, if possible, because the skins contain valuable fibre.

Fruit

Perhaps the ultimate convenience food, most fruits can be simply washed and eaten, and, as the nutrients are concentrated just below the skin, it is best to avoid peeling. Cooking fruit reduces valuable vitamins and minerals, so, if you can, eat it raw. Most fruit is now available all year round, but it is generally best when home-grown, organically produced and in season.

ORCHARD FRUITS

Orchard fruits offer an incredible range of colours and flavours.

Apples

There are thousands of varieties of apple, although the choice in shops is often restricted to a mere few. Some of the most well-liked eating varieties are Cox's Orange Pippin, Granny Smith, Gala, Braeburn, and Golden and Red Delicious. The Bramley Seedling, with its thick, shiny, green skin and tart flesh, is the most familiar cooking apple and is perfect for baking, or as the basis of apple sauce.

Apples are delicious when eaten raw with their skin on. This versatile fruit is often used in breakfast dishes, main meals, salads, desserts, pies and even soups. Large cooking apples are ideal puréed, stewed and baked, but their tartness means that sugar has to be added. Some varieties of eating apple are just as good cooked and don't need any added sugar.

When buying, choose bright, firm fruits without any bruises. Organic apples are more prone to blemishes than non-organic ones, and the fruits can look a little tatty, but the taste is often superior. Store in a cool place, away from direct sunlight.

Apples aid digestion and can remove impurities in the liver. They are a good source of vitamin C and fibre, if you eat the skin. Although low in calories, apples contain fructose, a simple sugar that is released slowly to supply the body with energy and balance blood sugar levels. Skin problems and arthritis are said to benefit if apples are eaten regularly.

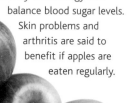

ABOVE: Large cooking apples (left) and eating apples

ABOVE: Apricots

Apricots

The best apricots are sunshine gold in colour and full of juice. They are delicious baked or used raw in salads. An apricot is at its best when truly ripe. Immature fruits are hard and tasteless, and never seem to reach the right level of sweetness. Apricots are extremely rich in beta carotene, minerals and vitamin A, and are a valuable source of fibre.

Cherries

There are two types: sweet and sour. Some are best eaten raw, such as the popular Bing variety, while others, such as Morello, are best cooked. Choose firm, bright, glossy fruits that have fresh, green stems. Discard any that are soft, or have split or damaged skin.

Cherries stimulate and cleanse the system, removing toxins from the kidneys. They are a remedy for gout and arthritis. Cherries also contain iron, potassium, vitamins C and B, as well as beta carotene.

Nectarines

Like a peach without the fuzzy skin, this sweet juicy fruit is named after the drink of the gods – nectar – and is delicious baked or used raw in salads.

When eaten raw, nectarines are especially rich in vitamin C. They aid digestion, effectively reduce high blood pressure and cleanse the body.

Peaches

These summer fruits are prized for their perfume and luscious juiciness. Peaches range in colour from gold to deep red, and the flesh can be orange or white. Peaches and nectarines are extremely fragile and bruise easily, so buy when slightly under-ripe. To ripen them quickly, place in a brown paper bag with an already ripened fruit. Store ripe nectarines and peaches in the refrigerator, but bring back to room temperature before eating.

Much of the vitamin C content of a peach lies in and just under its skin, so eat the fruit unpeeled. Peaches are an excellent source of the antioxidant beta carotene, said to lower the risk of heart disease and some cancers.

Pears

Late summer and autumn is when pears come into their own with the arrival of the new season's crops. Favourites are the green-and-brown-skinned Conference; Williams, with its thin, yellow skin and sweet, soft

flesh; plump Comice, which has a pale yellow skin with a green tinge; and Packham, excellent for cooking.

Some pears are good for cooking, others are best eaten raw, and a few varieties fit happily into both camps. Pears can be used in sweet and savoury dishes; they are excellent in salads, and can be baked, poached in syrup, and used in pies and tarts. They are unlikely to cause any allergic reactions, and so make ideal weaning food when cooked and puréed.

Choose firm, plump fruit that are just slightly under-ripe. Pears can ripen in a day or so, but they then pass their peak very quickly and become woolly or squashy. To tell if a pear is ripe, feel around the base of the stalk; it should give slightly when gently pressed, but the pear itself should be firm. Despite their high water content, pears contain useful amounts of vitamin C, fibre and potassium. In natural medicine, they are used as a diuretic and laxative.

Plums

Ranging from pale yellow to rich dark purple, plums come in many different varieties. They can be sweet and juicy, or slightly tart; the latter are best cooked in pies and cakes, or made into a delicious jam. Sweet plums can be eaten as

LEFT: From left to right, Conference, Comice and Williams pears

ABOVE: *Plums*

they are and in fruit salads, or puréed and combined with custard or yogurt to make a fruit fool.

Plums should be just firm, with shiny, smooth skin that has a slight 'bloom'. Store ripe plums in the refrigerator. Unripe fruits can be kept at room temperature for a few days to ripen. Plums relieve constipation and are said to stimulate the nerves.

Stoning fruit

1 To remove the stone (pit) from peaches, apricots or plums, cut around the middle of the fruit down to the stone with a paring knife. Twist each half of the fruit in opposite directions.

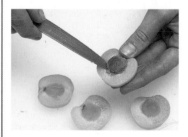

2 Prize out the stone using the tip of the knife, and discard. Rub the cut flesh with lemon juice.

BELOW: *Oranges*

CITRUS FRUITS

Juicy and brightly coloured, citrus fruits such as oranges, lemons and limes are best known for their sweet, slightly sour juice, which is rich in vitamin C. Invaluable in the kitchen, they add an aromatic acidity to many dishes, from sauces and soups to desserts. Try to buy organic fruit when you can, and eat within a week or two.

Look for plump, firm citrus fruit that feels heavy for its size. Fruits with bruises, brown spots, green patches (or yellow on limes) and soft, squashy skin should be avoided, as should dry, wrinkled specimens. Most citrus fruits are waxed or sprayed with fungicides, so scrub them thoroughly before using to remove any residues.

Oranges

Best eaten as soon as they are peeled, oranges start to lose vitamin C from the moment they are cut. Thin-skinned oranges tend to be the juiciest. Popular varieties include the Navel, which contains no pips and so is good for desserts; sweet, juicy Jaffa and Valencia; and Seville, a sour orange used to make marmalade.

Grapefruits

Grapefruit flesh ranges in colour from vivid pink and ruby red to white; the pink and red varieties are sweeter. Heavier fruits are likely to be juicier. Served juiced, halved or cut into slices, grapefruit can provide a refreshing start to the day. It also adds tang to salads or a contrast to rich foods. Cooking or grilling (broiling) mellows the tartness, but keep cooking times brief to preserve the nutrients.

Lemons

Both the juice and rind of this essential cooking ingredient can be used to enliven salad dressings, vegetables, marinades, sauces and biscuits. Lemon juice can also be used to prevent some fruits and vegetables from discolouring when cut. Lemons should be deep yellow in colour, firm and heavy for their size.

ABOVE: *Lemons*

Limes

Avoid limes with a yellowing skin, as this is a sign of deterioration. The juice has a sharper flavour than that of lemons; if you substitute limes for lemons in a recipe, you will need to use less juice. Limes are used a great deal in Asian cooking and the rind can be used to flavour an array of curries, marinades and dips. Coriander, chillies, garlic and ginger are natural partners.

Citrus nutrients

Eating an orange a day will generally supply an adult's daily requirement for vitamin C, but citrus fruits also contain phosphorus, potassium, calcium, beta carotene and fibre. Pectin, a soluble fibre that is found in the flesh and particularly in the membranes of citrus fruit, has been shown to reduce cholesterol levels. The membranes also contain bioflavonoids, which have powerful antioxidant properties. Try to choose fresh fruit juice when you can, as bottled, canned and concentrated citrus juices contain reduced levels of vitamin C.

BERRIES AND CURRANTS

These baubles of vivid red, purple and black are the epitome of summer and autumn, although they are now likely to be found all year round. Despite distinctive appearances and flavours, these soft fruits are interchangeable in their uses – jams, jellies, pies and tarts are some choices.

Strawberries

Strawberries do not need any embellishment. Serve ripe (avoid those with white or green tips) and raw, on their own, or with a little cream or some natural (plain) yogurt. Wash only if absolutely necessary and just before serving. Strawberries are rich in B complex vitamins and vitamin C.

Raspberries

Soft and fragrant, raspberries are best served simply and unadulterated. They are fragile and require the minimum of handling, so wash only if

BELOW: *Strawberries*

BELOW: *Raspberries*

ABOVE: *Blackberries*

really necessary. They are best eaten raw as cooking spoils their flavour and vitamin C content. Raspberries are a rich source of vitamin C. Store in the refrigerator for up to two days.

Blueberries

Dark purple in colour, ripe blueberries are plump and slightly firm, with a natural 'bloom'. Avoid any that are soft and dull-skinned, and wash and dry carefully to avoid bruising. Cultivated blueberries are larger than the wild variety. Both types are sweet enough to be eaten raw, but are also good cooked in pies and muffins, and used for jellies and jams. Unwashed blueberries will keep for up to a week in the bottom of the refrigerator. Blueberries are effective in treating urinary tract infections and can improve poor circulation.

Blackberries

These are a familiar sight in early autumn, growing wild in hedgerows. Cultivated blackberries have a slightly longer season and are generally much larger than the wild fruits. Juicy and plump, blackberries vary in sweetness, and are often cooked. Wash carefully to prevent bruising, then pat dry with kitchen paper. Use in pies and tarts, or make into jams and jellies. The berries

can also be lightly cooked, puréed and strained to make a sauce to serve with other fruits or ice cream.

Blackberries are high in fibre and contain a wealth of minerals, such as magnesium, iron and calcium. Rich in vitamin C, they are also one of the best low-fat sources of vitamin E. They are also rich in bioflavonoids, which act as antioxidants, inhibiting growth of cancer cells and protecting against cell damage by carcinogens.

Blackcurrants, redcurrants and whitecurrants

These delicate fruits are usually sold in bunches on the stem. To remove from the stalk, run the prongs of a fork down through the clusters, taking care not to damage the fruit. Wash the fruits carefully, then pat dry. Raw blackcurrants are quite tart, but this makes them ideal for cooking in sweet pies. They make delicious jams and jellies. Sweeter whitecurrants are a delightful addition to fruit salads.

Currants are high in antioxidants, vitamins C and E, and carotenes. They also contain fibre, calcium, iron and magnesium. Look for firm, glossy berries and currants. Make sure that they are not squashed or mouldy.

BELOW: *Blackcurrants*

GRAPES, MELONS, DATES AND FIGS

These fruits were some of the first ever to be cultivated and are available in an immense variety of shapes, colours and sizes, and, with the exception of melons, they can also be bought dried. As well as being a good source of nutrients, these fruits are high in soluble fibre.

ABOVE: *Galia melons (front left and back), cantaloupe (centre), and watermelon (right)*

Grapes

There are many varieties of grape, each with its own particular flavour and character. Most are grown for wine production. Grapes for eating are less acidic and have a thinner skin than those used for wine-making. Seedless grapes are easier to eat and contain less tannin than the seeded fruit. Grapes range in colour from deep purple to pale red, and from bright green to almost white. The finest eating grapes are Muscat grapes, which have a wonderful, perfumed flavour. They may be pale green or golden, or black or red. Italia grapes, another popular eating variety, have a luscious musky flavour and may be green or black. Unless they are organic, grapes should be thoroughly washed before eating because they are routinely sprayed with

pesticides and fungicides.

Serve grapes with cheese, in salads or as a topping for a tart. Before cooking them, remove the skin by blanching the grapes in boiling water for a few seconds, then peel with a small knife. Buy grapes that are plump and fairly firm. Unwashed fruit may be stored in the refrigerator for up to five days.

Melons

Watermelons are very low in calories because of their high water content, which is around 90 per cent. They contain less vitamin C than the fragrant, orange-fleshed varieties, such as the cantaloupe and Charentais. Avoid buying ready-cut melons because most of the vitamins will have been lost. Look for melons that feel heavy for their size and yield to gentle pressure at the stem end.

When they are eaten on their own, melons are easy to digest, and pass quickly through the system. But, when they are consumed with other foods requiring a more complex digestive process, they may actually inhibit the absorption of nutrients.

ABOVE: *Red and green grapes*

Figs

These delicate, thin-skinned fruits may be purple, brown or greenish-gold. Delicious raw, figs can also be poached or baked. Choose unbruised, ripe fruits that yield to gentle pressure, and eat on the day of purchase. If they are not too ripe, figs can be kept in the refrigerator for a day or two before eating. Figs are a well-known laxative and an excellent source of calcium.

Dates

Like figs, dates are one of the oldest cultivated fruits, possibly dating back as far as 50,000BC. Fresh dates are sweet and soft, and make a good natural sweetener: purée the cooked fruit, then add to cake or bread mixtures, or simply mix into natural yogurt to make a quick dessert. Always choose fresh dates that are plump and glossy. Medjool dates from Egypt and California have a wrinkly skin, but most other varieties are smooth. They can be stored in the refrigerator for up to a week. The sweetness of dried dates is even more intense. Both fresh and dried dates are high in vitamin C and a good source of potassium and soluble fibre.

TROPICAL FRUIT

This exotic collection of fruits ranges from the bananas and pineapples to papayas and passion fruit, with a diversity of colours, shapes and flavours sure to excite the tastebuds.

Pineapples

These distinctive fruits have a sweet, juicy and golden flesh. Unlike most other fruits, pineapples do not ripen after picking, but leaving a slightly unripe fruit for a few days at room temperature may reduce its acidity. Choose pineapples that have fresh green spiky leaves, are heavy for their size and are slightly soft to the touch. Store in the refrigerator when ripe.

Pineapple contains an antibacterial enzyme called bromelain, which has anti-inflammatory properties and should help arthritis sufferers. It also aids digestion.

Papayas

Also known as pawpaw, these pear-shaped fruits come from South America. When ripe, the green skin turns a speckled yellow and the pulp is

a glorious orange-pink colour. The numerous edible, small black seeds taste peppery when dried. Peel off the skin using a sharp knife or a vegetable peeler before enjoying the creamy flesh, which has a lovely perfumed aroma and sweet flavour. Ripe papaya is best eaten raw, while unripe green fruit can be used in cooking.

Papaya contains an enzyme called papain, which aids the digestion, but levels of this enzyme diminish with ripening. Skin, hair and nails all benefit from the generous amounts of vitamin C and beta carotene found in papaya. Iron, potassium and calcium are also present.

Mangoes

The skin of these luscious fruits can range in colour from green to yellow, orange or red. Their shape varies tremendously, too. An entirely green skin

LEFT: *Yellow-skinned bananas*

is a sign of an unripe fruit; in Asia, these are often used in salads. Ripe fruit should yield to gentle pressure and, when cut, it should reveal a juicy, orange flesh. Rich in vitamin C and beta carotene, mangoes are also reputed to cleanse the blood.

Bananas

These concentrated bundles of energy are full of valuable nutrients. The soft and creamy flesh can be blended into smooth, sweet drinks, or mashed and mixed with yogurt. Bananas can also be baked or barbecued whole. They make ideal weaning food because they rarely cause an allergic reaction.

Bananas are rich in dietary fibre, vitamins and minerals, especially potassium, which is important for the functioning of cells, nerves and muscles, and can relieve high blood pressure. Their high starch content makes them a good source of sustained energy, and they are an effective laxative. Bananas are rich in the amino acid tryptophan, known to lift the spirits and aid sleep. Bananas with patches of green can be ripened at room temperature. Avoid completely green bananas, as these rarely ripen properly. Store at a cool room temperature.

ABOVE: *Papayas*

RIGHT: *Mangoes*

Vegetables

Today, the choice of vegetables is immense, and growing demand for organic produce has meant that pesticide-free vegetables are now increasingly available. Vegetables, an essential part of a healthy diet, have numerous nutritional benefits. They are at their best freshly picked.

ROOTS AND TUBERS

Vegetables such as carrots, swedes (rutabagas), parsnips and potatoes are comforting and nourishing, and it is no surprise that they are popular in the winter. Their sweet, dense flesh provides sustained energy, valuable fibre, vitamins and minerals.

Carrots

The best carrots are not restricted to the cold winter months. Summer welcomes the slender sweet new crop, often sold with their green, feathery tops. (These are best removed after buying, as they rob the root of moisture and nutrients.) Buy organic carrots if you can; high pesticide residues have been found in non-organic ones. As an added bonus, organic carrots do not need peeling. Look for firm, smooth carrots – the smaller they are, the sweeter they are. They should be prepared just before use to preserve valuable nutrients.

ABOVE:
Fresh carrots with their green, feathery tops

A single carrot will supply enough vitamin A for an entire day and is reputed to cut the risk of lung cancer by half, even among ex-smokers. This may be due to the high level of the antioxidant beta carotene that carrots contain. This antioxidant may also reduce the risk of prostate cancer in men.

Beetroot (Beet)

Deep ruby-red in colour, beetroot adds a vibrant hue and flavour to all sorts of dishes. It is often pickled in vinegar, but is much better roasted, as this emphasizes its sweet earthy flavour. Raw beetroot can be grated into salads or used to make relishes. It can also be added to risottos or made into delicious soups. If cooking beetroot whole, wash carefully, taking care not to damage the skin, or the nutrients and colour will leach out. Trim the stalks to about 2.5cm/1in above the root. Small beetroot are sweeter and more tender than larger ones.

Beetroot has long been considered medicinally beneficial and is recommended as a general tonic. It can be used to help disorders of the blood, including anaemia, is an effective detoxifier and, because of its high fibre content, will relieve constipation. Beetroot contains calcium, iron and vitamins A and C – all at their highest levels when it is eaten raw.

Celeriac

This knobbly root is closely related to celery – its flavour is a cross between aniseed, celery and parsley. Celeriac is one of the few root vegetables that must be peeled before use. When grated and eaten raw in salads, it has a crunchy texture. It can be used in soups and broths, steamed, baked in gratins or combined with potatoes and mashed with butter or margarine and grainy mustard. Like celery, celeriac is a diuretic. It also contains vitamin C, calcium, iron, potassium and fibre.

BELOW: *Celeriac*

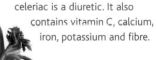

RIGHT:
Parsnips

Swede (Rutabaga)

The globe-shaped swede has pale orange flesh with a delicate sweet flavour. Trim off the thick peel, then treat as other root vegetables: grate raw into salads; dice and cook in soups and casseroles; or steam, then mash and serve as an accompaniment.

As cruciferous vegetables, swedes contain compounds that are believed to have antioxidant and cancer-fighting properties. They also contain vitamins A and C.

Parsnips

Parsnips have a sweet, creamy flavour and are delicious roasted, puréed or steamed. They are best purchased after the first frost of the year, as the cold converts their starches into sugar, enhancing their sweetness. Scrub before use, and peel only if tough. Avoid large roots, which can be woody. Parsnips are effective detoxifiers and are believed to fight some cancers. They contain vitamins C and E, iron, folic acid and potassium.

Turnips

This humble root vegetable has many health-giving qualities, and small turnips with their green tops intact are especially nutritious. Their crisp, ivory flesh, which is enclosed in white, green and pink-tinged skin, has a pleasant, slightly peppery flavour, the intensity of which depends on their size and the time of harvesting.

Small turnips can be eaten raw. Alternatively, steam, bake or use in casseroles and soups.

This cruciferous vegetable is said to halt the onset of certain cancers, particularly rectal cancer. It is also a digestive and maintains bowel regularity. The green tops are rich in beta carotene and vitamin C.

Potatoes

There are thousands of potato varieties, and many lend themselves to particular cooking methods. Small potatoes, such as Pink Fir Apple and Charlotte, and new potatoes, such as Jersey Royals, are best steamed. They have a waxy texture, which retains its shape after cooking, making them ideal for salads. Main crop potatoes, such as Estima and Maris Piper, are more suited to roasting, baking or mashing, and can be used to make chips (French fries). Discard any potatoes with green patches – these indicate the presence of toxic alkaloids called 'solanines'. Vitamins and minerals are stored in, or just below, the skin, so it is best to use potatoes unpeeled. New potatoes and salad potatoes need only be scrubbed. Potatoes are not in themselves fattening – it is added ingredients, such as cheese, and the cooking method, such as frying, that can bump up the calories. Steam rather than boil, and bake instead of frying, to retain valuable nutrients and keep fat levels down. Potatoes are high in complex carbohydrates, and include both protein and fibre, as well as vitamins B and C, iron and potassium.

Jerusalem artichokes

This small knobbly tuber has a sweet, nutty flavour. Peeling can be fiddly, but scrubbing and trimming is usually sufficient. Store in the refrigerator for up to one week. Use in the same way as potatoes; they make good creamy soups. Jerusalem artichokes contain vitamin C and fibre.

BELOW: *Jerusalem artichokes*

LEFT: *Potatoes*

BRASSICAS

This large group of vegetables boasts an extraordinary number of health-giving properties. Brassicas range from crinkly-leafed Savoy cabbages to small, walnut-sized Brussels sprouts.

Seek out bright, firm brassicas with no signs of discoloration or wilting. Store cabbages and Brussels sprouts in a cool, dark place for up to a week. Keep broccoli and cauliflower in the refrigerator for only 2–3 days. Chinese leaves and pak choi should be stored in the salad drawer of the refrigerator, and used within 1–2 days.

Broccoli

This nutritious vegetable should be a regular part of everyone's diet. Two types are commonly available: purple-sprouting, which has fine, leafy stems and a delicate head, and Calabrese, with a tightly budded top and thick stalk. Choose broccoli that has bright, compact florets. Yellowing florets, a limp woody stalk and a pungent smell all indicate overmaturity. Trim stalks before cooking, though young

BELOW: *Broccoli*

stems can be eaten, too. Serve raw in salads or with a dip. If you cook broccoli, steam or stir-fry it to preserve the nutrients and keep the cooking time brief.

Broccoli is a cruciferous vegetable, which studies have shown to be particularly effective in fighting cancer of the lung, colon and breast. Raw broccoli contains almost as much calcium as milk and also provides plenty of B vitamins, vitamin C, iron, folate, zinc and potassium.

Cauliflower

The cream-coloured compact florets should be encased in large, bright green leaves. To get the most nutrients from a cauliflower, eat it raw, or bake or steam lightly. Cauliflower is delicious tossed in a vinaigrette or combined with tomatoes and spices. It has many cancer-fighting qualities, particularly against cancer of the lung and colon. It also contains vitamin C, folate and potassium, and can be used as a natural blood purifier and laxative.

Cabbage

Frequently overcooked, cabbage is best eaten raw, or cooked until only just tender. There are several varieties:

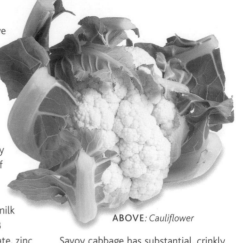

ABOVE: *Cauliflower*

Savoy cabbage has substantial, crinkly leaves with a strong flavour and is perfect for stuffing; firm white and red cabbages can be shredded and used raw in salads (as can Chinese leaves); while pak choi (bok choy) is best cooked in stir-fries or with noodles. Raw or juiced cabbage is particularly potent and has antiviral and antibacterial qualities. It is a valuable source of vitamins C and E, beta carotene, folate, potassium, thiamine and fibre.

Brussels sprouts

Basically miniature cabbages that grow on a long tough stalk, the best sprouts are small with tightly packed leaves – avoid any that are very large or turning yellow or brown. They are sweeter when picked after the first frost, and are best cooked very lightly. Either steam or stir-fry to keep their green colour and crisp texture, as well as to retain vitamins and minerals. Brussels sprouts contain significant amounts of vitamin C, folate, iron, potassium and some B vitamins.

GREEN LEAFY VEGETABLES

For years we have been told to eat up our greens, and now we are beginning to learn why. Research into their health benefits has indicated that eating dark green leafy vegetables such as spring greens (collards), spinach, chard and kale on a regular basis may protect us against certain forms of cancer.

Green, leafy vegetables do not keep well – up to 2 or 3 days at most. Eat soon after purchase to enjoy them at their best. Look for brightly coloured, undamaged leaves that are not showing any signs of yellowing or wilting. Wash the leaves thoroughly in cold water before use and eat them raw, or cook lightly, either by steaming or stir-frying to preserve their nutrients.

ABOVE:
Mixed Swiss chard

BELOW: *Spinach beet*

Spinach

This dark, green leaf is a superb source of cancer-fighting antioxidants. It contains about four times more beta carotene than broccoli. It is

also rich in fibre, which can help to lower harmful levels of LDL cholesterol in the body, reducing the risk of heart disease and stroke. Spinach does contain iron, but not in such rich supply as was once thought.

Furthermore, spinach contains oxalic acid, which inhibits the absorption of iron and calcium in the body. However, eating spinach with a vitamin C-rich food increases absorption. Spinach also contains vitamins C and B6, calcium, potassium, folate, thiamine and zinc.

ABOVE: *Spinach*

Nutritionally, it is most beneficial when eaten raw in a salad, but it is also good lightly steamed.

Swiss chard

A member of the beet family, Swiss chard has large, dark leaves and thick, white, orange or red edible ribs. It can be used in the same way as spinach, or the stems may be cooked on their own. Swiss chard is rich in vitamins and minerals – although, like spinach, it contains oxalic acid, and should therefore be combined with a vitamin C-rich food to increase absorption of these nutrients.

Spinach beet

Similar to Swiss chard, this form of the beetroot plant is grown only for its leaves and has a sweet, mild flavour. Use as you would spinach.

Spring greens (Collards)

These leafy, dark green young cabbages are full of flavour. Rich in vitamin C and beta carotene, spring greens contain indoles, one of the phytochemicals that are thought to protect the body against breast and ovarian cancer.

ABOVE: *Spring greens*

PUMPKINS AND SQUASHES

Pumpkins and squashes come in a tremendous range of shapes, colours and sizes. They are broadly divided into summer and winter types: cucumbers, courgettes (zucchini) and marrows fall into the summer category, while pumpkins, butternut and acorn squashes are winter varieties.

Winter squashes

These have tough inedible skins, dense, fibrous flesh and large seeds. Most winter squashes can be used in both sweet and savoury dishes. Acorn squashes are small to medium-sized. The orange flesh has a sweet flavour and slightly dry texture, and the skin ranges from golden to dark green. They are perfect for stuffing.

Butternut squash

This is a large, pear-shaped squash with a golden brown skin and vibrant orange flesh. The skin is inedible and should be removed along with the seeds. Roast, bake, mash or use in soups or casseroles. The flesh has a rich, sweet, creamy flavour when cooked and makes a good substitute for pumpkin.

RIGHT: Acorn, pattypan and butternut squashes

Pumpkins

These are native to America, where they are synonymous with Thanksgiving. Small pumpkins have sweeter, less fibrous flesh than the larger ones, which are perhaps best kept for making into lanterns. Deep orange in colour, pumpkin can be used in both sweet and savoury dishes, such as pies, soups, casseroles, soufflés and even ice cream. Avoid boiling pumpkin, as it can become waterlogged and soggy. The seeds are edible and highly nutritious.

Summer squashes

Picked when still young, summer squash have thin edible skins and tender, edible seeds. Their delicate flesh cooks quickly.

Pattypan squash

These pretty baby squash resemble mini flying saucers. Similar in taste to a courgette, pattypan squash are best steamed

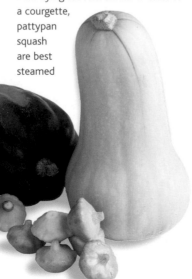

ABOVE: Courgettes

or roasted. They may be yellow or bright green. Pattypan squash will keep for only a few days in the refrigerator.

Courgettes (Zucchini)

At their best when small and young, courgettes' flavour diminishes when they are old and the seeds toughen. Young courgettes have a glossy, bright green skin and creamy coloured flesh. Extremely versatile, they can be steamed, grated raw into salads, stir-fried, griddled, puréed or used in soups and casseroles. Their deep yellow flowers are a delicacy and are perfect for stuffing.

Marrows (Large zucchini)

Marrows have a pleasant, mild flavour and are best baked either plain or with a stuffing. Spices, chillies and tomatoes are good flavourings.

Cucumbers

Probably cultivated as long ago as 10,000 BC, cucumbers were popular vegetables with the Greeks and the Romans. Their refreshing, mild flavour makes them perfect to use raw in salads or thinly sliced as a sandwich filling. They can also be pickled, steamed, baked or stir-fried. Look for firm, bright, unblemished cucumbers.

SHOOT VEGETABLES

This highly prized collection of vegetables, each honoured with a distinctive flavour and appearance, ranges from aristocratic asparagus to the flowerbud-like globe artichoke.

Fennel

Florence fennel is closely related to the herb and spice of the same name. The short, fat bulbs have a similar texture to celery and are topped with edible feathery fronds. Fennel has a mild aniseed flavour, which is most potent when eaten raw. Cooking tempers the flavour, giving it a delicious sweetness. When using fennel raw, slice it thinly or chop roughly, and add to salads. Alternatively, slice or cut into wedges and steam, or brush with olive oil and roast or cook on a griddle. Fennel is at its best when it is fresh and should be eaten as soon as possible.

Fennel is a diuretic and also has a calming and toning effect on the stomach. Low in calories, it contains beta carotene and folate, which is known to reduce the risk of spina bifida in the unborn child. Fennel seeds are good for the digestion.

Asparagus

Asparagus has been cultivated commercially since the 17th century. There are two main types: white asparagus is picked just before it sprouts above the surface of the soil;

LEFT: Fennel

green-tipped asparagus is cut above the ground and develops its colour when it comes into contact with sunlight. It takes three years to grow a crop from seed, which may account for its expense. Before use, scrape the stalk's lower half with a vegetable peeler, then trim off the woody end. Briefly poach whole spears in a frying pan with a little boiling salted water, or tie the spears in a bundle and boil upright in an asparagus boiler or tall pan.

Asparagus was used as a medicine long before it was eaten as a food. It is a rich source of vitamin C and also has diuretic and laxative properties. It contains the antioxidant glutathione, which has been found to prevent the formation of cataracts in the eyes.

Chicory

This shoot has long, tightly packed leaves. There are two kinds: white and red. Red chicory has

RIGHT: Chicory

BELOW: Asparagus

a more pronounced flavour, while the white variety has crisper leaves. The crisp texture and slightly bitter taste means that chicory is particularly good in salads. Chicory can also be steamed or braised, although in cooking, sadly, the red-leafed variety fades to brown. Before use, remove outer leaves and wash thoroughly, then trim the base. In natural medicine, chicory is sometimes used to treat gout and rheumatism. It is also a digestive and liver stimulant, and good for a spring tonic.

Celery

Like asparagus, celery was once grown primarily for medicinal reasons. Serve raw, steam or braise. Celery leaves have a tangy taste and are also useful for adding flavour to stocks. Low in calories, but rich in vitamin C and potassium, celery is a recognized diuretic and sedative.

Globe artichokes

Once cooked, the purple-tinged leaves of globe artichokes have an exquisite flavour. A good way to eat them is with the fingers, dipping each leaf into garlic butter or vinaigrette dressing, then drawing each leaf through the teeth and eating the fleshy part. The heart is then dipped in the butter or dressing, and eaten with a knife and fork. Globe artichokes are a good source of vitamins A and C, fibre, iron, calcium and potassium.

VEGETABLE FRUITS

By cultivation and use, tomatoes, aubergines (eggplants) and (bell) peppers are all treated as vegetables, but botanically they are classified as fruit. Part of the nightshade family, they have only recently become appreciated for their health-giving qualities.

Tomatoes

There are dozens of varieties to choose from, which vary in colour, shape and size. The egg-shaped plum tomato is perfect for cooking because it has a rich flavour and a high proportion of flesh to seeds – but it must be used when fully ripe. Too often, shop-bought tomatoes are bland and tasteless because they have been picked too young. Vine-ripened and cherry tomatoes are sweet and juicy and are good in salads or uncooked sauces. Large beefsteak tomatoes have a good flavour and are also excellent for salads. Sun-dried tomatoes add a rich intensity to sauces, soups and stews. Genetically engineered tomatoes are now sold in some countries, but at present they are only sold canned as a concentrated purée. Always check the label before buying.

Look for deep-red fruit with a firm, yielding flesh. Tomatoes that are grown and sold locally will have the best flavour. To improve the flavour of a slightly hard tomato, leave it to ripen fully at room temperature. Avoid refrigeration because this stops the ripening process and also adversely affects the taste and texture of the tomato.

Vine-ripened tomatoes are higher in vitamin C than those picked when they are still green. They are also a good source of vitamin E, beta carotene, magnesium, calcium and phosphorus. Tomatoes contain the bioflavonoid lycopene, which is believed to prevent some forms of cancer by reducing the harmful effects of free radicals.

RIGHT: *Aubergines*

Aubergines (Eggplants)

The dark-purple, glossy-skinned aubergine is the most familiar variety, although it is the small, ivory-white egg-shaped variety that has inspired the name 'eggplant' in the USA. There is also the bright-green pea aubergine that is used in Asian cooking, and a pale-purple Chinese aubergine. Known in the Middle East as 'poor man's caviar', aubergines give substance and flavour to spicy casseroles and tomato-based bakes, and are delicious roasted, griddled and puréed into garlic-laden dips. It is not essential to salt them to remove any bitterness; however, this method prevents the absorption of excessive amounts of oil during frying.

When buying, look for small to medium-size aubergines, which have sweet, tender flesh. Large specimens with a shrivelled skin are overmature

BELOW: *Red and green chillies*

ABOVE: *Tomatoes*

ABOVE: *Jalapeño chillies*

ABOVE: *Habañero chillies*

and are likely to be bitter and tough. Aubergines can be stored in the refrigerator for up to two weeks.

An excellent source of vitamin C, aubergines contain moderate amounts of iron and potassium, calcium and B vitamins, as well as bioflavonoids, which help to prevent strokes and reduce the risk of certain cancers.

Chillies

Native to America, this member of the capsicum family now forms an important part of many cuisines, including Indian, Thai, Mexican, South American and African. There are more than 200 different types of chilli, ranging from the long, narrow Anaheim to the lantern-shaped and incredibly hot habañero. Red chillies are not necessarily hotter than green ones – but they have probably been left for longer in the sun.

The heat in chillies comes from capsaicin, a compound found in the seeds, white membranes and, to a lesser extent, in the flesh. Chillies range in potency from mild and flavourful to blisteringly hot. Dried chillies tend to be hotter than fresh. Smaller chillies, such as bird's-eye chillies, contain proportionately more seeds and membrane, which makes them more potent than larger ones. Take care when using chillies, and wash your hands afterwards, as they can irritate the skin and eyes.

Chillies contain more vitamin C than an orange and are a good source of beta carotene, folate, potassium and vitamin E. They stimulate the release of endorphins, the body's 'feel-good' chemicals, and are a powerful decongestant, helping to open sinuses and air passages. They improve circulation, but if eaten to excess can irritate the stomach.

(Bell) Peppers

Like chillies, sweet peppers are members of the capsicum family.

BELOW: *Avocados*

They range in colour from green through to orange, yellow, red and even purple. Green peppers are fully developed but not completely ripe, which can make them difficult to digest. They have refreshing, juicy flesh with a crisp texture. Other colours of peppers are more mature, have sweeter flesh, and are more digestible than less ripe green peppers. Roasting or chargrilling peppers will enhance their sweetness. They can also be stuffed, sliced into salads or steamed.

Avocados

Although avocados have a high fat content, the fat is monounsaturated, and is thought to lower blood cholesterol levels in the body. Avocados also contain valuable amounts of vitamins C and E, iron, potassium and manganese.

BELOW: *Peppers*

PODS AND SEEDS

While most of these vegetables are delicious eaten fresh, many of them – peas, corn and broad and green beans, for example – can also be bought frozen. High in nutritional value, these vegetables can be enjoyed all year. Other pea types include mangetouts (snow peas) and sugar snap peas, which can be eaten whole – pod and all.

Peas

Peas are one of the few vegetables that taste just as good when frozen. As freezing takes place soon after picking, frozen peas often have a higher nutritional value than fresh. Another advantage is that frozen peas are readily available all year round. Peas in the pod have a restricted availability and their taste diminishes if not absolutely fresh, because their sugars rapidly turn to starch. However, when they are at the peak of freshness, peas are delicious and have a delicate, sweet flavour. Pop them from the pod and serve raw in salads or steam lightly. Delicious cooked with fresh mint, peas also make satisfying purées and soups, and can be added to risottos and other rice dishes.

BELOW: *Peas*

Broad beans (Fava beans)

When young and fresh these beans are a delight to eat. Tiny pods can be eaten whole; simply top and tail, and then slice. Usually, however, you will need to shell the beans as their skins can become tough. Elderly beans are often better skinned after they are cooked. Broad beans can be eaten raw or lightly cooked.

Green beans

French, runner and dwarf beans are eaten pod and all. They should be bright green and crisp-textured. Simply trim, and lightly cook or steam. Serve green beans hot, or leave to cool slightly and serve as a warm salad with a squeeze of fresh lemon juice or a vinaigrette dressing. Look for bright-green, smooth, plump pods, and keep in the refrigerator for no more than a day or two.

Peas and beans are a good source of protein and fibre. They are rich in vitamin C, iron, thiamine, folate, phosphorus and potassium.

Corn

Corn cobs are best eaten soon after

BELOW: *Corn*

picking, before their natural sugars start to convert into starch when the flavour fades and kernels toughen. Remove the green outer leaves and cook whole or slice off the kernels with a sharp knife. Baby corn cobs can be eaten raw, and are good in stir-fries. Look out for fresh, plump kernels with no signs of discoloration, wrinkling or drying.

Corn is a good carbohydrate food and is rich in vitamins A, B and C, and fibre. It has useful amounts of iron, magnesium, phosphorus and potassium. Baby corn is high in folate.

BELOW: *Broad beans are best eaten shelled unless they are really young and fresh.*

ABOVE: *Spring onions, red onions, shallots and white onions*

THE ONION FAMILY

Onions and garlic are highly prized as two of the oldest remedies known to man. Both contain allicin, which has been found to stimulate the body's antioxidant mechanisms, raising levels of beneficial HDL cholesterol and combating the formation of clogged arteries. What's more, they are indispensable in cooking.

Onions

An essential flavouring, onions offer a range of taste sensations, from the sweet and juicy red onion and powerfully pungent white onion, to the light and fresh spring onion (scallion). Pearl onions and shallots are the babies of the family. When buying, choose onions that have dry, papery skins and are heavy for their size. They will keep for 1–2 months when stored in a cool, dark place.

Eating half a raw onion a day is said to thin the blood, lower LDL cholesterol and raise beneficial HDL cholesterol by about 30 per cent. This means that cholesterol is transported away from the arteries, reducing the risk of heart disease and stroke. Whether raw or cooked, onions are antibacterial and antiviral, helping to fight off colds, relieve bronchial congestion, asthma and hay fever. They are also good for arthritis, rheumatism and gout.

Garlic

For centuries, this wonder food has been the focus of much attention. The flavour of garlic is milder when whole or sliced; crushing or chopping releases the oils, making the flavour stronger. Slow-cooking also tames the pungency of garlic, although it still affects the breath. Most garlic is semi-dried to prolong its shelf-life, yet the cloves should still be moist and juicy. Young garlic, available in early summer, has a long green stem and soft white bulb. It has a fresher flavour than semi-dried garlic, but can be used in the same ways. If stored in a cool, dry place and not in the refrigerator, garlic will keep for up to about eight weeks.

Although garlic's antiviral, antibacterial and antifungal qualities are most potent when it is eaten raw, cooking does not inhibit its anti-cancer, blood-thinning and decongestant capabilities. Garlic has been found to reduce high blood pressure, lower blood cholesterol, boost the immune system, act as an anti-inflammatory, lift mood and have a calming effect. It should be eaten on a daily basis.

Leeks

Leeks have their own distinct, subtle flavour. They are less pungent than onions, but are still therapeutically beneficial. Excellent in soups and casseroles, pies or flans, they are also delicious with a vinaigrette or stir-fried with a little garlic and ginger.

Choose firm leeks with bright-green leaves. Leeks have the same active constituents as onions, but in smaller amounts. They also contain vitamins C and E, iron, folate and potassium.

ABOVE: *Leeks*

MUSHROOMS

Thanks to their rich earthiness, mushrooms add substance and flavour to all sorts of dishes. There are more than 2,000 edible varieties but only a tiny proportion are readily available. These fall into three camps: common cultivated mushrooms, like the button (white); wild varieties that are now cultivated, such as the shiitake; and the truly wild types that have escaped cultivation, such as the morel. Buy mushrooms that smell and look fresh. Avoid ones with damp, slimy patches and any that are discoloured. Store in a paper bag in the refrigerator for up to 4 days. Mushrooms do not contain a wealth of nutrients but they are a useful source of vitamins B1 and B2, potassium, iron and niacin.

Button (white), cap and flat mushrooms

The most common cultivated variety of mushrooms, these are actually one type in various stages of maturity. The button mushroom is the youngest and has, as its name suggests, a tight, white, button-like cap. It has a mild

flavour and can be eaten raw in salads. Cap mushrooms are slightly more mature and larger in size, while the flat mushroom is the largest and has dark, open gills.

Flat mushrooms have the most prominent flavour and are good grilled (broiled) or baked on their own, or stuffed.

Chestnut mushrooms

The brown-capped chestnut mushroom looks similar to the cultivated button but has a more assertive, nutty flavour.

Portabello mushrooms

Similar in appearance to the cultivated flat mushroom, the portabello is simply a large chestnut mushroom. It has a rich flavour and a meaty texture and is good grilled. This wild mushroom has an intense, rich flavour. Its texture makes it ideal for grilling (broiling) and stuffing.

ABOVE: Chestnut (left) and portabello mushrooms

Chanterelles

This egg-yolk-coloured mushroom has a pretty, funnel shape and a fragrant but delicate flavour.

Cleaning mushrooms

Before use, wipe mushrooms with damp kitchen paper and trim the stem. Wild mushrooms often harbour grit and dirt, and may need to be rinsed briefly under cold running water, but dry thoroughly. Never soak mushrooms or they will become soggy. Peeling is not usually necessary.

RIGHT: Cultivated mushrooms come in a variety of sizes

BELOW: *Oyster mushrooms*

ABOVE: *Chanterelles*

Also known as the girolle, it is sold
fresh in season and dried all year
round. If buying fresh, eat as soon as
possible and wipe rather than wash
because the skin is very porous.
Sauté, bake or add to sauces.

Shiitake mushrooms
In Asia, these mushrooms are
recommended for a long and healthy
life. Research has shown that they
have antiviral properties that stimulate
the immune system. They may help
lower cholesterol, even curtailing
some of the side effects of saturated
fat. They have also been found to halt
the latter stages of certain cancers.

BELOW: *Shiitake mushrooms are thought
to have many medicinal properties.*

Ceps
These wild
mushrooms, which are also known by
their Italian name, porcini, have a
tender, meaty texture and a
distinctive, woody taste. Dried ceps
are used for their rich flavour.

Morels
These lightly sweet-flavoured
mushrooms have a distinctive
pointed honeycomb cap and a hollow
stalk. Due to their peculiar shape,
they can be fiddly to clean. Morels
are costly to buy fresh because they
have a short season, but they can be
bought dried.

Field blewitts
This wild mushroom is now widely
cultivated in caves in Britain, France
and Switzerland. It has a thick,
lilac-blue stem, which is topped with
a smooth, whitish cap. When they are
cooked, field blewitts have a dense,
meaty texture.

Enoki mushrooms
These Japanese mushrooms have a
pretty, tiny cap on an elegant, long
stalk. Sold in clusters, enoki have a
slightly lemony flavour. Use in
stir-fries or eat raw in salads.

Oyster mushrooms
Now cultivated and widely available,
oyster mushrooms have an attractive
shell-shaped cap and thick stalk. They
are usually a pale grey-brown in
colour, but there are also yellow and
pink varieties.

Dried mushrooms
These are a useful stand-by and have
a rich, intense flavour. To reconstitute
dried mushrooms, soak them in
boiling water for 20–30 minutes,
depending on the variety and size of
mushroom, until tender. Drain in a
sieve (strainer) or colander, and rinse
well to remove any grit and dirt.
Dried mushrooms often require
longer cooking than fresh ones.

SALAD LEAVES

It is only a few years since the most exotic lettuce available was the crisp-textured iceberg. Today, salad leaves come in a huge variety of shapes, sizes, colours and flavours, from bitter-tasting endive to peppery rocket (arugula) and red-leafed lollo rosso. Making a mixed leaf salad has never been so easy.

Salad leaves are best when they are very fresh and do not keep well. Avoid leaves that are wilted, discoloured or shrivelled. Store in the refrigerator, unwashed, for between 2 days and 1 week, depending on the variety. As salad leaves are routinely sprayed with pesticides, they should be washed thoroughly, but gently, to avoid damaging the leaves, and then dried with a dish towel. Better still, choose organically grown produce.

Although all types of salad leaves are about 90 per cent water, they contain useful amounts of vitamins and minerals, particularly folate, iron and the antioxidants, vitamin C and beta carotene. The outer, darker leaves tend to be more nutritious than the paler leaves in the centre. More importantly, like other green, leafy vegetables, their antioxidant content has been found to guard against the risk of many cancers. Salad leaves are usually eaten raw when nutrients are at their strongest. Lettuce is reputed to have a calming, sedative effect.

Cultivated for thousands of years, lettuces were probably first eaten as a salad vegetable during Roman times. Nutritionally, lettuce is best eaten raw, but it can be braised, steamed or made into a soup. Large-leafed varieties can be used to wrap around a filling.

ABOVE: *Lamb's lettuce*

Butterhead lettuce

This soft-leafed lettuce has an unassuming flavour and is good as a sandwich-filler.

Cos lettuce

Known since Roman times, the cos lettuce has long, sturdy leaves and a strong flavour. Little Gem is a baby version of cos and has firm, densely packed leaves.

Iceberg lettuce

This lettuce has a round, firm head of pale-green leaves with a crisp texture. Like the butterhead, it has a mild, slightly bitter flavour and is best used as a garnish. It is reputed to be one of the most highly chemically treated crops, so it is a good idea to choose organic iceberg lettuces if you can.

Oak leaf

This attractive lettuce has red-tinged, soft-textured leaves with a slightly bitter flavour. In salads, combine oak leaf with a mixture of green lettuces for a wonderful contrast of tastes and textures.

LEFT: *Clockwise from left: curly endive, oak leaf, cos, butterhead and iceberg lettuces*

BELOW: *Radicchio*

Lamb's lettuce

This tiny lettuce has a cluster of small, rounded, velvety leaves with a delicate flavour. Serve lamb's lettuce on its own, or mix with other salad leaves and lettuces.

Curly endive

Also known as frisée, curly endive has spiky, ragged leaves that are dark green on the outside and fade to an attractive pale yellow-green towards its centre. It has a distinctive bitter flavour that can be enhanced by a robust dressing.

Radicchio

A member of the chicory family, radicchio has deep-red, tightly packed leaves that have a bitter peppery flavour. It is good in salads and can be sautéed or roasted.

BELOW: *Rocket*

Rocket (Arugula)

Classified as a herb, rocket is a popular addition to many salads, or it can be served as a starter with thin shavings of Parmesan cheese. It has a very distinctive, strong, peppery flavour, which is more robust when the rocket is wild. Lightly steamed rocket has a milder flavour than the raw leaves but it is still equally delicious.

Sorrel

The long pointed leaves of sorrel have a refreshing, sharp flavour that is best when mixed in a salad with milder tasting leaves. This salad leaf contains oxalic acid, which, when cooked, will inhibit the body's absorption of iron. Sorrel also acts as an effective diuretic.

Watercress

The hot, peppery flavour of watercress complements milder tasting salad leaves and is classically combined with sweet fresh orange. It does not keep well and is best used within two days of purchase. Watercress is a member of the cruciferous family and shares its cancer-fighting properties.

BELOW: *Sorrel*

Lollo rosso

The pretty, frilly leaves of lollo rosso are green at the base and a deep, autumn-red around the edge. Its imposing shape means that it is best mixed with other leaves if used in a salad or as a base for roasted vegetables. Lollo biondo is a pale-green version.

BELOW: *Watercress*

Herbs

In cooking, herbs can make a significant difference to the flavour and aroma of a dish and they have the ability to enliven the simplest of meals.

Fresh herbs are widely available, sold loose, in packets or growing in pots. The packets do not keep for as long and should be stored in the refrigerator. Place stems of fresh herbs in a half-filled jar of water and cover with a plastic bag. Sealed with an elastic band, the herbs should keep in the refrigerator for a week. Growing herbs should be kept on a sunny windowsill. If watered regularly, and not cut too often, they will keep for months.

Basil

This delicate aromatic herb is widely used in Italian and Thai cooking. The leaves bruise easily, so are best used whole or torn, rather than cut with a

BELOW: Basil

knife. Basil is said to have a calming effect on the stomach, easing constipation, sickness and cramps, and aiding digestion.

Bay leaves

These dark-green, glossy leaves are best left to dry for a few days before use. They have a robust, spicy flavour and are an essential ingredient in bouquet garni. Studies show that bay has a restorative effect on the digestive system.

Chives

A member of the onion family, chives have a milder flavour and are best used as a garnish, snipped over egg or potato dishes, or added to salads or flans. Like onions, chives are an antiseptic and act as a digestive.

Coriander (Cilantro)

Warm and spicy, coriander is popular in Indian and Thai curries, stir-fries and salads. It looks similar to flat leaf parsley but its taste is completely different. It is often sold with its root intact. The root has a more intense flavour than the leaves and can be used in curry pastes. Coriander is an effective digestive, easing indigestion and nausea.

Dill

The mild, yet distinctive, aniseed flavour of dill goes well with potatoes, courgettes (zucchini) and cucumber. It makes a good addition to creamy sauces and can be added

ABOVE: *Chives (left) and bay leaves*

to a wide variety of egg dishes. It can also be used as a flavouring for dressings and marinades and is a good partner for mustard. An attractive herb with delicate, wispy leaves, add to dishes just prior to serving as its mild flavour diminishes with cooking. Dill is a popular herb for settling the stomach and is thought to reduce flatulence.

Kaffir lime leaves

These attractive glossy, green leaves are commonly used in Asian cuisines, lending a tantalizing citrus aroma and flavour to a wide variety of dishes. They are available fresh or frozen

BELOW: Kaffir lime leaves

HERBS 179

from Asian stores, or dried from large supermarkets. The fruit resembles a knobbly lime and its rind, which is rich in vitamin C, is used grated in Thai and Indonesian curries. The leaves can be used as a digestive.

Lemon balm
This herb makes a refreshing tea and is good in any sweet or savoury dish that uses lemon juice. It has antiviral, antibacterial and antidepressant qualities. The calming and sedative attributes of lemon balm are beneficial for those suffering from stress or nervous exhaustion.

Marjoram
Closely related to oregano, marjoram has a slightly sweeter flavour. It goes well in Mediterranean-style dishes such as ratatouille or in casseroles and tomato sauces. Add at the last minute as its flavour diminishes when heated. It also makes a good addition to a marinade.

RIGHT: *Thyme*

BELOW: *Parsley*

Mint
The most familiar types are spearmint and peppermint, but there are other distinct-flavoured varieties, such as apple, lemon and pineapple mint, which make a refreshing drink when infused in boiling water. Mint is used as a flavouring in a wide variety of dishes, from stuffings to fruit salads. It is a traditional cure for nausea and indigestion, and is also effective in stimulating and cleansing the system.

Oregano
This is a wild variety of marjoram, but has a more robust flavour that goes well with tomato-based dishes. It can relieve digestive problems.

Parsley
There are two types of parsley: flat leaf and curly. Both taste relatively similiar, but the flat leaf variety is preferable in cooked dishes. Parsley is an excellent source of vitamin C, iron and calcium. Chewing parsley after eating garlic or onions can neutralize the smell and freshen breath.

Rosemary
Wonderfully aromatic, rosemary is traditionally used in meat dishes, but it can also add a smoky

BELOW: *Tarragon*

flavour to hearty bean and vegetable dishes. Rosemary has a reputation for invigorating circulation and relieving headaches and respiratory problems.

Sage
The leaves of this herb, which may be silver-grey or purple, have a potent aroma, and only a small amount is needed. Sage is commonly added to meat dishes but, if used discreetly, it is delicious with beans, cheese, lentils and in stuffings. Sage is seen as a tonic for the stomach, kidneys and liver.

Thyme
This robustly flavoured aromatic herb is good in tomato-based recipes, and with roasted vegetables, lentils and beans. It is an essential ingredient in a bouquet garni. It aids the digestion and works as a powerful antiseptic.

Tarragon
Tarragon has an affinity with all egg- and cheese-based dishes. The French variety has a warm, aniseed flavour and is considered superior to Russian tarragon. Tarragon has diuretic properties and can relieve indigestion. In a herbal tisane, it soothes sore throats and promotes restful sleep.

Sea vegetables

The West has only relatively recently acknowledged the extraordinary variety and remarkable health benefits of sea vegetables, which have been an essential part of the Asian diet for centuries.

Sea vegetables are highly versatile and can be used as the main component of a dish, to add texture and substance, or as a seasoning. Some sea vegetables, such as wakame, hijiki and kombu (or kelp) can be used in soups, stews and stir-fries; others, such as agar-agar and carrageen, are used as a setting agent in jellies, mousses and cheesecakes.

Sea vegetables are usually sold dried and will keep for months. Once the packet is opened, transfer the sea vegetables to an airtight jar. Fresh sea vegetables may be stored in the refrigerator, but will only remain fresh for 1–2 days. Rinse well before use.

The health benefits of sea vegetables have been recognized for centuries and range from improving the lustre of hair and clarity of the skin to reducing cholesterol levels in the body. Sea vegetables are rich in the antioxidant beta carotene. They contain some of the B complex vitamins, and significant amounts of the major minerals, such as calcium, magnesium, potassium, phosphorus and iron, as well as useful amounts of trace elements, such as selenium, zinc and iodine.

ABOVE: *Laver*

The rich mineral content of sea vegetables benefits the nervous system, helping to reduce stress. It also boosts the immune system, aiding the metabolism, while the iodine content prevents goitre and helps thyroid function. Research shows that alginic acid found in some seaweeds, notably kombu, arame, hijiki and wakame, binds with heavy metals, such as cadmium, lead, mercury and radium, in our intestines and helps to eliminate them.

Nori

This useful sea vegetable has a delicate texture and mild flavour. It is sold in thin purple-black sheets, which turn a pretty, translucent green when toasted or cooked. It is one of the few sea vegetables that does not require soaking. Nori is processed by being chopped, flattened and dried on frames, like paper. In Japanese cooking, the sheets are used as wraps for sushi. Once toasted and crisp, nori is crumbled and used as a garnish.

ABOVE: *Nori sheets*

Laver

A relation of nori, laver is commonly found around the shores of Britain. Unlike Japanese nori, it is not cultivated. Laver is used in traditional regional cooking – particularly in Wales, Scotland and Ireland. It is cooked into a thick dark purée, which can be spread on hot toast or mixed with oatmeal to make the Welsh delicacy, laverbread. It can also be added to sauces and stuffings. Available ready-cooked in cans from health food shops, laver has a stronger flavour than the more delicate nori and a higher concentration of vitamins and minerals.

Arame

Sold in delicate, black strips, arame has a mild, slightly sweet flavour and, if you haven't tried sea vegetables before, it is a good one to start with. It needs to be soaked before using in stir-fries or salads, but if using in moist or slow-cooked dishes, such as noodles and soups, it can be added straight from the packet. Arame has been used to treat female disorders and is also recommended for high blood pressure. It is rich in iodine, calcium and iron.

RIGHT: *Kombu or kelp*

RIGHT: *Wakame*

cooking will soften them and increase their digestibility as well as their nutritional value. Kombu is richer in iodine than other sea vegetables, and also contains calcium, potassium and iron.

Hijiki

This sea vegetable looks similar to arame but is thicker and has a slightly stronger flavour. Once soaked, hijiki can be sautéed or added to soups and salads, but it does require longer cooking than most sea vegetables. It expands considerably during soaking, so only a small amount is needed. It is particularly rich in calcium and iron.

Dulse

A purple-red sea vegetable, dulse has flat fronds, which have a chewy texture and spicy flavour when cooked. For hundreds of years, dulse was popular in North America and northern Europe and was traded on both sides of the Atlantic. It needs to be soaked until soft before adding to salads, noodle dishes, soups and vegetable dishes. It can also be toasted and crumbled to make a nourishing garnish. Dulse is rich in several minerals – potassium, iodine, phosphorus, iron and manganese.

Wakame

This sea vegetable is often confused with its relative kombu because it looks very similar until it is soaked, when it changes colour from brown to a delicate green. Wakame has a mild flavour and is one of the most versatile sea vegetables. Soak briefly and use in salads and soups, or toast, crumble and use as a garnish. It is rich in calcium and vitamins B and C.

Kombu

Known as kelp in the West, kombu is now farmed in the UK. It is a brown sea vegetable and is usually sold dried in strips. In Japan it is available in a multitude of forms. It has a very strong flavour and is used in slowly cooked dishes, soups and stocks – it is an essential ingredient in the Japanese stock, dashi. A small strip of kombu added to beans while they are

Agar-agar

The vegetarian equivalent to the animal-derived gelatine, agar-agar can be used as a setting agent in both sweet and savoury dishes. Known as kanten in Japan, it can be bought as flakes or strands, both of which need to be dissolved in water before use. Agar-agar has a neutral taste and its gelling abilities vary according to the other ingredients in a dish, so you may need to experiment, if substituting it for gelatine in a recipe, to achieve the best results. It is more effective than gelatine, so only a small amount is needed. It is said to be an effective laxative.

Carrageen

This fern-like seaweed, also known as Irish moss, is found along the Atlantic coasts of America and Europe. Like agar-agar, it has gelling properties, but produces a softer set, making it useful for jellies and mousses, and as a thickener in soups and stews. Carrageen is used for treating colds and bronchial problems, as well as digestive disorders.

BELOW: *Carrageen (left) and agar-agar flakes*

Sprouted seeds, pulses and grains

Sprouts are quite remarkable in terms of nutritional content. Once the seed (or pulse or grain) has germinated, the nutritional value rises dramatically. There are almost 30 per cent more B vitamins and 60 per cent more vitamin C in the sprout than in the original seed, pulse or grain.

Supermarkets and health food shops sell a variety of sprouts, but it is easy to grow them at home – all you need is a jar, some clean muslin (cheesecloth) and an elastic band.

When buying, choose fresh, crisp sprouts with the seed or bean still

BELOW: *Mung beansprouts*

BELOW: *Chickpea sprouts*

attached. Avoid any that are slimy or musty-looking. Sprouts are best eaten on the day they are bought but, if fresh, they will keep, wrapped in a plastic bag, in the refrigerator for 2–3 days. Rinse and pat dry before use.

Sprouted seeds, pulses and grains supply rich amounts of protein, B vitamins and vitamins C and E, potassium and phosphorus which, due to the sprouting process, are in an easily digestible form.

Mung beansprouts

The most commonly available beansprouts, mung beansprouts are popular in Chinese and Asian cooking, where they are used in soups, salads and stir-fries. They are fairly large, with a crunchy texture and a delicate flavour.

Alfalfa sprouts

These tiny, wispy white sprouts have a mild, nutty flavour. They are best eaten raw to retain their crunchy texture.

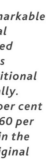

Wheat berry sprouts

Sprouts grown from wheat berries have a crunchy texture and sweet flavour and are excellent in breads. If left to grow, the sprouts become wheatgrass, a powerful detoxifier that is usually made into a juice.

Chickpea sprouts

Sprouts grown from chickpeas have a nutty flavour and add substance to dishes.

BELOW: *Wheat berry sprouts*

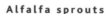

ABOVE: *Lentil sprouts*

ABOVE: *Aduki beansprouts*

Lentil sprouts

These sprouts have a slightly spicy, peppery flavour and thin, white shoots. Use only whole lentils when growing these: split lentils won't sprout because they are actually halved lentils.

Aduki beansprouts

These fine wispy sprouts have a sweet nutty taste. Use aduki beansprouts in fresh salads and vegetable stir-fries.

Cereal grains

Grains have been cultivated throughout the world for centuries. The seeds of cereal grasses, they are packed with concentrated goodness and are an important source of complex carbohydrates as well as protein, vitamins and minerals.

ABOVE: *Wheat flakes*

The most popular types of grain, such as wheat, rice, oats, barley and corn or maize, come in various forms, from whole grains to flours. Inexpensive and readily available, grains are incredibly versatile and should form a major part of our diet.

WHEAT

Wheat is the largest and most important grain crop in the world and has been cultivated since 7,000BC. The wheat kernel comprises three parts: bran, germ and endosperm. Wheat bran is the outer husk of the kernel, while wheat germ is the

BELOW: *Wholewheat berries*

nutritious seed from which the plant grows. Sprouted wheat is an excellent food, highly recommended in cancer prevention diets. The endosperm, the inner part of the kernel, is full of starch and protein and forms the basis of wheat flour. In addition to flour, wheat comes in various other forms.

Wheat berries

These are whole-wheat grains with the husks removed and they can be bought in health food shops. Wheat berries may be used to add a sweet, nutty flavour and chewy texture to breads, soups and stews, or can be combined with rice or other grains. Wheat berries must be soaked overnight, then cooked in boiling salted water until tender. If they are left to germinate, the berries sprout into wheatgrass, a powerful detoxifier and cleanser.

Wheat bran

Wheat bran is actually the outer husk of the wheat kernel and is a by-product of white flour production. It is very high in soluble dietary fibre, which makes it nature's most effective laxative. Wheat bran makes

a healthy addition to bread doughs, breakfast cereals, cakes, muffins and biscuits (cookies), and it can also be used to add substance to stews and bakes.

Cooking wheat berries
Wheat berries make a delicious addition to salads, and they can also be used to add texture to breads, soups and stews.

1 Put the wheat berries in a bowl and cover with cold water. Soak overnight, then rinse thoroughly and drain in a colander.

2 Put the wheat berries in a pan with water. Bring to the boil, then cover and simmer for 1–2 hours until tender, replenishing with extra water when necessary.

ABOVE: *Wheat germ*

ABOVE: *Bulgur wheat*

Wheat flakes

Steamed and softened berries that have been rolled and pressed are known as wheat flakes or rolled wheat. They are best used on their own or mixed with other flaked grains in porridge, as a base for muesli, or added to breads and cakes.

Cracked wheat

Made from crushed wheat berries, cracked wheat retains all the nutrients of wholewheat. Often confused with bulgur wheat, cracked wheat can be used in the same way as wheat berries (but cooks in less time), or as an alternative to rice and other grains. When cooked, it has both a slightly sticky and pleasant crunchy texture. Use it in salads and pilaffs, or serve it as an accompaniment to a main dish.

Wheat germ

The nutritious heart of the whole wheat berry, wheat germ is a rich source of protein, vitamins B and E, and iron. It is used in much the same way as wheat bran and lends a pleasant, nutty flavour to breakfast cereals and porridge. It is available toasted or untoasted. Store in an airtight container in the refrigerator to avoid it becoming rancid.

Bulgur wheat

Unlike cracked wheat, this grain is made from cooked wheat berries, which have the bran removed, and are then dried and crushed. This light, nutty grain is simply soaked in water for 20 minutes, then drained — some

BELOW: *Couscous*

BELOW: *Semolina*

manufacturers specify cold water but boiling water produces a softer grain. It can also be cooked in boiling water until tender. Bulgur wheat is the main ingredient in the Middle Eastern salad tabbouleh, where it is combined with chopped parsley, mint, tomatoes, cucumber and onion, and dressed with lemon juice and olive oil.

Semolina

Made from the endosperm of durum wheat, semolina can be used to make a hot milk pudding or it can be added to cakes, biscuits and breads to give them a pleasant grainy texture.

Couscous

Although this looks like a grain, couscous is a form of pasta made by steaming and drying cracked durum wheat. Couscous is popular in North Africa, where it forms the basis of a dish of the same name. Individual grains are moistened by hand, passed through a sieve (strainer) and then

Coeliac disease

This is caused by an allergy to gluten, a substance found in bread, cakes, pastries and cereals. It is estimated that millions of people suffer from the disease, many without diagnosis. Symptoms may include anaemia, weight loss, fatigue, depression and diarrhoea. Wheat, rye, barley and oats are the main culprits and sufferers are usually advised to remove these completely from their diet. Rice, soya, buckwheat, quinoa, millet and corn are gluten-free substitutes.

RIGHT: *Wheat flour (left) and malted brown flour, which contains flour from malted wheat grains.*

steamed in a couscousière, suspended over a bubbling vegetable stew, until light and fluffy. Nowadays, the couscous that is generally available is the quick-cooking variety, which simply needs soaking, although it can also be steamed or baked. Couscous itself has a fairly bland flavour, which makes it a good foil for spicy dishes.

Wheat flour

This is ground from the whole grain and may be wholemeal (whole-wheat) or white, depending on the degree of processing. Hard, or strong flour is high in a protein called gluten, which makes it ideal for bread making, while soft flour is lower in gluten but higher in starch and is better for light cakes and pastries. Durum wheat flour comes from one of the hardest varieties of wheat and is used to make pasta. Most commercial white flour is a combination of soft and hard wheat, which produces an 'all-purpose' flour.

As the refining process robs many commercial flours of most of their nutrients, lost vitamins and minerals are synthetically replaced. When buying flour, look out for brands that are unbleached and organically produced, as these have fewer chemical additives. Nutritionally, stoneground wholewheat flour is the best buy because it is largely unprocessed and retains all the valuable nutrients. It produces slightly heavier breads, cakes and pastries than white flour, but it can be combined with white flour to make lighter versions – although the nutritional value will not be as high.

Seitan

Used as a meat replacement, seitan is made from wheat gluten and has a firm, chewy texture. Found in health food shops, it has a neutral flavour that benefits from marinating. Slice or cut into chunks and stir-fry, or add to stews and pasta sauces during the last few minutes

of cooking time. Seitan does not need to be cooked for a long time, just heated through.

Buy wheat-based foods from shops with a high turnover of stock. Wheat berries can be kept for 6 months, but wholewheat flour should be used within 3 months, as its oils turn rancid. Always decant grains into airtight containers and store in a cool, dark place. Wheat germ deteriorates very quickly at room temperature; store in an airtight container in the refrigerator for no more than a month.

Wheat is most nutritious when it is unprocessed and in its whole form. (When milled into white flour, wheat loses a staggering 80 per cent of its nutrients.) Wheat is an excellent source of dietary fibre, B vitamins and vitamin E, as well as iron, selenium and zinc. Most of the fibre in whole-wheat is concentrated in the bran. Eating bran is recommended to relieve constipation. Studies show fibre could inhibit colon and rectal cancer, varicose veins, haemorrhoids and obesity. Phytoestrogens found in wholegrains may also ward off breast cancer.

RIGHT: *Seitan*

RICE

Throughout Asia, a meal is considered incomplete without rice. It is a staple food for over half the world's population, and almost every culture has its own repertoire of rice dishes, ranging from risottos to pilaffs.

To ensure freshness, always buy rice from shops that have a regular turnover of stock. Store in an airtight container in a cool, dry, dark place to keep out moisture and insects. Wash before use to remove any impurities. When reheating, cooked rice should be cooled quickly, then chilled and reheated thoroughly before serving.

Rice is a valuable source of complex carbohydrates and fibre. In its whole form it is a good source of B vitamins. White rice is deprived of much of its nutrients because the bran and germ have been removed. The starch in rice is absorbed slowly, keeping blood sugar levels on an even keel and making it an important food for diabetics. Research shows that rice may benefit sufferers of psoriasis. It can also be used to treat digestive disorders, calm the nervous system, prevent kidney stones and reduce the risk of bowel cancer. However, the phytates found in brown rice can inhibit absorption of iron and calcium.

Long grain rice

The most widely used type of rice is long grain rice, where the grain is five times as long as it is wide. Long grain brown rice has had its outer husk removed, leaving the bran and germ intact, which gives it a chewy nutty flavour. It takes longer to cook than white rice, but contains more fibre, vitamins and minerals.

Long grain white rice has had its husk, bran and germ removed, taking most of the nutrients with them and leaving a bland-flavoured rice that is light and fluffy when cooked. It is often whitened with chalk, talc or other preservatives, so rinsing before cooking is essential.

Easy-cook long grain white rice, sometimes called parboiled or converted rice, has been steamed under pressure. This process hardens the grain and makes it difficult to overcook, and some nutrients are transferred from the bran and germ into the kernel during this process.

Easy-cook brown rice cooks more quickly than normal brown rice.

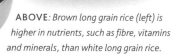

ABOVE: *Brown long grain rice (left) is higher in nutrients, such as fibre, vitamins and minerals, than white long grain rice.*

Cooking long grain brown rice
There are many methods and opinions on how to cook rice. The absorption method is one of the simplest and as a bonus also retains valuable nutrients that would otherwise be lost in cooking water that is drained away.

Different types of rice have different powers of absorption; however, the general rule of thumb for long grain rice is to use double the quantity of water to rice. For example, use 1 cup of rice to 2 cups of water; 200g/7oz/1 cup long grain rice is sufficient for about four people as a side dish.

1 Rinse the rice in a sieve (strainer) under cold, running water. Put in a heavy pan and add the measured cold water. Bring to the boil, uncovered, then reduce the heat and stir the rice. Add salt, to taste, if you wish.

2 Cover the pan with a tight-fitting lid. Simmer for 25–35 minutes, without removing the lid, until the water is absorbed and the rice tender. Remove the pan from the heat and leave to stand, covered, for 5 minutes before serving.

BELOW: *Jasmine fragrant rice*

Jasmine rice

The soft, sticky texture and mildly perfumed flavour of this rice accounts for its other name, fragrant rice. It is a long grain rice that is widely used in Thai cooking, where its delicate flavour tempers strongly spiced food.

Basmati rice

This is a slender long grain rice, which is grown in the foothills of the Himalayas. It is aged for a year after

BELOW: *White and brown basmati rice*

harvest, giving it a characteristic light, fluffy texture and aromatic flavour. Its name means 'fragrant'.

Both white and brown types of basmati rice are available. Brown basmati contains more nutrients and has a slightly nuttier flavour than the white variety. Widely used in Indian cooking, basmati rice has a cooling effect on hot and spicy curries. It is also excellent for biryanis and for rice salads, when you want very light, fluffy separate grains.

Red rice

This rice comes from the Camargue in France and has a distinctive chewy texture and a nutty flavour. It is an unusually hard grain, which retains its shape even after long cooking. Cooking intensifies its red colour, making it a distinctive addition to salads and stuffings.

Wild rice

This is not a true rice but an aquatic grass grown in North America. It has dramatic, long, slender brown-black grains that have a nutty flavour and chewy texture. It takes longer to cook than most types of rice – from 35–60 minutes, depending on whether you like it chewy or tender – but you can reduce the cooking time by soaking it in water overnight. Wild rice is extremely nutritious. It contains all eight essential amino acids and is particularly rich in lysine.

It is a good source of fibre, low in calories and gluten free. Use in stuffings, serve plain or mix with other rices in pilaffs and rice salads.

Valencia rice

Traditionally used for making Spanish paella, this short grain rice is not as sturdy as risotto rice and needs to be

BELOW: *Valencia rice*

BELOW: *Red rice*

BELOW: *Wild rice*

RIGHT: Clockwise from left, Arborio, Carnaroli and Vialone Nano risotto rice

handled with care because it breaks down easily. The best way of cooking paella is to leave the rice unstirred once all the ingredients are in the pan.

Risotto rice

To make Italian risotto, it is essential that you use a special fat short grain rice. Arborio rice, which originates from the Po Valley region in Italy, is the most widely sold variety of risotto rice, but you may also find varieties such as Carnaroli and

BELOW: Pudding rice

Vialone Nano in specialist shops. When cooked, most rice absorbs around three times its weight in water, but risotto rice can absorb nearly five times its weight, and the result is a creamy grain that still retains a slight bite.

Pudding rice

This rounded short grain rice is suitable for milk puddings and rice desserts. The grains swell and absorb a great deal of milk during cooking, which gives the pudding a soft, creamy consistency. Brown pudding rice is also available.

Glutinous rice

This rice is almost round in shape and has a slightly sweet flavour. Despite its name, the rice is gluten-free. The grains stick together when cooked due to their high starch content, making the rice easier to eat with chopsticks. Glutinous rice, which can be either white, black or purple, is used in many South-east Asian

Rice products

Rice flakes These are made by steaming and rolling whole or white grains. They are light and quick-cooking, and can be added raw to muesli or used to make porridge, creamy puddings, bread, biscuits (cookies) and cakes.

Rice bran Like wheat and oat bran, rice bran comes from the husk of the grain kernel. It is high in soluble dietary fibre and useful for adding texture and substance to bread, cakes and biscuits, and stews.

Rice flour Often used to make sticky Asian cakes and sweets, rice flour can also be used to thicken sauces. Because rice flour does not contain gluten, cakes made with it are rather flat. It can be combined with wheat flour to make cakes and bread, but produces a crumbly loaf. Glutinous or sweet rice flour is made from short grain rice, and is most often used for thickening sauces. Rice powder is a very fine rice flour, found in Asian shops.

BELOW: Clockwise from top left: Rice bran, rice flour, rice powder and rice flakes

ABOVE: *White and black glutinous rice*

countries to make sticky, creamy puddings. It is also ground into a fine flour and commonly used to thicken sauces and sometimes for desserts.

In China, white glutinous rice is often wrapped in lotus leaves and steamed to make a very popular dim sum dish.

Japanese sushi rice

Similar to glutinous rice, this is cooked and cooled, then mixed with rice vinegar to make the Japanese speciality sushi. Most of the sushi rice eaten in the West is actually grown in California.

ABOVE: *Sushi rice*

Japanese rice products

The Japanese are very resourceful when it comes to exploiting the vast potential of rice.

Sake Japan's national drink, this spirit can also be used in cooking.

Mirin Sweet rice wine that is delicious in marinades and savoury dishes, and a key teriyaki ingredient.

Rice vinegar Popular throughout Asia, this ranges in colour from white to brown. Japanese rice vinegar has a mild, mellow flavour. The Chinese version is far harsher.

Amasake A healthful rice drink made by adding enzymes from fermented rice to wholegrain pudding rice. Similar to soya 'milk', it can be flavoured. Amasake may be used for baking or desserts. It is an easily digestible weaning food.

RIGHT: *Clockwise from top left: Amasake, mirin, rice vinegar and sake*

OTHER GRAINS

Wheat and rice are undoubtedly the most widely used grains, yet there are others such as oats, rye, corn, barley, quinoa and spelt that should not be ignored. They provide variety in our diet and are packed with nutrients.

Oats

Available rolled, flaked, as oatmeal or oatbran, oats are warming and sustaining when cooked. Like rye, oats are a popular grain in northern Europe, particularly Scotland, where they are commonly turned into porridge, oatcakes and pancakes.

Whole oats are unprocessed with the nutritious bran and germ remaining intact. Oat groats are the hulled, whole kernel, while rolled oats are made from groats that have been heated and pressed flat. Quick-cooking rolled oats have been pre-cooked in water and then dried, which diminishes their nutritional value. Medium oatmeal is best in cakes and breads, while fine is ideal in pancakes, and fruit and milk drinks.

Oatmeal and oat flour contain very little gluten so should be mixed with wheat flour to make leavened bread. Oat bran can be sprinkled over breakfast cereals and mixed into plain or fruit yogurt.

Oats are perhaps the most nutritious of all the grains. Recent research has focused on the ability of oat bran to reduce blood cholesterol (sometimes with dramatic results), while beneficial HDL cholesterol levels increase. For the best results, oat bran should be eaten daily at regular intervals.

High in fibre, oats are an effective laxative and also feature protease inhibitors, a combination that has been found to inhibit certain cancers. Oats also contain vitamin E, some B vitamins, iron, calcium, magnesium, phosphorus and potassium.

Rye

The most popular grain for bread-making in Eastern Europe, Scandinavia and Russia, rye flour produces a dark,

ABOVE: *Rye grain and flour*

dense and dry loaf that keeps well. It is a hardy grain, which grows where most others fail – hence its popularity in colder climates.

Rye is low in gluten, and as a result rye flour is often mixed with high-gluten wheat flours to create lighter textured breads; the colour of these breads is sometimes intensified using molasses. The whole grain can be soaked overnight, then cooked in boiling water until tender; however, the flour, with its robust, full flavour and greyish colour, is the most commonly used form of rye. The flour ranges from dark to light, depending on whether the bran and germ have been removed.

Rye is a good source of vitamin E and some B vitamins, as well as protein, calcium, iron, phosphorus and potassium. It is also high in fibre, and is used in natural medicine to help to strengthen the digestive system.

ABOVE: *Clockwise from top left: Rolled oats, oatmeal, whole oats and oat bran*

Corn

Although we are most familiar with yellow corn or maize, blue, red, black and even multicoloured varieties can also be found. Corn is an essential store-cupboard ingredient in the USA, Caribbean, South America and Italy.

Masa harina

Maize meal, or masa harina, is made from the cooked whole grain, which is ground into flour and commonly used to make the flat bread tortilla.

Cornmeal

In the Caribbean, cornmeal is used to make puddings and dumplings. The main culinary uses for cornmeal are cornbread, a classic, southern American bread, and polenta, which confusingly is both the Italian name for cornmeal as well as a dish made with the grain. Polenta (the cooked dish) is a thick, golden porridge,

BELOW: *Clockwise from top left: Blue and yellow cornmeal, cornflour, popcorn, masa harina and polenta*

which is often flavoured with butter and cheese or chopped herbs. Once cooked, polenta can also be left to cool, then cut into slabs and fried, barbecued or griddled until golden brown. It is delicious with roasted vegetables. Ready-to-slice polenta is available from some supermarkets.

Polenta grain comes in various grades, ranging from fine to coarse. You can buy polenta that takes 40–45 minutes to cook or an 'instant' part-cooked version that can be cooked in less than 5 minutes.

Cornflour (Cornstarch)

This fine white powder is a useful thickening agent for sauces, soups and casseroles. It can also be used in cakes.

Hominy

These are the husked whole grains of corn. Cook in boiling water until softened, then use in stews and soups, or add to cakes and muffins.

Making polenta

Polenta makes an excellent alternative to mashed potato. It needs plenty of seasoning and is even better with a knob of butter and grated cheese, such as Parmesan, Gorgonzola or Taleggio. Serve with stews or casseroles. It is available in standard and quick-cook forms.

1 Pour 1 litre/1³/₄ pints/4 cups water into a heavy pan and bring to the boil. Remove from the heat.

2 In a steady stream, gradually add 185g/6¹/₂oz/1¹/₂ cups instant polenta and mix with a balloon whisk to avoid any lumps forming.

3 Return the pan to the heat and cook, stirring constantly with a wooden spoon, until the polenta is thick and creamy and starts to come away from the sides of the pan – this will take only a few minutes if you are using instant polenta.

4 Season to taste with salt and plenty of ground black pepper, then add a generous knob of butter and mix well. Remove from the heat and stir in the cheese, if using.

BELOW: *Clockwise from left: Pot barley, barley flakes and pearl barley*

Grits

Coarsely ground, dried yellow or white corn is known as grits. Use for porridge and pancakes or add to baked goods.

Popcorn

This is a separate strain of corn that is grown specifically to make the popular snack food. The kernel's hard outer casing explodes when heated. Popcorn can easily be made at home and flavoured sweet or savoury according to taste. The shop-bought types are often high in salt or sugar.

Barley

Believed to be the oldest cultivated grain, barley is still a fundamental part of the everyday diet in Eastern Europe, the Middle East and Asia. Pearl barley, the most usual form, is husked, steamed and polished to give it its characteristic ivory-coloured appearance. It has a mild, sweet flavour and chewy texture, and can be added to soups, stews and bakes. It is also used to make barley water.

Pot barley is the whole grain with just the inedible outer husk removed.

It takes much longer to cook than pearl barley. Barley flakes, which make a satisfying porridge, and barley flour are also available.

Pot barley is more nutritious than pearl barley, because it contains extra fibre, calcium, phosphorus, iron, magnesium and B vitamins. Barley was once used to increase potency and boost physical strength. More recently, studies have shown that its fibre content may help to prevent constipation and other digestive problems, as well as heart disease and certain cancers. In addition, the protease inhibitors in barley have been found to suppress cancer of the intestines, and eating barley regularly may also reduce the amount of harmful cholesterol produced by the liver.

Quinoa

Hailed as the supergrain of the future, quinoa (pronounced 'keen-wa') is a grain of the past. It was called the 'mother grain' by the Incas, who cultivated it for hundreds of years, high in the Andes, solely for their use.

Nowadays, quinoa is widely available. The tiny, bead-shaped grains have a mild, slightly bitter taste and firm texture. It is cooked in the same way as rice, but the grains quadruple in size, becoming translucent with an

unusual white outer ring. Quinoa is useful for making stuffings, pilaffs, bakes and breakfast cereals.

Quinoa's supergrain status hails from its rich nutritional value. Unlike other grains, quinoa is a complete protein because it contains all eight essential amino acids. It is an excellent source of calcium, potassium and zinc as well as iron, magnesium and B vitamins. It is particularly valuable for people with coeliac disease as it is gluten-free.

Millet

Although millet is usually associated with bird food, it is a highly nutritious grain. It once rivalled barley as the main food of Europe and remains a staple ingredient in many parts of the world, including Africa, China and India.

BELOW: *Quinoa*

BELOW: *Millet*

ABOVE: *Plain buckwheat, buckwheat flour and toasted buckwheat*

Its mild flavour makes it an ideal accompaniment to spicy stews and curries, and it can be used as a base for pilaffs or milk puddings. The tiny, firm grains can also be flaked or ground into flour. Millet is gluten-free, so it is useful for people with coeliac disease. The flour can be used for baking, but needs to be combined with high-gluten flours to make leavened bread.

Millet is an easily digestible grain. It contains more iron than other grains and is a good source of zinc, calcium, manganese and B vitamins. It is believed to be beneficial to those suffering from candidiasis, a fungal infection caused by *Candida albicans*.

Buckwheat

In spite of its name, buckwheat is not a type of wheat, but actually related to the rhubarb family. Available plain or toasted, it has a nutty, earthy flavour. It is a staple food in Eastern Europe as well as Russia, where the triangular grain is milled into a speckled-grey flour and used to make blini. The flour is also used for soba noodles and for pasta. The whole grain, which is also known as kasha, makes a fine porridge or a creamy pudding. Buckwheat is a complete protein. It contains all eight essential amino acids as well as rutin, which aids circulation and helps treat high blood pressure. It is rich in both iron and some of the B complex vitamins. It is also reputed to be good for the lungs, the kidneys and the bladder. Buckwheat is gluten-free.

Amaranth

This plant can be eaten as both a vegetable and a grain. Amaranth is considered a supergrain due to its excellent nutritional content. The tiny pale seed or 'grain' has a strong and distinctive, peppery flavour. It is best used in stews and soups, or it can be ground into a gluten-free flour to make bread, pastries and biscuits (cookies). Amaranth has more protein than pulses and is rich in amino acids, particularly lysine. It is also high in iron and calcium.

Kamut

An ancient relative of wheat, this grain has long, slender, brown kernels with a creamy, nutty flavour. It is as versatile as wheat and, when ground into flour, can be used to make pasta, breads, cakes and pastry. Puffed kamut cereals and kamut crackers are available in health food shops. Kamut has a higher nutritional value than wheat and is easier to digest.

Sorghum

This grain is best known for its thick sweet syrup, which is used in cakes and desserts. It is similar to millet and can be used much like rice. The ground flour is used for unleavened bread. Sorghum is a useful source of calcium, iron and B vitamins.

Spelt

This grain looks very similar to wheat and its flour can be substituted for wheat flour in bread. Spelt is richer in vitamins and minerals than wheat, and they are in a more readily digestible form.

BELOW: *Amaranth*

BELOW: *Kamut*

Lentils, peas and beans

Known as pulses (legumes), lentils, peas and beans provide a diverse range of flavours and textures. A staple food in the Middle East, South America, the Mediterranean and India, they are also used in classic recipes throughout the world, from Boston baked beans in the USA to lentil dhal in India. In Mexico, they are used for spicy refried beans; in China they are fermented for black bean and yellow bean sauces.

Low in fat and high in complex carbohydrates, vitamins and minerals, pulses are also an important source of protein for vegetarians and, when eaten with cereals, easily match animal-based sources.

LENTILS AND PEAS

The humble lentil is one of our oldest foods. It originated in Asia and north Africa, and continues to be cultivated in those regions, as well as in France and Italy. Lentils are hard even when fresh, so they are always sold dried. Unlike most other pulses, they do not need soaking first.

Lentils and peas can be kept for up to a year, but toughen with time. Buy them from shops with a fast turnover of stock, and store in airtight containers in a cool, dark place. Look for bright, unwrinkled pulses that are not dusty. Rinse well before use.

Lentils and peas share an impressive range of nutrients, including iron, selenium, folate, manganese, zinc, phosphorus and some B vitamins. Extremely low in fat and richer in protein than most pulses, lentils and peas are reputed to be important in fighting heart disease by reducing harmful LDL cholesterol in the body. They are high in fibre, which aids the functioning of the bowels and colon.

ABOVE: *Puy lentils*

ABOVE: *Green and brown lentils*

Red lentils

Orange-coloured red split lentils, sometimes known as Egyptian lentils, cook in just 20 minutes, eventually disintegrating into a thick purée. Ideal for thickening soups and casseroles, when cooked with spices, they make a delicious dhal. In the Middle East, red or yellow lentils are mixed with spices and vegetables to form balls known as kofte.

Yellow lentils

The less well known yellow lentils taste very similar to the red variety and are used in much the same way.

Green and brown lentils

Sometimes referred to as continental lentils, these disc-shaped pulses retain their shape when cooked, unlike red and yellow split lentils, but they do become mushy if overcooked. They also take longer to cook than split lentils – from 40–45 minutes – and are ideal for adding to warm salads, casseroles and stuffings. Alternatively, green and brown lentils can be cooked and blended with herbs or spices to make a nutritious pâté.

BELOW: *Red lentils*

have a sweeter flavour and cook more quickly. Like split lentils, split peas do not hold their shape when cooked, making them perfect for dahls, purées, casseroles and soups. They take about 45 minutes to cook. Marrow fat peas are larger in size and are used to make the traditional British dish 'mushy' peas. Like other whole peas, they require soaking overnight before use.

Puy lentils

These tiny dark blue-green marbled lentils grow in the Auvergne region in central France. They are considered to be far superior in taste and texture to other varieties, and they retain their beadlike shape during cooking, which takes 25–30 minutes. Puy lentils are a delicious addition to simple dishes such as warm salads, and are also good braised in wine and flavoured with fresh herbs.

Peas

Dried peas come from the field pea not the garden pea, which is eaten fresh. Unlike lentils, peas are soft when young and require drying. They are available whole or split; the latter

BELOW: *Marrow fat peas*

Cooking lentils
Lentils are easy to cook and there is no need to soak them first. Split red and green lentils cook down to a soft, purée-like consistency, while whole lentils hold their shape when cooked.

Green, brown and Puy lentils

1 Put 250g/9oz/generous 1 cup whole lentils in a sieve (strainer), and rinse well under cold running water. Transfer into a heavy pan.

2 Cover with water and bring to the boil. Simmer for 25–30 minutes until tender, topping up the water if necessary. Drain, and season with salt and ground black pepper.

Split red and yellow lentils

1 Put 250g/9oz/generous 1 cup split lentils in a sieve (strainer), and rinse well under cold running water. Transfer into a heavy pan.

2 Cover with 600ml/1 pint/2 1/2 cups water; bring to the boil. Simmer for 20–25 minutes, stirring occasionally, until the water is absorbed and the lentils are tender. Season to taste.

BEANS

These are edible seeds from plants belonging to the legume family. They are packed with protein, vitamins, minerals and fibre, and are extremely low in fat. They can be used as the base for an infinite variety of dishes. Most beans require soaking overnight in cold water before use, so plan ahead if using the dried type.

Look for plump, shiny beans with unbroken skin. Beans toughen with age so, although they will keep for up to a year in a cool, dry place, buy in small quantities. Avoid dusty or dirty beans, and store in airtight containers in a cool, dark, dry place.

Beans are packed with protein, soluble and insoluble fibre, iron, potassium, phosphorous, manganese, magnesium, folate and B vitamins. The soya bean is the most nutritious. Rich in high-quality protein, this wonder pulse contains all eight essential amino acids that cannot be synthesized by the body, but are vital for the renewal of cells and tissues.

Aduki beans

Also known as adzuki beans, these tiny deep-red beans have a sweet, nutty flavour. In Chinese cooking, they form the base of red bean paste. Aduki beans are reputed to be good for the liver and kidneys. They cook quickly and can be used in casseroles and bakes, or ground into flour for cakes, breads and pastries.

Black beans

These black kidney-shaped beans are often used in Caribbean cooking. With a sweetish flavour and distinctive colour, they add a dramatic touch to soups, bean salads or casseroles.

Black-eyed beans

Also known as black-eye peas or cow peas, these beans are a key ingredient in Creole cooking and some spicy Indian curries. They are characterized by the black spot on their sides. Good in soups, salads, bakes and casseroles, they can also be used in place of haricot or cannellini beans.

Borlotti beans

These oval beans have red-streaked pinkish-brown skin and a bittersweet flavour. Tender and moist when cooked, they are good in Italian bean and pasta soups, as well as hearty vegetable stews. They are interchangeable with red kidney beans in most recipes.

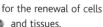

LEFT: Black beans (left), black-eyed beans (centre) and borlotti beans (below right)

ABOVE: *Butter beans*

Broad (Fava) beans

These large beans are usually eaten fresh. They change in colour from green to brown when dried, making them difficult to recognize in their dried state. The outer skin can be very tough and chewy; some people prefer to remove this after cooking. They can also be bought ready-skinned.

Butter beans and lima beans

Similar in flavour and appearance, both butter beans and lima beans are characterized by their flattish kidney shape and soft, floury texture. In Greek cooking, butter beans are baked with tomato, garlic and olive oil until tender and creamy. The lima bean is the main ingredient in succotash. Both types are good with creamy herb sauces. Be careful not to overcook either lima or butter beans, as they become pulpy and mushy.

Cannellini beans

These small, white, kidney-shaped beans have a soft, creamy texture when cooked. When dressed with olive oil, lemon juice, crushed garlic and fresh chopped parsley, they make an excellent warm salad.

Chickpeas

Also known as garbanzo beans, robust chickpeas have a nutty flavour and creamy texture. They are much used in Mediterranean and Middle Eastern cooking. In India, they are known as 'gram' and are ground into flour for fritters and flatbreads. Gram flour, also called besan, is sold in health food shops and Asian grocery stores.

Flageolet (Small cannellini) beans

These young haricot beans are removed from the pod before they are fully ripe, hence their delicate flavour. A pretty, mint-green colour, they are best treated simply. Cook until tender, then season and drizzle with a little olive oil and lemon juice.

Haricot beans

Most commonly used for canned baked beans, these versatile ivory-coloured beans are oval in shape. Called navy or Boston beans in the USA, they suit slow-cooked dishes, such as casseroles and bakes.

BELOW: *Clockwise from left: Haricot, red kidney, flageolet and pinto*

Pinto beans

A smaller, paler version of the borlotti bean, the pinto has an attractive speckled skin; it is aptly called the painted bean. Pinto beans feature extensively in Mexican cooking, most familiarly in refried beans, when they are cooked until tender and fried with garlic, chilli and tomatoes, then mashed.

Red kidney beans

Red kidney beans retain their colour and shape when cooked. Much used in South American cooking, kidney beans must always be boiled vigorously for the first 10–15 minutes of their cooking time, as they contain a substance that otherwise causes severe food poisoning.

Ful medames

A member of the broad bean family, these small Egyptian beans form the base of the dish of the same name, in which they are flavoured with ground cumin, baked with olive oil, garlic and lemon, and served topped with hard-boiled egg. Soak overnight in cold water, then cook slowly for 1 hour until soft.

Soya beans

These small oval beans vary in colour from creamy-yellow through brown to black. They need to be

LEFT AND BELOW: *White and black soya beans*

BELOW: *Mung beans*

soaked for 12 hours before cooking. Soya beans combine well with robust ingredients such as garlic, herbs and spices, and make a healthy addition to soups, casseroles, bakes and salads. Soya beans are also used to make tofu, tempeh, soy sauce, flour and textured vegetable protein (TVP).

Mung beans

Instantly recognizable as beansprouts in their sprouted form, mung or moong beans are small, olive-coloured beans native to India. Soft and sweet when cooked, they are used in spicy moong dahl. Soaking is not essential, but soaking overnight reduces the usual 40 minutes' cooking time by half.

Soya bean products

Soya beans are incredibly versatile and are used to make an extensive array of products, including tofu, tempeh, textured vegetable protein, flour, miso and a variety of sauces.

ABOVE: *Clockwise from top: Beancurd skins, firm tofu, deep-fried tofu and silken tofu*

The soya bean is the most nutritious bean of all. Rich in high-quality protein, it is one of the few vegetarian foods that contains all eight essential amino acids, which are vital for the renewal of the body's cells and tissues.

Soya is rich in minerals, particularly iron and calcium, it is also low in saturated fat and is cholesterol-free. It can help to reduce osteoporosis, blood pressure and blood cholesterol, and there is evidence to suggest that it helps to reduce the risk of cancer as it contains hormone-like substances called 'phytoestrogens'.

TOFU

Also known as beancurd, tofu is made in a similar way to soft cheese. The beans are boiled, mashed and sieved (strained) to make soya 'milk', which is then curdled using a coagulant. The resulting curds are drained and pressed to make tofu.

Firm tofu

Sold in blocks, firm tofu can be cubed or sliced, and used in vegetable stir-fries, kebabs, salads, soups and casseroles. Alternatively, mash it and use it in bakes and burgers. Its bland flavour is improved by marinating, as its porous texture absorbs flavours.

Silken tofu

Soft with a silky, smooth texture, this type of tofu is ideal for use in sauces, dressings, dips and soups. It is a useful dairy-free alternative to cream, soft cheese or yogurt, and can be used to make creamy desserts.

Other forms of tofu

Smoked, marinated and deep-fried tofu are all readily available in health food stores and Oriental shops, as well as some larger supermarkets. Deep-fried tofu is fairly tasteless on its own, but it has an interesting texture. It puffs up during cooking and is white and soft underneath the golden, crisp coating. It easily absorbs the flavours of other ingredients and it can be used in much the same way as firm tofu; as it is fried in vegetable oil, it is suitable for vegetarian cooking.

All types of fresh tofu can be kept in the refrigerator for up to 1 week. Firm tofu should be kept covered in water, which must be changed regularly. Freezing tofu is not recommended because it alters the texture. Silken tofu is often available in vacuum packs, which do not have to be refrigerated and have a much longer shelf life.

TEMPEH

This Indonesian speciality is made by fermenting cooked soya beans with a cultured starter. Tempeh is similar to tofu, but has a nuttier, more savoury flavour. It can be used in the same way as firm tofu and also benefits from marinating. Some types of tofu are used as a dairy replacement, but tempeh's firm texture means that it can be used instead of meat.

You can buy tempeh chilled or frozen from health food stores and Oriental shops. Chilled tempeh can be stored in the refrigerator for up to a week. Frozen tempeh can kept in the freezer for 1 month; defrost before use.

ABOVE: *Minced and cubed TVP*

ABOVE: *Soya flour*

BELOW: *Light soy sauce and dark soy sauce*

BEANCURD SKINS AND STICKS
Made from soya 'milk', dried beancurd skins and sticks, like fresh beancurd, rapidly absorb the flavour of seasonings and other ingredients when cooked. Beancurd skins and sticks need to be soaked until pliable before use. Beancurd skins need to be soaked in cold water for an hour or two, and can be used to wrap a variety of fillings. Beancurd sticks are soaked for several hours or overnight. They can be chopped and used in soups, stir-fries and casseroles.

TVP
Textured vegetable protein, or TVP, is a useful meat replacement and is usually bought in dry chunks or as mince. Made from processed soya beans, TVP is first rehydrated in boiling water or vegetable stock, then used in stews, curries or pie fillings.

SOYA FLOUR
This is a finely ground high-protein flour that is also gluten-free. It is often mixed with other flours in bread and pastries, adding a pleasant nuttiness, or it can be used as a thickener in sauces.

SOY SAUCE
Soy sauce originated over 2,000 years ago. Made by combining crushed soya beans with wheat, salt, water and a yeast-based culture called koji, it is left to ferment for between 6 months and 3 years.

There are two basic types of soy sauce: light and dark. Light soy sauce is slightly thinner and saltier. It is used in dressings and soups. Dark soy sauce is heavier and sweeter, with a more rounded flavour, and is used in marinades, stir-fries and sauces. Try to buy naturally brewed soy sauce. as many other kinds are now chemically prepared to hasten fermentation.

Shoyu
Made in Japan, shoyu is aged for 1–2 years, resulting in a full-flavoured sauce that can be used in the same way as dark soy sauce. You can buy it from Oriental and health food stores.

Tamari
This form of soy sauce is a natural by-product of making miso, although it is often produced in the same way as soy sauce. Most tamari is made without wheat, making it gluten-free. It has a rich, robust flavour and is used in cooking or as a condiment.

MISO
A thick paste made from a mixture of cooked soya beans, rice, wheat or barley, salt and water, miso is left to ferment for up to 3 years. It is used to add flavour to soups, stocks, stir-fries and noodle dishes. There are three main types: kome, or white miso, the lightest and sweetest; medium-strength mugi miso, with a mellow flavour ideal for everyday use; and hacho miso, which has a thick texture and a strong flavour.

ABOVE: *Tamari (left) and shoyu*

BELOW: *Mugi miso (left) and hacho miso*

Dairy foods and non-dairy alternatives

Some people may question including dairy products in a wholefood cookbook. While it would be foolish to advocate the consumption of vast quantities of high-fat milk, cream and cheese, a diet that includes moderate amounts of dairy products does provide valuable vitamins and minerals. There is little reason to reject dairy products wholesale, as they can enrich vegetarian cooking. And for those who choose to avoid dairy foods, there are plenty of alternatives.

MILK, CREAM AND YOGURT

This wide group of ingredients includes milk, cream and yogurt made from cow's, goat's and sheep's milk, as well as non-dairy products such as soya 'milk' and 'cream', and other non-dairy 'milks', which are made from nuts and grains.

Milk

Cow's milk remains the most popular type, although, with the growing concern about saturated fat and cholesterol, semi-skimmed (low-fat) and skimmed milks now outsell the full-fat version. Skimmed milk contains half the calories of full-fat milk and only a fraction of the fat, but nutritionally it

is on a par, retaining its vitamins, calcium and other minerals. Buy organic milk, if you can, because it comes from cows that have been fed on a pesticide-free diet and are not routinely treated with hormones, antibiotics or BST (bovine somatotrophin), which is used in some countries to boost milk yield.

When buying milk, cream and cream-related products, don't forget to check the 'best before' or 'sell-by' date. The fat content, nutritional information and ingredients are also detailed. Try to avoid products with unnecessary additives or flavourings.

Milk is an important source of calcium and phosphorus, both of which are essential for healthy teeth and bones, and are said to prevent osteoporosis. Milk also contains significant amounts of zinc and the B vitamins, including B12, along with a small amount of vitamin D. Numerous studies have revealed that,

BELOW: *From left: Goat's milk, cow's milk, sheep's milk and soya 'milk'*

ABOVE: *Smetana*

due to its high calcium content, milk fortified with vitamin D may have a role in preventing colon cancer. The antibodies found in milk may help gastrointestinal problems and boost the immune system, and skimmed milk may reduce the amount of cholesterol produced by the liver.

Goat's and sheep's milk

These milks make useful alternatives for people who are intolerant to cow's milk. The lactose in cow's milk can cause severe indigestion, and an intolerance to dairy products often manifests itself in eczema or sinus congestion. Goat's and sheep's milk are nutritionally similar to cow's milk, but easier to digest. Goat's milk has a distinctive, musky flavour; sheep's milk has a less assuming flavour.

Cream

Cream's high fat content means that it should not be eaten on a daily basis. Used with discretion, however, cream lends a richness to soups, sauces, bakes and desserts.

The fat content of cream ranges enormously: pouring (half-and-half) contains about 12 per cent, single (light) cream 18 per cent, double (heavy) cream 48 per cent, and clotted cream, which is the highest, about 55 per cent.

Sour cream

This thick-textured cream is treated with lactic acid, which gives it its characteristic tang. Full-fat sour cream contains about 20 per cent fat, although low- and non-fat versions are available. It can be used in the same way as cream. Care should be taken when cooking, as it can curdle if heated to too high a temperature.

BELOW: *Clockwise from bottom left: Whipping cream, single cream and whipped double cream*

ABOVE: *Clockwise from top left: Thick cow's milk yogurt, thin cow's milk yogurt, Greek-style yogurt, soya yogurt, goat's milk yogurt and sheep's milk yogurt*

Crème fraîche

This rich cultured cream is similar to sour cream, but its high fat content (around 35 per cent) means that it does not curdle when cooked.

Buttermilk

Traditionally made from the milky liquid left over after butter making, buttermilk is now more likely to be made from skimmed milk, mixed with milk solids, then cultured with lactic acid. Its creamy, mild sour taste adds a distinctive tang to desserts. Used in baking, buttermilk gives cakes and soda bread a moist texture.

Smetana

Originally made in Russia, this rich version of buttermilk is made from skimmed milk and single cream with an added culture. It has a similar fat content to Greek (US strained plain) yogurt (about 10 per cent), and should be treated in the same way. Smetana can curdle if overheated.

Yogurt

Yogurt varies in fat content from virtually fat-free to those made from whole milk. Greek (US strained plain) and Greek-style yogurt, made from cow's or sheep's milk, has less fat than cream. Lower fat yogurts can also be used instead of cream, but are best in uncooked dishes. Look for 'live' on the label when buying yogurt. This means that it has been fermented with a starter culture bacteria, ensuring that it is easily digestible. Yogurt is rich in calcium, phosphorus and B vitamins.

SOYA SUBSTITUTES

Soya 'milk', a cholesterol-free milk alternative, is made from pulverized soya beans. Suitable for cooking and drinking, it is used to make yogurt, cream and cheese. Soya 'cream' is slightly thicker. Both are valuable sources of protein, calcium, iron, magnesium, phosphorus and vitamin E, and the 'milk' is low in calories.

SOFT AND HARD CHEESES

The selection of cheeses in this section is a mere fraction of the extensive range that is available in good cheese shops and supermarkets. Some, like mozzarella and feta, are more often cooked in pies or on pizzas, or used in salads, while others, such as the soft, white, Camembert-type goat's cheeses, make a good addition to a cheese board.

Hard cheeses are best stored in a cool larder; however, if kept in the refrigerator, the cheese should be left at room temperature for at least an hour before eating. Cheese starts to dry out as soon as it is cut, so always keep it loosely wrapped in foil or baking parchment.

Semi-soft cheeses, such as mozzarella, and hard cheeses, such as Parmesan and Cheddar, contain valuable amounts of calcium, protein, vitamins and minerals. Hard cheeses are also high in saturated fat. When buying hard cheeses, choose a mature, good-quality type, as the strong flavour means that relatively small quantities are needed to add

BELOW: Mozzarella

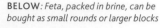

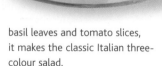

flavour to a dish. Saturated fat is known to increase blood cholesterol, which can lead to heart disease and stroke, so always eat cheese in moderation. On the plus side, research shows that cheese – particularly a waxy, hard cheese such as Cheddar – eaten after a meal, may reduce the likelihood of tooth decay by as much as 50 per cent.

Mozzarella

This delicate, silky-white cheese is usually made from cow's milk, although authentically it should be made from buffalo's milk and eaten fresh on the day it is made. This is not practical for most of us, though, so most mozzarella is sold stored in brine or vacuum-sealed packages. It is also available smoked. The sweet milky balls of cheese have excellent melting qualities, hence its use on pizzas and in bakes, but it is equally delicious served in salads. When it is combined with fresh

BELOW: Feta, packed in brine, can be bought as small rounds or larger blocks

basil leaves and tomato slices, it makes the classic Italian three-colour salad.

Feta

Believed to be one of the first cheeses, authentic feta is curdled naturally without the addition of rennet. Although it was once made with goat's or sheep's milk, it is now more often made with milk from cows. It is preserved in brine, hence its saltiness, and has a firm, crumbly texture. It is used in the classic Greek salad with cucumber, tomatoes and olives. To reduce the salty taste of feta, rinse it in water, then leave to soak in cold water for 10 minutes.

BELOW: Halloumi

BELOW: *Goat's cheese comes in a multitude of different forms*

Goat's cheese

Indispensable for those intolerant or allergic to cow's milk, goat's cheese varieties range from soft, mild and creamy, through a Camembert-type, which has a soft centre and downy rind, to the firm Cheddar alternative. Similarly, the flavour of goat's cheese spans from fresh, creamy and mild, to sharp and pungent.

Halloumi

This ancient cheese was first made by nomadic Bedouin tribes. Halloumi is commonly sold in small blocks, and is often sprinkled with mint. It has a firm, rubbery texture and retains its shape when grilled (broiled) or fried. Some people consider halloumi cheese to be a tasty vegetarian alternative to bacon.

BELOW: *Parmesan*

Cheddar

Unfortunately, much of the Cheddar sold today is made in factories and bears little resemblance to authentic, traditional Cheddar cheese. Avoid these fairly tasteless, rubbery blocks, and instead look out for traditional farmhouse Cheddar, which is matured for between 9 and 24 months, resulting in the classic rich, strong savoury flavour.

Parmesan

Allowed to mature for at least 18 months and up to four years, this richly flavoured cow's milk cheese may be high in fat – although not as high as Cheddar – but a little goes a long way. Authentic Parmesan cheese is labelled Parmigano-Reggiano, after the region in Italy where it is traditionally made. Avoid ready-grated Parmesan, and opt for a freshly cut chunk. It keeps for a long time in the refrigerator and is excellent grated and added to pasta, risottos and bakes, or shaved over salads.

Non-dairy cheeses

Soya cheese is the most common non-dairy variety. It can lack the depth of flavour of cheese made from cow's, goat's or sheep's milk, but it is nevertheless a valuable alternative for people who prefer not to buy dairy products or who are lactose-intolerant. Soya cheese is made from a blend of processed soya beans and vegetable fats, and may be flavoured with herbs and spices. Other non-dairy cheeses include a Parmesan-type cheese made from rice and a spice-flavoured cheese produced from nuts.

BELOW: *A selection of non-dairy cheeses*

FRESH UNRIPENED CHEESES

As their name suggests, fresh unripened cheeses are young and immature. Their light, mild taste readily accepts stronger flavoured ingredients, such as herbs and spices. Fresh cheeses can be used in both savoury dishes and desserts.

Fresh unripened cheeses do not keep for very long and are best bought in small quantities and eaten soon after purchase. Store in an airtight container in the refrigerator. They generally have a lower fat content than hard cheeses and are less likely to trigger migraines. They also provide plenty of protein, calcium and vitamin B12.

Quark

This low-fat curd cheese is usually made with semi-skimmed (low-fat) or skimmed milk. Its mild, slightly tangy flavour and light, creamy texture make it perfect in cheesecakes and desserts, or it can be diluted with milk to make an

BELOW: Clockwise from left: Ricotta, fromage frais, quark, cream cheese and cottage cheese

alternative to cream. In northern European countries, it is used as a spread instead of butter.

Fromage frais

This smooth, fresh cheese has the same consistency as thick yogurt, but is less acidic. It can be used in the same way as yogurt – mixed with fruit purée to make fools, combined with dried fruit, nuts and grains, or in sweet and savoury flans. The fat content varies from almost nothing to about 8 per cent. Full-fat fromage frais is the best choice for cooking.

Cottage cheese

Lower in fat than most other cheeses (between 2 and 5 per cent), cottage cheese is not usually used for cooking, but is good for salads and dips. It makes a fine accompaniment to soft fruits and is best eaten as fresh as possible.

Ricotta

A soft low-fat unsalted cheese that can be made from sheep's, goat's or cow's milk, ricotta has a slightly granular texture and is widely used in Italian cooking. Its mild,

Making fresh soft cheese

Fresh soft cheese can be made using soured milk (made from milk mixed with yogurt) or soured cream. Use plain or sweeten with honey, orange flower water or fresh soft fruit. Alternatively, mix with fresh chopped herbs and garlic.

1 Put 1 litre/1¾ pints/4 cups semi-skimmed (low-fat) milk and 120ml/4fl oz/½ cup live yogurt or soured cream in a pan. Mix well. Bring to the boil, then simmer for 5 minutes or until the milk curdles, stirring constantly.

2 Line a metal sieve (strainer) or colander with muslin (cheesecloth), and place over a large bowl. Pour the milk mixture into the sieve or colander and leave to drain for 1 hour or until it stops dripping. Alternatively, gather together the edges of the muslin, tie with string, and suspend over the bowl for about 1 hour until it stops dripping.

3 The solid residue left behind in the muslin is the soft unripened cheese. It will keep in the refrigerator for 3–4 days if stored in a covered bowl. Use as needed.

clean flavour means that it is very versatile. It makes a neutral base for pancake fillings, and can be used as a stuffing for pasta, when it is often combined with spinach. Ricotta is also good in tarts, cakes and cheesecakes, or it can be served on its own with fruit. Mixed with herbs and garlic, it makes a tasty sandwich filling.

Cream cheese

Commonly used in cheesecakes, dips, spreads and even icing (frosting), cream cheese has a rich, velvety consistency, mild flavour and a high fat content – about 35 per cent. It is possible to buy lower-fat alternatives made from skimmed milk, but these are not suitable for all recipes.

Non-dairy soft cheeses

Like non-dairy hard cheeses, a range of soft soya-based cheeses is available from health food stores. They are a good alternative for those who prefer not to buy dairy products or who are lactose-intolerant. They can be used as sandwich fillers as well as in many desserts.

Butter versus margarine

Whether butter is better than margarine has been the focus of much debate. The taste, especially of good-quality, farmhouse butter, is certainly superior to margarine. However, butter, which contains 80 per cent saturated fat, has the ability to raise cholesterol levels in the body.

Vegetable margarine contains the same amount of fat as butter, but the fat is polyunsaturated, which was once considered to give margarine greater health benefits. Unfortunately, margarine manufacturing processes change the fats into trans fats, or hydrogenated fats. Studies have shown that trans fats may be more likely than the saturated fat in butter to damage the heart and blood vessels. In addition, cooking removes many of the health benefits of polyunsaturated fats.

Lower fat margarines are known as spreads. They contain less than 80 per cent fat, and those that are under 65 per cent fat can be classified as reduced-fat. When the fat content falls below 41 per cent,

a spread can be called low-fat or half-fat. Very low-fat spreads may contain gelatine, and their high water content means that they are not suitable for cooking. Olive-oil based spreads are rich in monounsaturated fats and are said to reduce cholesterol levels. They can be used for cooking.

When buying margarine and spreads, always choose good-quality brands that contain no hydrogenated fats. Butter, margarines and spreads

absorb other flavours, so they need to be kept well wrapped. Always store these products in the refrigerator; unsalted butters will keep for up to 2 weeks, other butters for up to 1 month, and margarines and spreads will keep for about 2 months.

BELOW: *There is a wide variety of different butters, margarines and spreads available. Whichever option you choose to use, remember not to consume too much of these high-fat foods.*

Eggs

An inexpensive, self-contained source of nourishment, hen's eggs offer the cook tremendous scope, whether served simply solo or as part of a dish.

There are several different types, but the best are organic, free-range eggs from a small producer. Freshness is paramount when buying eggs. Buy from a shop that has a high turnover of stock, and reject any eggs that have a broken, dirty or damaged shell. Most eggs are date stamped, but you can check if an egg is fresh by placing it in a bowl of cold water: if it sinks and lays flat it is fresh. The older the egg, the more it will stand on its end. A really old egg will float and should not be eaten. Store eggs in their box in the main part of the refrigerator and not in a rack in the door as this can expose them to damage. The shells are porous, so eggs can be tainted by strong smells. Eggs should be stored large-end up for no longer than 3 weeks.

Eggs have received much adverse publicity due to their high cholesterol levels, but attention has moved from dietary cholesterol to cholesterol that is produced in the body from saturated fats. Saturated fats are now claimed to play a bigger role in raising cholesterol levels. As eggs are low in saturated fat, they have been somewhat reprieved. They should, however, be eaten in moderation, and people with raised cholesterol levels should take particular care. Nutritionists recommend that we eat no more than four eggs a week. Eggs provide B vitamins, especially B12, vitamins A and D, iron, choline and phosphorus. Cooking does not alter their nutritional content significantly.

Battery eggs

Battery eggs are laid by hens that are kept in cages with minimum space in which to move. Hens are debeaked to prevent them pecking each other. These eggs are the cheapest to buy.

Barn or perch eggs

These eggs are produced by hens that are kept indoors. Hens can roam around in the barn, but have no access to the outside. Barn or perch eggs are more expensive than battery eggs, but cheaper than free-range eggs.

Organic free-range eggs

These eggs are from hens that are fed on a natural pesticide-free diet that has not had hormones or artificial colorants added. The hens are able to roam on land that has

ABOVE: *Organic free-range eggs*

not been treated with chemical fertilizers and is certified organic. Free-range hens have the same indoor conditions as barn hens, but also have daytime access to the open air – although the term 'access' has been open to abuse. Organic free-range hens are said to have better conditions than other free-range hens, and are not routinely debeaked.

Fourgrain eggs

These eggs are produced by hens that are fed a diet based on barley, oats, wheat and rye. Hens have the same living conditions as barn or perch hens, in that they are kept indoors without access to the outside.

Misleading labels

The labels on egg boxes often have phrases such as 'farm fresh', 'natural' or 'country-fresh', which conjure up images of hens roaming around in the open, but they may well refer to eggs that are laid by birds reared in battery cages. It is advisable to avoid eggs that are labelled with such claims.

The store cupboard

The following section features a diverse range of foods that can enrich and add variety to a vegetarian diet. Some ingredients may be familiar, others less so, but all are useful to keep in the store cupboard. Each mentioned food comes with notes on choosing, storage and preparation, when necessary, as well as nutritional or medicinal properties.

NUTS

With the exception of peanuts, nuts are the fruits of trees. The quality and availability of fresh nuts varies with the seasons, although most types are sold dried, either whole or prepared ready for use. Shelled nuts come in many forms: they may be whole, blanched, halved, sliced, shredded, chopped, ground or toasted.

Always buy nuts in small quantities because, if kept for too long, they can turn rancid. Nuts in their shells should feel heavy for their size. Store nuts in airtight containers in a cool, dark place or in the refrigerator, and they should keep fresh for 3 months. When buying a coconut, make sure that there is no sign of mould or a rancid smell. Give it a shake – it should be full of liquid. Keep coconut milk in the refrigerator or freezer once opened. Desiccated (dry unsweetened shredded) coconut can be stored in an airtight container, but don't keep it too long because its high fat content means that it is prone to rancidity.

Rich in B complex vitamins, vitamin E, potassium, magnesium, calcium, phosphorus and iron, nuts offer the vegetarian an abundance of nutrients, although they contain a hefty number of calories. Most nuts are rich in monounsaturated and polyunsaturated fats, with the exception of Brazil nuts and coconuts, which are high in saturated fat, but do not contain cholesterol.

Numerous studies highlight the substantial health benefits of walnuts. According to one study, the essential fatty acids found in walnuts can decrease cholesterol levels and may reduce the risk of heart disease by 50 per cent. Almonds and hazelnuts have similar properties.

Of all foods, Brazil nuts are the richest in selenium, which is a known mood enhancer. Apparently, a single Brazil nut each day will ensure that you are never deficient in this vital mineral.

Nuts are one of the richest vegetable sources of the important antioxidant vitamin E, which has been associated with a lower risk of heart disease, stroke and certain cancers.

Almonds

There are two types of almond: sweet and bitter. The best sweet varieties are the flat and slender Jordan almonds from Spain. Heart-shaped Valencia almonds from Portugal and Spain, and the flatter Californian almonds, are also widely available. For the best flavour, buy shelled almonds in their skins and blanch them yourself: cover with boiling water, leave for a few minutes, then drain and the skins will peel off easily. Almonds are available ready-blanched, flaked and ground. The latter adds a richness to cakes, tarts, pastry and sauces. Bitter almonds are much smaller and are used in almond oil and extract. They should not be eaten raw, as they contain traces of the lethal prussic acid.

ABOVE: *Blanched, whole and shelled almonds; shelled cashew nuts; and shelled and whole Brazil nuts*

Brazil nuts

These are, in fact, seeds, and are grown mainly in the Amazon regions of Brazil and neighbouring countries. Between 12 and 20 Brazil nuts grow, packed snugly together, in a large brown husk, hence their three-cornered wedge shape. Brazil nuts have a sweet, milky taste and are used mainly as dessert nuts. They have a high fat content, and so go rancid very quickly.

Cashew nuts

These are the seeds of the 'cashew apple' – an evergreen tree with bright-orange fruit. Cashew nuts have a sweet flavour and crumbly texture. They make delicious nut butters or can be sprinkled into stir-fries or over salads. They are never sold in the shell and undergo an extensive heating process that removes the seed from its outer casing.

Chestnuts

Raw chestnuts are not recommended. They are not only unpleasant to eat, but also contain tannic acid, which inhibits the absorption of iron. Most chestnuts are imported from France and Spain and are excellent after roasting.

RIGHT:
Chestnuts

Unlike other nuts, they contain very little fat. Out of season, chestnuts can be bought dried, canned or puréed. Add whole chestnuts to winter stews, soups, stuffings or pies. The sweetened purée is delicious in desserts.

Coconuts

This versatile nut grows all over the tropics. The white dense flesh is made into desiccated (dry unsweetened shredded) coconut, blocks of creamed coconut and a thick and creamy milk. A popular ingredient in Asian, African and South American cuisines, coconut lends a sweet, creamy flavour to desserts, curries, soups and casseroles. Use in moderation, as it is high in fat.

Hazelnuts

Grown in the USA, Britain, Turkey, Italy and Spain, hazelnuts are usually sold dried, and can be bought whole, shelled and ground. They can be eaten raw, and the shelled nuts are especially good toasted. Hazelnuts can be grated or chopped for use in cakes and desserts, but they are also tasty in savoury dishes and can be added to salads, stir-fries and pasta.

Macadamia nuts

This round nut, about the size of a large hazelnut, is native to Australia, but is now grown in California, Hawaii and South America. Macadamia nuts are commonly sold shelled (the shell is extremely hard to crack). They have a crisp texture, a rich, buttery flavour and a high fat content.

ABOVE: Hazelnuts

BELOW:
Macadamia nuts

Peanuts

Not strictly nuts but a member of the pulse family, peanuts bury themselves just below the earth after flowering – hence their alternative name, groundnuts. They are a staple food in many countries, and are widely used in South-east Asia, notably for satay sauce, and in African cuisines, where they are used as an ingredient in

---

Nut allergy

Any food has the potential to cause an allergic reaction, but peanuts, as well as walnuts, Brazil nuts, hazelnuts and almonds, are known to be common allergens. In cases of extreme allergy, nuts can trigger a life-threatening reaction known as anaphylaxis. Symptoms include facial swelling, shortness of breath, dizziness and loss of consciousness, so it is essential that sufferers take every precaution to avoid nuts.

stews. In the West, peanuts are a popular snack food; the shelled nuts are frequently sold roasted and salted, and they are used to make the ever-popular peanut butter. Peanuts are particularly high in fat and should be eaten in moderation.

Pecan nuts

A glossy, reddish-brown, oval-shaped shell encloses the pecan kernel, which looks like an elongated walnut, but has a sweeter, milder flavour.

This native American nut is a favourite in sweet pies, especially the classic pecan pie, but is also good eaten on its own or added to salads. However, pecan nuts should be eaten only as an occasional treat because they have the highest fat content of any nut, with a calorie content to match.

Pine nuts

These are actually not nuts, but the fruit of the Mediterranean stone pine tree. They have a rich, aromatic flavour, which lends itself to toasting. Buy in small quantities because their high oil content quickly turns them rancid. Pine nuts are a key ingredient in Italian pesto sauce, where they are pounded with garlic, olive oil and basil, and in the Middle Eastern sauce tarator, in which toasted pine nuts are combined with bread, garlic, milk and olive oil to make a creamy paste that has a similar consistency to hummus.

Pistachio nuts

Incredibly 'moreish' when served as a snack, pistachio nuts have pale-green flesh and thin, reddish-purple skin. Sold shelled or in a split shell, these mild nuts are often used chopped as a colourful garnish, sprinkled over both sweet and savoury foods. Pistachio nuts have a wonderful flavour and are widely used in Middle Eastern cuisines. They are also good in all manner of desserts and can be made into a delicious ice cream. Pistachio nuts are widely used in Turkish and Arabic sweets, notably nougat and Turkish delight. Check before buying pistachio nuts for cooking, as they are often sold salted.

Walnuts

Most walnuts are imported from France, Italy and California, but they are also grown in the Middle East, Britain and China. This versatile nut has been around for hundreds of years. When picked young, walnuts are referred to as 'wet' and have fresh, milky-white kernels, which can be eaten raw, but are often pickled.

Dried walnuts have a delicious bittersweet flavour and can be bought shelled, chopped or ground. They can be used to make cakes and biscuits, as well as rich pie fillings, but are also good added to savoury dishes such as stir-fries and salads – the classic Waldorf salad combines whole kernels with sliced celery and apples in a mayonnaise dressing.

ABOVE: *Peanuts*

ABOVE: *Pecan nuts*

ABOVE: *Walnuts*

ABOVE: *Pine nuts*

ABOVE: Tahini (left) and black and white sesame seeds

SEEDS

They may look very small and unassuming, but seeds are nutritional powerhouses, packed with vitamins and minerals, beneficial oils and protein. They can be used in a huge array of sweet and savoury dishes, and will add an instant healthy boost, pleasant crunch and nutty flavour when added to rice and pasta dishes, salads, stir-fries, soups and yogurt.

Seeds are best bought in small quantities from shops. Purchase whole seeds, rather than ground, and store them in a cool, dark place as they are prone to turning rancid. After opening the packet, decant the seeds into an airtight container.

Seeds contain valuable amounts of the antioxidant vitamin E, which enhances the immune system and protects cells from oxidation. Vitamin E also improves blood circulation, and promotes healing and normal blood clotting, as well as reducing infections associated with ageing. Numerous studies show that the vitamin works in tandem with beta carotene and vitamin C to fight off certain cancers and heart disease, as well as slow the progression of Alzheimer's disease.

For their size, seeds contain a lot of iron. Sesame seeds are particularly rich – just 25g/1oz provides nearly half the daily requirement of iron, and 50g/2oz pumpkin seeds provides almost three-quarters of the iron we need each day.

Seeds, particularly sunflower seeds, may help to reduce the body's blood cholesterol levels because they contain plentiful amounts of linoleic acid (also known as omega-6 fatty acid).

Sesame seeds

These tiny, white or black seeds are a feature of Middle Eastern and Oriental cooking. In the Middle East they are ground into tahini, a thick paste that is a key component of hummus. Sesame seeds are also ground to make halvah, a sweet confection from Greece, Israel and Turkey. Gomassio, or gomashio, is the name of a crushed sesame seed condiment used in Japan. It can easily be made at home: toast the seeds, then crush with a little sea salt using a mortar and pestle. Try a ratio of one part salt to five parts sesame seeds.

Sesame seeds' flavour is improved by roasting them in a dry frying pan; it gives them a distinctive nuttiness. Toasted seeds make a good addition to salads and noodle dishes. Unroasted seeds can be used as a topping for breads, buns, cakes and biscuits (cookies), or added to pastry dough.

When buying sesame seeds, try to find seeds that have been mechanically rolled – the telltale sign is a matt appearance. Seeds that have undergone other processing methods, such as salt-brining or a chemical bath, are usually glossy. Salt brining can affect the flavour of the seeds, as can chemical processing, which also damages their nutritional value.

Quick ideas for seeds

• Sprinkle over breads, cakes and biscuits just before baking, or add to flapjacks, wholemeal scones or pastry.
• Combine with dried or fresh fruit, chopped nuts and natural yogurt.
• Add a spoonful of seeds to rissoles, vegetable burgers or casseroles.
• Mix with rolled oats, flour, butter or margarine, and sugar to make a sweet crumble topping. Omit the sugar to make a savoury topping and combine with chopped fresh or dried herbs.
• Scatter over a mixed green salad or vegetable stir-fries or noodle dishes just before serving.

BELOW: Sunflower seeds

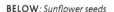

ABOVE:
Pumpkin seeds

RIGHT: *Black
and white
poppy seeds*

Sunflower seeds

These are the seeds of the sunflower, a symbol of summer and an important crop throughout the world. The impressive golden-yellow flowers are grown for their seeds and oil; the leaves are used to treat malaria and the stalks are made into fertilizer. Rich in vitamin E, the pale-green, tear-drop-shaped seeds have a semi-crunchy texture and an oily taste that is much improved by dry-roasting. Sprinkle sunflower seeds over salads, rice pilaffs and couscous, or use in bread dough, muffins, casseroles and baked dishes.

Poppy seeds

These are the seeds of the opium poppy, but without any of the habit-forming alkaloids. Poppy seeds can be blue (usually described as black) or white.

RIGHT: *Linseeds (left)
and hemp seeds*

The black variety looks good sprinkled on the top of cakes and breads, adding a pleasant crunch. Black poppy seeds can be used to make delicious seed cakes and teabreads, and they are also used in German and Eastern European pastries, strudels and tarts. In India, the ground white seeds are used to thicken sauces, while adding a distinctively nutty flavour.

Linseeds

Also known as flaxseeds, linseeds are a rich source of polyunsaturated fat, including the essential linoleic acid. They can be added to muesli as well as other breakfast cereals, mixed into bread dough or sprinkled over salads to add an interesting texture.

Pumpkin seeds

Richer in iron than any other seed and an excellent source of zinc, pumpkin seeds are a nutritious snack. They are also delicious lightly toasted, tossed

in a little toasted sesame seed oil or soy sauce, and stirred into a mixed leaf or rice salad. Pumpkin seeds are widely used in South American cooking, where they are generally roasted and ground, and added to a variety of sauces.

Hemp seeds

The cultivation of hemp has a long history, but for various reasons it fell out of fashion. Today, hemp is making a comeback as a food. Hemp seeds are best roasted, as this enhances their nutty flavour. They can be used in either sweet or savoury dishes.

Roasting seeds

The flavour of seeds is greatly improved by 'roasting' them in a dry frying pan. Obviously, black poppy seeds won't turn golden brown, so watch them carefully to make sure that they don't scorch.

1 Spread out a spoonful or two of seeds in a thin layer in a large non-stick frying pan and heat gently.

2 Cook the seeds for 2–3 minutes over medium heat, tossing frequently, until they are golden brown.

SPICES AND SEASONINGS

If you are new to wholefood vegetarian cooking, you may find you need to rethink your approach to seasonings of all kinds. Spices play a vital role in healthy and appetizing vegetarian cooking, and organic and wholefood ingredients taste so good that to mask their flavours would be a sin.

Spices

More than 60 different kinds of spices are regularly used in cooking around the world, ranging from allspice to vanilla, and there are too many to go into great detail in this book. About 20 of these are easily available organically grown. Try to find and use organic spices where you can because non-organic ones have often been heavily sprayed with pesticides. Most of these plants are grown in

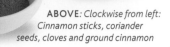

ABOVE: Clockwise from left: Cinnamon sticks, coriander seeds, cloves and ground cinnamon

developing countries where non-organic farming practices can undermine farmers' health and the environment. Until recently, dried spices with organic certification were quite difficult to track down. Now they are much more readily available, in good health food stores, direct from the packers or through mail-order companies.

Spices are almost always used dried, when their flavours are condensed. However, fresh versions of chillies and ginger, and even turmeric, are also popular. Organic dried chillies are a useful ingredient to have in the store cupboard. They come whole, powdered or in flakes, and tend to be hotter than fresh chillies.

Fry dried spices before adding them to a dish. Heat a pan with or without oil and fry or toast the spices for about 1 minute, until they release their aroma. Shake the pan often to prevent them sticking. Most spices should be toasted whole, then crushed with a pestle in a mortar, or in a coffee grinder. Such spices as nutmeg and cinnamon, however, are too large or bulky to be heated whole. Crush cinnamon bark or grate whole nutmeg just before toasting it. These spices retain more flavour when they are stored whole.

Grinding spices

Whole spices ground by hand provide the best flavour and aroma. Grind as you need them, and do not be tempted to grind too much because they tend to lose their potency and flavour over time. Some spices such as mace, fenugreek, cloves, turmeric and cinnamon are difficult to grind at home, and these are better bought ready-ground.

BELOW: Grind whole spices in a mortar using a pestle – or use an electric coffee grinder if you prefer.

LEFT: Cardamom pods

BELOW: Fresh root ginger

ABOVE: *Ground and fresh turmeric*

Fresh organic root ginger is smaller and has a more intense flavour than the swollen and sometimes watery non-organic spice. Ginger and galangal add a hot yet refreshing flavour to sweet and savoury dishes, including marinades, stir-fries, fresh vegetables, poached fruit and cakes and bakes.

The five spices most often used in Indian cooking are coriander, cumin, turmeric, pepper and chilli. Many other spices are used alongside this quintet, including star anise and fenugreek. Try adding nutmeg to savoury dishes such as pumpkin soup and baked fish, as well as more traditional sweet dishes such as Christmas pudding or rice pudding. The powerful essential oils in this spice have slightly euphoric properties, so they lift the spirits. No wonder nutmeg is a popular spice in mulled wine and other festive Christmas treats. Add caraway seeds to sauerkraut or bean stews, as they help to ease flatulence. Coriander seeds can help to cool an otherwise hot and spicy dish, as well as adding their distinctive flavour. Chilli powder acts like cornflour (cornstarch), thickening stews and curries, while pepper adds accent to almost anything, including strawberries.

Pepper

Undoubtedly the oldest, most widely used spice in the world, pepper is a very useful seasoning because it not only adds flavour of its own to a dish, but also brings out the flavour of the other ingredients. Pepper is a digestive stimulant, as well as a decongestant and antioxidant.

Black peppercorns are the dried green berries of the vine pepper and they are relatively mild. They are best when freshly ground in a peppermill as you need them because they quickly lose their aroma. White pepper is less aromatic than black pepper and is generally used in white sauces and other dishes to avoid dark specks of black pepper.

Green peppercorns are unripened berries and have a milder flavour than black or white peppercorns. They may be dried or preserved in brine. They are sometimes used to make a spicy peppercorn sauce. Pink peppercorns are pretty pink berries and not a true pepper. They are the processed berries of a type of poison ivy and should be used in small amounts as they are mildly toxic.

ABOVE: *White, black and pink peppercorns*

Salt
Moderate amounts of salt are needed by the body, but it is easy to consume too much, as salt is already added to many processed foods. Too much salt can lead to high blood pressure and water retention, and may increase the risk of heart disease. Used in small amounts, however, salt can enhance the flavour of food. Use rock or sea salt rather than refined table salt.

ABOVE: *Table salt (top), rock salt (right) and sea salt (left)*

PASTA

Once considered a fattening food, pasta is now recognized as an important part of a healthy diet. The variety of shapes is almost endless, from the numerous tiny soup pastas to huge shells used for stuffing. Pasta can be plain, made with egg or flavoured with ingredients such as tomato or spinach. Low in fat and high in complex carbohydrates, it provides plenty of long-term energy. Corn and buckwheat varieties are also available, as is wholewheat pasta, which is high in fibre.

Pasta is one of our most simple, yet most versatile foods. A combination of wheat flour and water produces the basic dough, which can then be formed into an infinite number of shape variations. Alter the type of flour, add fresh eggs or a vegetable purée, and the options are even greater. Although pasta is itself a low-fat food, it is important to take care when choosing the accompanying sauce, as overloading on cheese or cream can soon transform pasta dishes into a high-fat food.

BELOW: *Buckwheat pasta spirals (left) and short-cut pizzoccheri*

Buying pasta

The quality of pasta varies tremendously — choose good-quality Italian brands of pasta made from 100 per cent durum wheat. Try to visit your local Italian delicatessen to buy fresh pasta, rather than buying it from the supermarket. Dried pasta will keep almost indefinitely, but, if you decant the pasta into a storage jar, it is a good idea to use it all before adding any from a new packet.

Fresh pasta from a delicatessen is usually sold loose and is best cooked the same day, but can be kept in the refrigerator for a day or two. Fresh pasta from a supermarket is likely to be packed in plastic packs and bags, and these will keep for 3–4 days in the refrigerator. Fresh pasta freezes well and should be cooked from frozen. Packs and bags of supermarket pasta have the advantage of being easy to store in the freezer.

Pasta for health

Pasta provides the body with fuel for all kinds of physical activity, from running a marathon to walking to the bus stop. High in complex carbohydrates, pasta is broken down slowly, providing energy over a long

BELOW: *Corn or maize pasta comes in a variety of shapes, from elbow macaroni to fusilli and three-coloured radiatori*

period of time. Wholewheat pasta is the most nutritious, with a richer concentration of vitamins, minerals and fibre. Still, all pasta is a useful source of protein, as well as being low in fat. Buckwheat is very nutritious; it contains all eight essential amino acids, making it a complete protein. It is also particularly high in fibre.

Durum wheat pasta

This is the most readily available type of pasta and can be made with or without egg. Plain wheat pasta is used for straight long shapes, such as spaghetti, while long shapes made with egg pasta are traditionally packed in nests or compressed into waves because it is more delicate. Lasagne can be made with either plain or egg pasta. At one time, almost all short pasta shapes were made from plain pasta, but egg pasta shapes are now becoming increasingly available. Pasta made with egg has several advantages over plain pasta: it is more nutritious, many people consider it to have a superior flavour, and it is more difficult to overcook.

ABOVE:
*Pasta can be
coloured and flavoured in various ways,
such as plain, spinach and tomato varieties*

Coloured and flavoured pasta

A variety of ingredients can be added to the pasta dough to give it both flavour and colour. The most common additions are tomato and spinach, but beetroot (beet), saffron, fresh herbs such as basil, and even chocolate are used. Mixed bags of pasta are also available – the traditional combination of plain and spinach-flavoured pasta is called paglia e fieno, meaning 'straw and hay', but there are many other mixtures to be found.

ABOVE: *Spinach and
wholewheat lasagne and
plain cannelloni*

Wholewheat pasta

This substantial pasta is made using wholemeal (whole-wheat) flour, and it contains more fibre than plain durum wheat pasta. It takes longer to cook, and has a slightly chewy texture and nutty flavour. Wholewheat spaghetti (bigoli), a traditional variety from the area around Venice known as the Veneto, can be found in good Italian delicatessens, health food shops and supermarkets. There is an increasing range of wholewheat shapes, from tiny soup pastas to rotelle (wheels) and lasagne.

Buckwheat pasta

Pasta made from buckwheat flour has a nutty taste and is darker in colour than wholewheat pasta. Pizzoccheri from Lombardy is the classic shape. Traditionally sold in nests like tagliatelle, these thin, flat noodles are also available cut into short strips. Other buckwheat pasta shapes are available in health food shops and supermarkets. Buckwheat pasta is not only gluten-free, but also contains calcium, zinc and B vitamins.

Corn pasta

Made with corn or maize flour, this gluten-free pasta is made in a wide range of shapes, including spaghetti, fusilli (spirals) and conchiglie (shells), as well as more unusual varieties. Plain corn pasta is a sunshine-yellow colour, and may be flavoured with spinach or tomato. It is available from health food stores and supermarkets.

Choosing the right shape

While you don't need to stick rigidly to hard-and-fast rules, some pasta shapes definitely work better than others with particular sauces.
• Long pasta shapes such as spaghetti, linguine, tagliatelle and fettuccine suit smooth cream- or olive oil-based sauces, or vegetable sauces where the ingredients are very finely chopped.
• Hollow shapes such as penne (quills), fusilli (spirals) and macaroni work well with robust sauces, such as cheese, tomato and vegetable.
• Stuffed pasta shapes such as ravioli and cappelletti are good with simple sauces made with butter, extra virgin olive oil or tomatoes.
• In soups, the delicate small shapes, risi (rice), orzi (barley) and quadrucci (squares) suit lighter broths, while the more substantial conchigliette (little shells) and farfalline (little butterflies) go well in heartier vegetable soups.

NOODLES

The fast food of the East, noodles can be made from wheat flour, rice, buckwheat flour or mung bean flour. Both fresh and dried noodles are readily available in health food stores and Asian shops, as well as good supermarkets. Like pasta, noodles are low in fat and high in complex carbohydrates, and so provide long-term energy. Wholewheat noodles are the most nutritious, containing a richer concentration of vitamins, minerals and fibre. Nevertheless, all noodles are a useful source of protein, as well as being low in fat. Buckwheat noodles are made from buckwheat flour, which contains all eight essential amino acids, making it a complete protein. It is also high in fibre. Cellophane noodles are made from mung bean starch, which is reputed to be a powerful detoxifier.

Packets of fresh noodles are found in the chiller cabinets of Asian shops. They usually carry a use-by date and must be stored in the refrigerator. Dried noodles will keep for many months if stored in an airtight container in a cool, dry place.

BELOW: *Rice noodles*

ABOVE: *Udon noodles*

Egg noodles

Far more common than the plain wheat variety, egg noodles are sold both fresh and dried. The Chinese type come in various thicknesses. Very fine egg noodles, which resemble vermicelli, are usually sold in coils. Wholewheat egg noodles are widely available from larger supermarkets.

ABOVE: *Dried and fresh egg noodles*

Udon noodles

These thick, egg-free Japanese noodles can be round or flat, and they are available fresh, pre-cooked or dried. Wholewheat udon noodles have a more robust flavour.

Somen noodles

Sold in bundles, held together by a paper band, these thin, white noodles are available from Oriental stores.

Ramen noodles

These Japanese egg noodles are sold in coils and are often cooked and served with an accompanying broth.

Cooking wheat noodles

Wheat noodles are very easy to cook. Both dried and fresh noodles are cooked in a large pan of boiling water – how long depends on the type of noodle and the thickness of the strips. Dried noodles need about 3 minutes' cooking time, while fresh ones will often be ready in less than a minute. Fresh noodles may need to be rinsed quickly in cold water to prevent them overcooking.

BELOW: *Wholewheat egg noodles*

Rice noodles

These fine, delicate noodles are made from rice and are an opaque white. Like wheat noodles, they come in various widths, from very thin strands known as rice vermicelli, which are popular in Thailand and southern China, to thicker rice sticks, which are used more in Vietnam and Malaysia. A huge range of rice noodles is available dried in Oriental grocers, and fresh ones are occasionally found in the chiller cabinets. As all rice noodles are pre-cooked, they need only to be soaked in hot water for a few minutes to soften them before use in stir-fries and salads.

BELOW: *Cellophane noodles*

Wheat noodles

There are two main types of noodle: plain and egg. Plain wheat noodles are made from strong flour and water. They can be flat or round, and come in various thicknesses.

Cellophane vermicelli and noodles

Made from mung bean starch, these translucent noodles, also known as bean thread vermicelli and glass noodles, come in different thicknesses and are only available dried. Although very fine, the strands are firm and fairly tough. Cellophane noodles don't need to be boiled, but simply soaked in boiling water for 10–15 minutes. They have a fantastic texture, which they retain when cooked, never becoming soggy. Cellophane noodles are almost tasteless unless combined with other strongly flavoured foods and seasonings. They are never eaten on their own, but used as an ingredient in varous dishes. They are very good in vegetarian dishes, and as an ingredient in spring rolls.

Buckwheat noodles

Soba noodles are the best-known type of buckwheat noodles. They are a much darker colour than wheat noodles – almost brownish grey. In Japan, soba noodles are traditionally served in soups or stir-fries with a variety of sauces.

Quick ideas for noodles

• To make a simple broth, dissolve mugi miso in hot water, add cooked soba noodles; sprinkle with chilli flakes and sliced spring onions (scallions).

• Cook ramen noodles in vegetable stock. Add a splash of dark soy sauce, shredded spinach and grated ginger (above). Serve sprinkled with sesame seeds and fresh coriander (cilantro).
• Stir-fry sliced shiitake and oyster mushrooms in garlic and ginger, then toss with rice or egg noodles. Scatter with fresh chives and a little roasted sesame oil.
• In a food processor, blend together some lemon grass, chilli, garlic, ginger, kaffir lime leaves and fresh coriander. Fry the paste in a little sunflower oil. Combine with cooked ribbon noodles, sprinkling fresh basil and chopped spring onions on top before serving.

OIL

There is a wide variety of cooking oils, and they are produced from a number of different sources: from cereals, such as corn; from fruits, such as olives; from nuts, such as walnuts, almonds and hazelnuts; and from seeds, such as rapeseed, safflower and sunflower. They can be extracted by simple mechanical means, such as pressing or crushing, or by further processing, usually heating. Virgin oils, which are obtained from the first cold pressing, are sold unrefined, have the most characteristic flavour and are the most expensive.

Olive oil

Indisputably the king of oils, olive oil varies in flavour and colour, depending on how it is made and where it

LEFT: *Extra virgin olive oil*

BELOW: *Groundnut (peanut) oil (left) and almond oil*

comes from. Climate, soil, harvesting and pressing all influence the end result – generally, the hotter the climate, the more robust the oil. Thus oils from southern Italy, Greece and Spain have a stronger flavour and a darker colour than those from the rest of Italy and from France. Olive oil is rich in monounsaturated fat, which has been found to reduce cholesterol, thereby reducing the risk of heart disease. There are different grades to choose from, such as extra virgin olive oil which has a low acidity – less than 1 per cent. It is excellent in salad dressings. Virgin olive oil is also a pure first-pressed oil; this has a slightly higher level of acidity than extra virgin olive oil, and can be used in much the same way.

Other oils

There is a wide range of light, processed oils on the market that are all relatively taste-free and have a variety of uses in the kitchen, such as corn oil, safflower oil, sunflower oil, rapeseed (canola) oil and soya oil.

ABOVE: *Walnut, sesame and hazelnut oils*

Groundnut oil is also known as peanut oil, is relatively tasteless and useful for frying, cooking and dressings.

Speciality oils such as sesame oil, walnut oil, hazelnut oil and almond oil are richly flavoured and are therefore used in small quantities, often as a flavouring ingredient for salad dressings and marinades.

Essential Fats

We all need some fat in our diet. It keeps us warm, adds flavour to our food, carries essential vitamins A, D, E and K around the body, and provides essential fatty acids, which cannot be produced in the body, but are vital for growth and development, and may reduce the risk of heart attacks.

What is more important is the type and amount of fat that we eat. Some fats are better for us than others, and we should adjust our intake accordingly. It is recommended that fat should make up no more than 35 per cent of our diet.

VINEGARS

One of our oldest condiments, vinegar is made by acetic fermentation, a process that occurs when a liquid containing less than 18 per cent alcohol is exposed to the air. Most countries produce their own type of vinegar, usually based on their most popular alcoholic drink – wine in France and Italy; sherry in Spain; rice wine in Asia; and beer and cider in Great Britain. Commonly used as a preservative in pickles and chutneys, it is also an ingredient in marinades and salad dressings.

Wine vinegars

These can be made from white, red or rosé wine. The quality of the vinegar depends on the quality of the original ingredient. The finest wine vinegars are made by the slow and costly Orleans method. Cheaper and faster methods of fermentation

LEFT: *Balsamic vinegar*

BELOW: *Sherry vinegar*

ABOVE: *Rice vinegar (left) and brown malt vinegar*

involve heating, which produces a harsher vinegar. Use in dressings, mayonnaise, sauces, stews and soups.

Balsamic vinegar

Rich, dark and mellow, this vinegar originates from northern Italy. Made from grape juice (predominantly from Trebbiano grapes), it is fermented in vast wooden barrels for a minimum of four to five years and up to 40 or more years, resulting in an intensely rich vinegar with concentrated flavour. Balsamic vinegar is delicious in dressings or sprinkled over roasted vegetables.

Sherry vinegar

This vinegar can be just as costly as balsamic vinegar and, if left to mature in wooden barrels, can be equally good. Sweet and mellow, it is used in the same way as balsamic.

Malt vinegar

Made from soured beer, malt vinegar is used for pickling onions and other vegetables, or for sprinkling over chips (French fries). It can be clear, but is often sold coloured with caramel. Malt vinegar's robust, harsh flavour is not suitable for salad dressings.

Cider vinegar

Made from cider and praised for its health-giving properties, cider vinegar has a slight apple flavour, but is too strong and sharp to use in the same ways as wine vinegar. It can be used for salad dressings, but is perhaps best for pickling fruits such as pears.

Rice vinegar

There are two kinds of rice vinegar: the type from Japan is mellow and sweet, and most often used to flavour sushi rice, but it can also be added to dressings, stir-fries and sauces; Chinese rice vinegar is much sharper. Rice vinegar is usually a clear pale-brown colour.

BELOW AND RIGHT: *Red and white wine vinegars*

TEAS AND TISANES

A popular reviving drink for centuries, tea comes in many different forms, from traditional teas such as green and black tea to fragrant fruit infusions and healing herbal tisanes.

The latest research shows that drinking about five cups of tea a day may help to prevent heart disease, stroke and certain cancers. These benefits have been attributed to a group of antioxidants found in tea called 'polyphenols' or 'flavonoids'. Flavonoids have antiviral, antibacterial and anti-inflammatory properties. Green tea contains the highest amount of flavonoids and black tea the lowest. Antioxidants help to mop up harmful free radicals, which cause damage to the body's cells and may cause cancer.

ABOVE:
Green tea

ABOVE: Black tea

Green tea

This tea is popular with the Chinese and Japanese, who prefer its light, slightly bitter but refreshing flavour. It is produced from leaves that are steamed and dried, but not fermented, a process that retains their green colour.

Black tea

This is the most widely available tea and is made by fermenting withered tea leaves, then drying them. It produces a dark brown brew that has a more assertive taste than green tea. Darjeeling and English breakfast tea are two examples.

Fruit teas

These are made from a blend of fruit flavours, such as rosehip, raspberry, strawberry and lemon, along with fruit pieces and sometimes herbs or real tea. Check the packaging to ensure the 'tea' is naturally, rather than artificially, flavoured. Fruit teas make refreshing caffeine-free drinks. They are ideal for pregnant women, and also suitable for diabetics because of their low sugar content.

Herbal tisanes

Herbal tisanes have been used for centuries for a multitude of ailments. Made from the leaves, seeds and flowers of herbs, they vary in strength and effectiveness.

ABOVE: *Naturally flavoured fruit teas are caffeine-free with hardly any calories*

Shop-bought teas are generally mild in their medicinal properties, but some varieties are not recommended for young children and pregnant women. Teas prescribed by herbalists can be incredibly powerful and should be taken with care. Popular types include peppermint tea (good as a digestive), camomile tea, rosehip tea, dandelion and lemon verbena.

Coffee

Although coffee is generally viewed as unhealthy, largely due to its high level of caffeine, studies have shown that it can enhance concentration and elevate mood. Drinking more than six cups a day, however, can increase the risk of heart disease and high blood pressure.

SWEETENERS

Nutritionists have wide-ranging, often extreme opinions on sugar and sugar alternatives. Some maintain that these products cause hyperactivity in children; others believe that sugars can induce relaxation and sleep. Many recipes, from breads and cakes to desserts and puddings, contain different types of sugar and/or sugar substitutes such as molasses, honey, malt and grain syrups, as well as dried fruit, and wouldn't be palatable without them. Provided that a diet is well balanced and varied, moderate amounts of sugar are nutritionally acceptable.

Molasses

This rich, syrupy liquid is a by-product of sugar refining. Blackstrap molasses, which contains less sugar than lighter alternatives, is the most nutritionally valuable. It may be better, however, to choose organically produced molasses, which do not contain the additives that are used in the sugar-refining process.

LEFT: Honey

Honey

The colour, flavour, consistency and quality of honey depends on the source of nectar, as well as the method of production. In general, the darker the colour, the stronger the flavour. Many commercial brands of honey are pasteurized and blended to give a uniform taste and texture, but, from the point of view of flavour and health, it is best to buy raw unfiltered honey from a single flower source.

Honey offers negligible nutritional benefits, but it is much sweeter than sugar, so less is needed; it is also lower in calories. Today, honey retains its reputation as an antiseptic. Recent studies show that, applied externally, honeys such as Manuka are effective in healing and disinfecting wounds.

Carob

This caffeine-free alternative to chocolate is made from the fleshy bean pod of a Mediterranean tree. Carob powder (flour) looks and tastes similar to cocoa powder and can be used in hot drinks, confectionery and baked goods. It is naturally sweeter, lower in fat and more nutritious than cocoa powder.

Maple syrup

This is made from the sap of the maple tree. Look for pure varieties rather than maple-flavoured syrup, which contains additives. Maple syrup has a rich, distinctive flavour and is sweeter than sugar, so less is required in cooking.

Grain syrups

Corn, barley, wheat and rice can be transformed into syrups that are used in place of sugar in baked goods and sauces. Grain syrups tend to be easier to digest and enter the bloodstream more slowly than other refined sugars, which cause swings in blood sugar levels. Malt extract, a by-product of barley, has a more intense flavour.

Fruit juice

Freshly squeezed fruit juice is a useful alternative to sugar in baked goods, sauces, pies and ice cream. Fruit juice concentrates such as apple and pear with no added preservatives or sugar are available from health food shops.

Dried fruit

Dates made into a rich-flavoured syrup can be used to sweeten cakes. Puréed dried fruits such as apricots, prunes and figs can also replace sugar in pies and cakes. Dried fruit can be added to sweet and savoury foods.

BELOW: Blackstrap molasses

BELOW: Dried fruit

Index